The Falklands War

THE INSIGHT TEAM of *The Sunday Times* was created twenty years ago and since then has acquired a world-wide reputation for its investigative journalism. Among Insight's best-selling books have been: *The Yom Kippur War, Ulster* and *Siege!*

PAUL EDDY is thirty-seven. He has been a member of the Insight team since 1976 and its editor for three years. He was co-author of *Destination Disaster, The Hughes Papers, The Plumbat Affair* and *Siege!* He has been with *The Sunday Times* for ten years.

MAGNUS LINKLATER is forty and has worked on *The Sunday Times* for thirteen years, as editor of Spectrum, The Colour Magazine, News Editor and Assistant Editor (Features). He is co-author of two previous *Sunday Times* books: *Hoax, the Story of the Clifford Irving/Howard Hughes Affair* and *Jeremy Thorpe – A Secret Life.* He is the author of *Massacre: The Story of Glencoe.*

PETER GILLMAN is forty. A *Sunday Times* feature writer, he was formerly with the Insight team and was co-author of *Eiger Direct, The Plumbat Affair, Siege!* and *Collar the Lot!* He has been with *The Sunday Times* for fifteen years.

The Falklands War

Written and edited by: Paul Eddy and Magnus Linklater
with Peter Gillman

The Insight team: John Ball
Michael Bilton (Washington)
Robin Morgan

**With the British task
force: In Argentina:** John Shirley
Isabel Hilton

**Defence
correspondent:** Jon Connell

Contributors: Ian Jack
Simon Winchester

Additional reporting: Will Ellsworth Jones (New York),
Michael Jones, Mark Hosenball
(Washington), Keith Richardson
(Brussels), George Rosie, Jon
Swain (Paris), Tony Terry, John
Witherow (of *The Times*) and
Mary Beale (London Weekend
Television)

Researchers: Lee Chester and Therese Stanton

Graphics: Gordon Beckett, Phil Green,
Peter Sullivan and
John Grimwade

Picture design: David Gibbons

SPHERE BOOKS LIMITED
30–32 Gray's Inn Road,
London WC1X 8JL

First published in Great Britain by
Sphere Books Ltd 1982

Copyright © by Times Newspapers Ltd 1982

Published simultaneously in hardback by
Andre Deutsch Ltd

Set in Plantin

Printed and bound in Great Britain by Collins, Glasgow.

Contents

The Falklands War

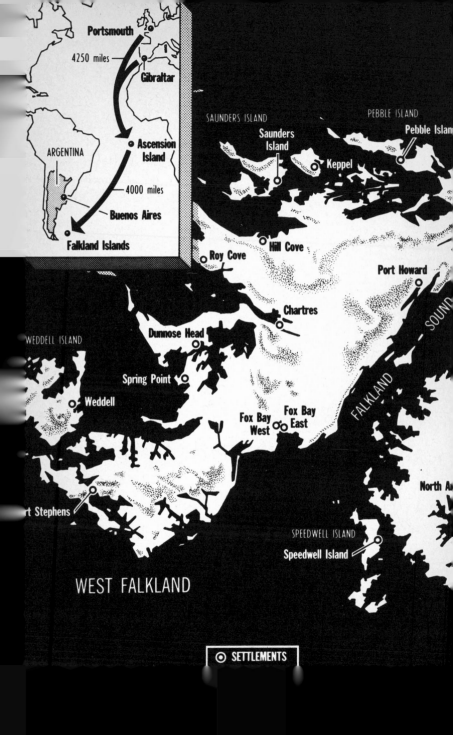

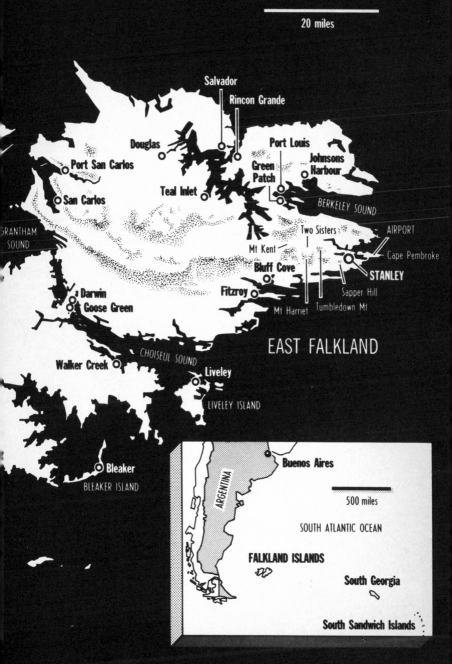

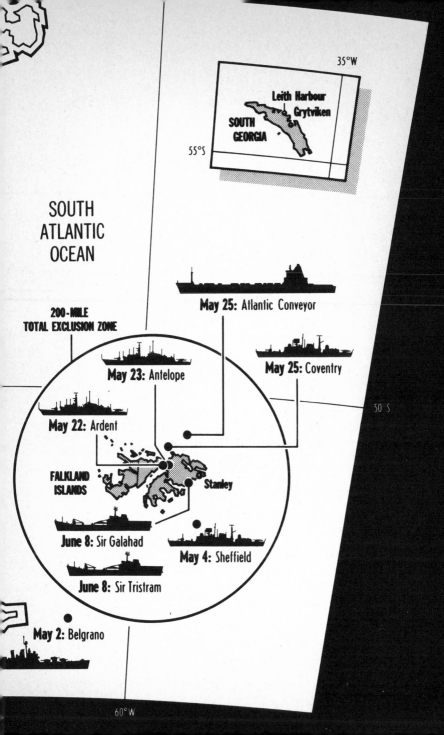

SOUTH
ATLANTIC
OCEAN

35°W

Leith Harbour
Grytviken
SOUTH
GEORGIA

55°S

200-MILE
TOTAL EXCLUSION ZONE

May 25: Atlantic Conveyor

May 23: Antelope

May 25: Coventry

May 22: Ardent

50°S

FALKLAND
ISLANDS

Stanley

June 8: Sir Galahad

May 4: Sheffield

June 8: Sir Tristram

May 2: Belgrano

60°W

Introduction

Even now that it is all over it is hard to grasp the enormity of what has happened: in the last quarter of the twentieth century, Great Britain has been to war and has fought on a scale and in a manner not seen by this country since the Second World War. A naval task force of 100 ships has sailed 8,000 miles to the South Atlantic to engage an enemy invasion force off the last outpost of a forgotten empire. Planes, helicopters, and missiles, many never deployed in combat before, have been thrown into a battle testing them to the limits of their capability. In the course of it more than 1,000 men have lost their lives.

But the reverberations of the Falklands War were felt far beyond the shores of Britain alone. They affected NATO, Europe and the United Nations; shook the United States's relations with Latin America; tested the tactics and hardware of armed forces throughout the world; threw the political structure of Argentina into chaos.

At *The Sunday Times* we covered the events of those hectic weeks from the day Argentina invaded the Falkland Islands – April 2 1982 – to the day she surrendered them – June 14. In the course of it, we devoted four or five pages a week, often in diary form, to the cut and thrust of diplomacy and of battle. This book stems from that coverage, but aims higher.

We have gone back to those sources and contacts we established during the war and tried, through their diaries and recollections, to piece together the full story of what happened. In addition we have managed to talk to many who were unable, unwilling or simply unavailable to discuss the affair while its outcome was still in doubt. The result is an account which traces decisions taken in the corridors of Whitehall right through to the marine advancing in darkness through an Argentinian minefield. In very few wars has one been able to chronicle cause and effect with quite the same starkness. What emerges at the same time is how many of the key decisions were taken, not in London or Buenos Aires, but by men in isolated command posts struggling to make sense of unforeseen and haphazard events. It was a horrifying war, as all wars are, but to study it at close quarters was to learn much about politics, about men under arms, and about human nature.

In Chapter Seven we have analysed the reasons why the war began. We do not wish to pre-empt the findings of the British Government's inquiry currently under way, merely to suggest an important part of its agenda.

There are many people we would like to thank for their help. The interest, even enthusiasm, shown by most of those whom we interviewed, mainly from the armed forces, but also some from the diplomatic and political field, and the Falkland Islanders themselves, has been, at times, overwhelming. We are grateful to them all. Without their co-operation the book could never have been contemplated.

At the same time, we depended heavily on the skills of our co-author, Peter Gillman, and many of our other colleagues. In particular we wish to thank three:

John Shirley sailed with the task force, endured the air attacks, landed at San Carlos and marched most of the way to Stanley. Unlike his fellow war correspondents, he then volunteered to return to Britain the slow way, on board *Canberra*, with many of the officers and men who had played such a crucial part in the war; much of the richness of military detail in this book was his, and our, reward.

Isabel Hilton spent the war in Argentina, filing the best dispatches of any foreign correspondent. She, too, stayed on for the aftermath and gained extraordinary access to Argentina's political and military hierarchy.

Simon Winchester was in the Falklands when Argentina invaded. Doubtless he would have continued his brilliant coverage of these events but for the fact that a week or so later he was arrested in Argentina on demonstrably false accusations of espionage, and jailed for the rest of the war. Despite that ordeal, when Stanley – and he – were liberated, he insisted on returning to the Falklands to finish the article he was writing when, as he put it, he was 'so rudely interrupted'.

Finally, we have some personal debts to pay. Our thanks to:

John Lovesey and David Gwyn Jones for allowing us to borrow three of the best reporters from *The Sunday Times* news department for far longer than any of us imagined.

To Christopher Hird, Don Berry and Liam McAuley for doing our respective jobs as well as their own, while we did this one. To Lee Chester and Therese Stanton for working above and beyond the call of duty, especially in the final hectic days before our production deadline.

To Frank Giles, Editor of *The Sunday Times*, who holds the view that journalists should write for newspapers not books but who agreed that this story merited the exception. For that, for his constructive comments on the manuscript and for his support, we are deeply grateful.

Paul Eddy, Insight Editor
Magnus Linklater, Assistant Editor (Features)
The Sunday Times, London: September 1982

PART 1

CHAPTER ONE

Surrender (I)

'We've never surrendered before.
It's not part of our training.'
– Major Mike Norman, April, 1982

East Falkland, April 2, 1982

The British forces immediately opposed to the Argentinian invasion of the Falklands were positioned in a spot overlooking York Bay. They numbered two. Marines Roderick Wilcox and Leslie Milne, both Scots, had drawn the short straw because they could ride motorcycles, considered the best available transport for crossing the sand dunes in which the two men now lay hidden. Below them was the beach, code-named Purple, where the first wave of the invasion was expected to land sometime before dawn. The beach had been booby-trapped with nothing more than barbed wire because that was all the marines had. There was only enough for one stretch of sand. The next beach, just around York Point and codenamed Orange, was completely unguarded.

The orders were to give the Argentinians 'a bloody nose' and, to inflict it, Wilcox and Milne were armed with a machine-gun and, as Milne remembers it, 1,600 rounds of ammunition. Wilcox thinks it was only 800 rounds. Either way, they had no spare barrel for the gun and after 500 rounds or so the heat would cause the barrel to expand, and the gun would jam.

At which point the two men were to 'withdraw'. (The word 'retreat' is not in a marine's vocabulary.) The plan called for them to escape on their motorbikes across the dunes to a nearby cove where they were supposed to have hidden a canoe. But, of the two canoes they had been offered, one had a leak and the other had lost its rudder, so Wilcox and Milne had decided to rely on just their bikes – and their luck. They knew they would need a great amount of it. Milne remembers he was 'scared shitless' because 'I couldn't see how we were going to get out of there.' Wilcox says: 'We had resigned ourselves to the fact we were going to die.'

That was a widely shared expectation. Major Mike Norman, the commanding officer of the Falklands garrison, known as Naval Party

8901 – a post he had assumed just twenty hours before – had told his men he expected them to fight until there was diplomatic intervention, or until they were overrun. Since his sixty-eight marines were likely to be outnumbered twenty to one, and hopelessly outgunned, and since, if the invasion did take place then the highest diplomacy would have failed, that meant, in all probability, to the death. Norman was surprised how well his men took it. He was also surprised by his own response: when he considered the prospect that he too was about to die, he found he didn't really mind.

Corporal Stefan York reckoned that the marines' high morale was directly attributable to Norman's 'impressive performance' at the final briefing which had taken place at Moody Brook barracks around midnight. Coming from York, that was quite a compliment: the last time Norman had spoken to him was back in England when the corporal had received a severe dressing down for being drunk; the two men did not like each other and it had taken special pleading from other officers to get York included in the Falklands detachment. What impressed York at Moody Brook was the determination Norman somehow managed to inspire, and the confidence that they would indeed give the Argentinians 'a bloody nose'. The men went off making jokes at each other's expense, enjoying the fact that for once no one at the armoury was rationing weapons, and no one was asking for signatures; they could take what they could carry. Wilcox remembers Major Norman's last exhortation: 'Remember, you are not fighting for the Falklands, you're fighting for yourselves.'

But inevitably, as the marines waited in the darkness in their various positions around the capital of Stanley, their confidence began to evaporate. The warning from London had come far too late. There had been no time to put the runway at Stanley airport out of action; the clerk of works said he could do it but it would take a week, so the only obstacle to an airborne invasion was the airport's fire truck which had been left parked in the middle of the runway. There had been no time to improvise mortars (the only one the marines had was cracked); no time to improvise claymore mines for the beaches; no time to block the approaches to the harbour; no time to rouse all the members of the islands' volunteer defence force who might have acted as snipers but for the fact that only twenty-three out of more than 100 had reported for duty, and they were needed to guard important buildings such as the radio station, and the cable and wireless office; no time to interrogate the thirty or so Argentinian civilians in Stanley, at least some of whom might have been privy to the invasion plan; and so, crucially, no time to do more than guess where and how the invasion would come, and, as the orders had it, 'make your dispositions accordingly'.

Purple beach was the most obvious spot for a landing because the approaches were free of rock and kelp – the thick brown seaweed that chokes most of the water around the Falklands – and because it had almost no gradient, allowing landing craft to get within feet of the sand. (Infantrymen are never more vulnerable than when they have a long wade ashore.) It was certainly the place Norman would have chosen to land. But he would also have chosen to send a second wave in helicopters to the airport which stands immediately behind Purple beach. So Corporal 'Figgy' Duff and his five marines dug themselves in alongside the hangar, ready to pour rifle fire into any helicopters that might try to land. (More than one commanding officer of the Falklands garrison had requested 81mm mortars for just such an eventuality, but they had never been provided.) Like Wilcox and Milne, Duff and his men had orders eventually to 'withdraw' and head back for Stanley. Strung out along the route were four more sections, six men in each, waiting to provide covering fire. They in their turn would fall back section by section until they reached Government House, on the western edges of the town. There they would make their last stand.

The plan was flawed because neither Purple beach nor the airport was Argentina's first choice, but in the scale of this war that was only a minor military miscalculation. Since Britain had misread or ignored all the warning signs until it was far too late to send reinforcements, nothing could alter the certainty that before the day was out the Argentinian flag would fly over the Falklands. The only remaining question was, how many men would die.

As an Alamo, Government House left a lot to be desired. For one thing, the northern face of the house – which overlooked the modest gardens, the road to Stanley and beyond that, the harbour – had windows of a conservatory running almost its entire length. The glass provided magnificent views, but, of course, no protection whatsoever. Indeed, in the entire house there was only one room, the ante-room to the governor's office, which was considered even reasonably protected from bullets. And the gardens, too, lacked any decent cover.

On the other hand, anyone attacking Government House had available all the cover and firing positions they could want. To the south, at the back of the house – beyond the vegetable garden and the staff quarters – there was a carefully cultivated copse of practically the only trees growing on the Falklands, and beyond that a steep, boulder-strewn ridge. It was, as the governor said, a ridiculous place to try to defend.

But when he said that he was looking at it from the military viewpoint. From a political viewpoint it was, as the seat of British government, the one place on the islands that *had* to be defended, no matter what the cost. So, the marines would fight for Government House – and so, too, would the governor, His Excellency Rex Hunt.

He intended to do that with his shotgun. But when Hunt went to

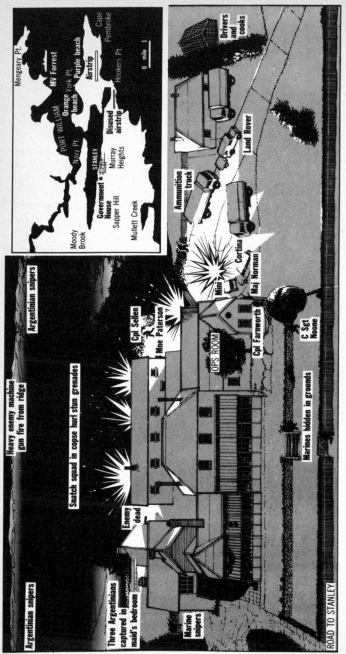

The battle for Government House, April 2 1982

arm himself, he found the gun had been commandeered by his chauffeur-cum-major-domo, Don Bonner, who had positioned himself in the rod room, where Hunt kept his fishing tackle and his golf clubs. From the window, Bonner had a good view of the ceremonial flagpole: the Union Jack atop it had not been lowered at sunset, as was customary; and Bonner was insistent that he would 'shoot the first Argie bastard who tries to take it down'. Hunt had to settle for a 9mm automatic, loaned by the marines. He spent much of the night practising how to load and cock the gun, but he never really got the hang of it.

Hunt was also given a personal bodyguard and from the moment invasion became inevitable, Marine Hugh Dorey never left his side. Dick Baker, the islands' chief secretary, went to the house sometime before midnight to find the governor and his wife sitting down to dinner in the formal dining room, surrounded by historic portraits and the ornate official silver, with Marine Dorey just inside the door, thrusting his rifle at any one who came through it. Baker found it a forlorn sight, 'my esteemed boss sitting there trying to sum up the enthusiasm to eat some dinner, terribly quiet, terribly depressed'. In fact, Baker felt like an intruder and refused Hunt's offer of something to eat or even a drink. He had not seen all the cables from London but he was pretty sure that the general thrust of the final messages to Hunt had been 'you're on your own, Jack'; and Baker could sense the weight of that bearing down on Hunt. 'The truth was, the responsibility was all his, and however much the rest of us wanted to help him or support him, the poor bugger was on his own.'

Baker had gone to see Hunt to get the governor's blessing for a couple of bits of navigational sabotage which he hoped might disrupt the invasion. First, a Canadian named Bill Curtis – who, as a matter of irony, had moved his family to the Falklands to escape the threat of war – had volunteered to tamper with the radio direction beacon at the airport which the Argentinians might use as a landing aid. Curtis, who had once been an air traffic controller, thought he could adjust the beacon's signal in such a way that anyone who followed it would land in the sea. But, was that permissible? After all, the beacon was Argentinian property. Second, Baker wanted to turn off the lantern in the Cape Pembroke lighthouse which warned of fearsome rocks that had made that bit of the South Atlantic the graveyard of more than a dozen ships since the Falklands became British. Hunt gave his consent for both schemes, and Baker went off to organise them – though, in the event, Curtis found he could not adjust the signal; he smashed the beacon with a sledge hammer.

Meanwhile, when their forlorn dinner was over, Hunt packed off his wife, and his seventeen-year-old son, Tony, to the comparative safety of Baker's house. (Family relations were somewhat strained: Tony was unhappy because he had failed to talk himself into a job as a dispatch

11

rider, with the islands' defence force; Mavis Hunt was furious with her husband for even allowing their son to volunteer.) Then, there being nothing else to do but wait, the governor went to bed for an hour or so's sleep.

At 3.15 a.m. precisely, the first Argentinian ship was sighted – or, at least Jack Sollis thought so. He was, at this moment, the sole representative of British naval power in the Falklands, because *HMS Endurance*, a converted ice-breaker – which was supposed to provide some deterrent to an Argentinian invasion – was 430 miles away, returning from South Georgia. So, the job of keeping a radar watch for the invasion fleet had been given to Sollis and his eighty-six foot motor vessel, *Forrest*. Sollis had, in fact, claimed a radar sighting some forty-five minutes earlier, and had hurriedly returned to port. Major Norman had thought that precipitate and ordered him back to sea. Sollis refused because now, from his berth in Port Stanley, he could actually see an aircraft carrier to the south, in Surf Bay.

The marines' operations room, now established at Government House, radioed Corporal David 'Lew' Armour who was in charge of Section One at Hookers Point. From their position on that isthmus – which joins the airport peninsula with the rest of East Falkland – Section One had an excellent view of Surf Bay: could they see the aircraft carrier?

No, said Corporal Armour, but he could see the wreck of the *Lady Elizabeth*, a hundred-year-old sailing ship abandoned in 1913. And from where Sollis was looking, with the blazing lights of Stanley oil refinery superimposed on her skeleton, she just might appear to be something more sinister.

Suitably reassured, Sollis agreed to return to sea and resume his watch.

But, by then, any vestige of hope that the Argentinians would not come had finally been removed. At 3.30 a.m., Governor Hunt was informed by London that President Ronald Reagan had personally telephoned President Galtieri to persuade him to call off the invasion – and had been rebuffed.

As a result, Hunt telephoned Baker. Since the previous day Major Norman had wanted to intern all Argentinian civilians in Stanley, and in particular seventeen young and suspiciously brawny 'gas workers' who had arrived from the mainland just a couple of days before. They said they had come to install some additional oil storage cylinders (under a 1974 agreement, Argentina supplied the Falklands with all of its fuel except diesel) but Norman suspected they might be part of the invasion plan; there, perhaps, to snatch the governor. Hunt, on London's advice, had decided to delay a round-up until 'the last possible moment' for fear of giving Argentina the remotest excuse to invade. The last possible moment having now arrived, Hunt asked

Baker – together with a party of sailors from *Endurance* who had been left behind when she sailed to South Georgia – to begin the arrests.

Even as the sailors were banging on the doors of the Upland Goose Hotel, where the gas workers were staying, Hunt went on the air to broadcast the state of emergency that would allow internment. Or rather, he tried to. Patrick Watts, who ran Falklands Radio, had earlier installed a microphone and a transmitter in the operations room at Government House for just such a purpose, but it now refused to work. Fortunately, Hunt had arranged for the Stanley telephone switchboard operator to remain on duty all night. He cranked the handle of his phone to rouse her and asked to be put through to the radio station, apologising for the fact that he could not remember the number. Once connected, he read out his message which Watts broadcast live. Hunt declared the emergency, and added: 'Anyone seen on the streets will be arrested. The morale of the Royal Marines and the Falkland Islands Defence Force is terrific. I am proud to be their commander-in-chief.'

In fact, Major Norman for one was becoming distinctly edgy. He is a rock of a man, six foot two inches and solid, someone who, in the words of a fellow officer, 'reinforces his arguments' and 'doesn't like being messed about'; his nickname is 'Punchy'. At 4.30 a.m. he was on Lookout Rocks, the nearest good vantage point to Government House, fed up with the waiting, hoping he just might see the first evidence of the invasion. But in the event, it was his ears and not his eyes that gave the warning.

Coming from the direction of Mullett Creek, a good two miles to the south, Norman *thought* he could hear the sound of rotor blades chopping through the night air. Helicopters? It might have been. It might also have been a trick of the wind, or merely his imagination.

Marine Michael Berry, keeping a lone vigil on Sapper Hill and much closer to Mullett Creek, also thought he could hear helicopters, but he was not sure either. At Purple beach, Wilcox and Milne were sure, but they couldn't report the fact because, they discovered, their Racal radio would not transmit.

From Lookout Rocks, Norman consulted by radio a fellow officer, and a firm friend, Major Gary Noott, who had been the commanding officer of the Falklands garrison until the previous morning when he handed over to Norman, and when he and his men were supposed to have packed their bags for home. Indeed, some of Noott's men had already left. Noott was at Government House in charge of the operations room and of communications with London – which proved to be fragmentary because the equipment kept playing up. He and Norman knew that if the Argentinians were landing at Mullet Creek then the defence plan which they had evolved together was in ruins. For one thing, the Argentinians would – by coming in the back door, as

13

it were – avoid the ambushes waiting for them at Purple beach and at the airport. But worse, they might also have scuppered the final element of the plan, which was for Major Noott to 'go covert': while Norman's men resisted, Noott and some of his men who knew the island well would slip away into the countryside – the Camp as Falklanders call it – and, hopefully, mount a guerrilla war against the occupation. To aid that, caches of food and ammunition had been stored in the Camp, and Noott had memorised the hiding places. But had their escape route now been cut?

One way to find out, of course, was to send some of the marines towards Mullett Creek. But if that turned out to be a wild goose chase, if the sound of helicopters had been no more than a trick of the wind, and if the invasion did then come at Purple beach or the airport, the thin blue line, already absurdly stretched, would provide even less resistance. Norman and Noott decided it was a gamble they could not afford; the marines should stay where they were until there was more solid evidence of the Argentinians' whereabouts.

It was provided, at 5.15 a.m., by Jack Sollis – and this time there was no mistake. He reported that *Forrest*'s radar had picked up three large ships off Mengeary Point, all heading west towards Stanley. As *Forrest* did the same with all the speed she could make, Basil Biggs, the lighthouse keeper, who was watching from the darkened tower at Cape Pembroke, reported that he could see the unmistakable bulk of Argentina's aircraft carrier, the flagship of her fleet, the *Veintecinco de Mayo*. A few minutes later, Biggs reported that he could now see what looked like a landing craft, heading towards York Point.

But the vessel did not, as expected, turn in towards Purple beach. Instead it sailed on, heading towards the narrows that mark the entrance to Port Stanley – and a nasty surprise. For at Navy Point, a finger of land that sticks into the narrows, Corporal York and his section were waiting with anti-tank guns, the heaviest weaponry the marines had. They prepared to fire. In the pre-dawn gloom York could hardly make out the vessel, let alone her exact position, so he sent up a flare – which instantly revealed that the supposed landing craft was in fact the *Forrest*. 'Hold your fire,' York shouted, only just in time.

At Government House Rex Hunt cranked the telephone once more, got through to the radio station and announced over the air that the Argentinian invasion fleet was in sight. He said it would not be long now.

Norman's ears had not deceived him. At approximately 4.30 a.m. helicopters *had* landed at Mullett Creek with the first invaders – 120 men of the *Buzo Tactico*, specialist commandos who are the Argentinian equivalent of the British Special Boat Squadron. Clad all in black, they had stealthily made their way due north, skirting Sapper Hill and Marine Berry's observation post, and then divided into two sections. One, a small advance party, had headed east to reconnoitre Government House. The other, larger group had turned west, for the barracks at Moody Brook. And, at 6.08 a.m., it launched a murderous attack.

Later, when it was all over, the Argentinian government made much of the claim that its troops had gone to great lengths to ensure that the invasion was 'bloodless'. That was indeed largely the result but what happened at Moody Brook suggests it was not the intention. For without warning, the *Buzo Tactico* mounted what is mundanely called a 'house clearance' of the barracks. The term is not an adequate description of the technique: the commandos burst into the building through all the entrances and systematically kicked down every door, hurled in a grenade and followed that with a burst of indiscriminate automatic fire. The Argentinians used phosphorus grenades, which burst with a blinding flash and are liable to incinerate anyone within their immediate range. And then they had literally riddled each room with bullets. It was purely fortuitous that Norman and Noott had decided the barracks should be abandoned.

The commotion could be heard miles away. Norman, still on Lookout Rock, knew instantly that his worst fears had been realised and that, having outflanked the defences by landing so far south, the Argentinians could now reach Government House unopposed. He ordered the sections at the airport and at Hookers Point to fall back to the house immediately, and then raced there himself.

So too did Chief Secretary Dick Baker and his naval escort. But they had not yet completed their round-up of Argentinian civilians, largely because the 'gas workers' had been compliant but tardy. 'They kept asking bloody stupid questions, like could they bring their toothbrushes and should they pay their hotel bills,' said Baker. He was sure it had been a time-wasting ploy. And, as a result, several important Argentinians were still free. Hunt asked Baker if he would mind going out again to finish the job, this time on his own because the sailors were needed to reinforce the defences. Baker agreed and headed for the door. When he opened it, he was met with a hail of machine-gun bullets. He dodged back inside and told the governor he was sorry but he didn't think he could make it to his car. Hunt said not to worry; perhaps there would be a lull later on and Baker could then try again.

Norman did not immediately comprehend what was going on. He had got back to Government House without incident just moments before and he thought it was his own men – deployed in sniper positions around the building and in the gardens – who had started shooting. He ran out of the house shouting: 'Who fired those guns?' He very quickly realised the answer. The machine-gunner who had opened up on Baker had been one of the small advance party of *Buzo Tactico* sent to keep the heads down at Government House. Now the main party had arrived, after finishing their work at Moody Brook.

And now the attack began in deadly earnest.

From the ridge behind the house, hails of automatic fire peppered the building and, inside it, the water pipes, sending water cascading down into the kitchen. Those in the operations room got down on to the floor and looked for cover. Brian Wells, the governor's cypher clerk, tried to get under a sofa but his bulk was too large, so he joined Hunt who had found sanctuary under the table. The governor clutched his automatic pistol in one hand, determined to shoot anyone who came into the room, thinking: 'Hell, I just hope it isn't one of ours. I was just worried that I'd just shoot the wrong chap.' The cacophony of noise was stunning. Hunt found himself calmly contemplating his fate: 'I thought, well I've had a good enough life, the kids are just about off my hands and Mavis will be much happier without me dragging her around all these parts of the world when all she wants to do is to get back and settle in her house in Sunningdale and look after the garden, and I don't blame her, and she'll be able to do that. So I worked all this out and I was quite resigned.' Then, as the bedlam continued, Hunt reached for the telephone and asked the operator to put him through to the radio station once more, and Baker, who was lying on the floor, thought, 'How bloody bizarre, lead is flying about and there he is underneath the desk talking to this girl as if it's an ordinary Monday afternoon in the office.'

Outside, the thirty-three marines defending Government House were firing back at the ridge but with no great expectation because the Argentinians' guns were fitted with flash eliminators, and the British therefore had no clues as to where their targets were. Then from the copse, unseen hands began to hurl stun grenades.

In the brief light provided by the deafening explosions that followed, Corporal Mick Sellen, who had taken cover near the side of the staff quarters, saw three black-clad figures vault the wall of the vegetable garden and run towards the house. Sellen and two other marines cut them down with automatic fire. They did not see three more Argentinians who made it to the house, and climbed in through a window.

Suddenly, after twenty-five minutes, the firing from the ridge stopped. If the Argentinian plan had been for the *Buzo Tactico* alone to eliminate the marines and snatch the governor, thus allowing the main force to land 'peacefully', it had clearly failed. It was time for the reinforcements to be called in.

At Purple beach\Wilcox and Milne watched uneasily as a large ship, 'a black-masted thing', headed slowly towards them. At Navy Point Corporal York and his section could see it too, 'something that looked at first like people walking along the hilltop, gradually getting taller and taller until they turned into the masts of a ship.'

The ship did not stop off Purple beach, as the defence plan had predicted, but continued slowly on towards York Point, sailing parallel to the shore. Wilcox and Milne contemplated opening fire on it but they did not have a tripod for their machine-gun and, without that, the ship was probably out of their effective range. Instead they watched it pass beyond York Point, out of their sight, and then they heard the engines stop. They guessed – correctly, as it turned out – that the Argentinians intended to land at Orange beach, the one that had been left totally unguarded. Once that happened Wilcox and Milne would be cut off. They decided to 'withdraw' immediately.

They raced their motorbikes across the sand dunes to the airport – now abandoned since Corporal Duff and his section had, with some difficulty, withdrawn to Government House – and then continued on the road to Stanley. They did not see a soul until they reached the town where, in the main street outside the post office, a Land Rover and two sections of marines were blocking the road. Corporal 'Lew' Armour waved them down and told them that Government House was surrounded. Wilcox and Milne abandoned their bikes and joined up with Corporal David Carr's section with the ambition of breaking through the enemy cordon. As they approached Government House they heard voices and hid themselves in someone's front garden. From there they could make out a voice shouting in English: 'Mr Hunt, we know you are a sensible man. You are surrounded. There is no escape. Come out with your hands up.' There was a pause of a few seconds and then someone replied: 'Fuck off you spic bastards' – and there was a long burst of automatic rifle fire.

The marines, now numbering sixteen, decided to try and work their way around to the back of the ridge where the Argentinians were positioned, and then charge down to Government House, hopefully taking the enemy by surprise. But as they moved through the edges of the town they came under fire at every street corner and it was eventually so heavy they had to abandon their plan. There was also the sound of more firing coming from Government House. In the occasional silences, though, Wilcox could still hear shouted appeals: 'Mr Hunt, do be sensible ...'

The sixteen headed back for the post office but en route Corporal Armour decided that he and his section would have one more try at getting to Government House. Everyone thought he was crazy. Wilcox watched as the six men set off on the first part of their journey which took them across the town's football pitch, and almost immediately a machine-gun opened up on them, and Wilcox heard one of the men shout: 'You bastard, Armour, what have you got us into now.' But to everyone's surprise they made it to the safety of a hedgerow – and eventually, to Government House.

There, the battle had resumed as a sniping contest and now that dawn had arrived the Argentinians had lost some of their advantage in that the marines could at least see their targets. But it remained a desperately dangerous business. Norman, lying in the main doorway, spotted one enemy sniper on the ridge and told his radio operator, Robbie Farnworth, to shoot him. Farnworth duly let off three rounds, the barrel of his gun so close to Norman's ear it practically deafened him. 'Stop it, Farnworth, let him live,' he said. There was another very loud bang: 'If you fire that bloody weapon again, I'll wrap it round your neck,' said Norman. Farnworth protested that *he* was not the culprit – and pointed out a smoking hole in the woodwork, no more than an inch from Norman's head.

Colour Sergeant Bill Muir who had taken charge of the ammunition truck, and cover behind it, heard a hissing noise that sounded like the fuse of something explosive. It turned out to be air escaping from one of the tyres that had been hit by rifle fire. But afterwards he discovered that the truck itself was riddled and even the grenades had holes drilled through them; he could not imagine why he hadn't been blown sky high.

Inside the house Dick Baker sat on the floor and found himself worrying about utterly inconsequential things: the damage that he was doing to his Marks & Spencer suit; the fact that during the lull in the fighting he had nodded off to sleep.

In contrast the governor, from his position under the desk, tirelessly made telephone calls to conveniently placed islanders to monitor the enemy's progress. At 7.10 a.m. he called the radio station yet again to announce the very disturbing news that the Argentinian reinforcements on their way to Government House now included Amtracs – tracked armoured personnel carriers – fitted with 30mm cannons.

They had first been reported by Marine Berry, still maintaining his lone vigil on Sapper Hill. He saw them grinding ashore at Orange beach, and eventually counted eighteen of them. As they headed off in the direction of Stanley, Berry saw helicopters landing at the airport bringing in wave after wave of steel-helmeted troops.

The Amtracs' route to Government House inevitably took them through a section of Stanley known as White City where Lieutenant Bill Trollope and Section Two were now covering the airport road. The governor had decreed that, for the sake of civilians, there was to be no fighting in Stanley itself but since White City consisted of just five prefabricated bungalows – all painted white, hence the name – Trollope decided it was permissible to make a stand. His men waited until the leading Amtrac was no more than 300 yards from them, and then opened up with an anti-tank gun and rockets. They hit it twice, and saw no one emerge from the wreckage before they hastily withdrew through the prefabs' rear gardens. (Return fire from the surviving Amtracs hit the five houses but, luckily, none of the civilians inside was hurt.)

But plainly the struggle was now so thoroughly unequal that resistance could not last very much longer. At the post office, Corporal Carr's section, supplemented by Wilcox and Milne, learned of the advancing Amtracs and troop reinforcements, and realised they were trapped unless they could somehow get across Stanley Harbour and take to the hills. They could see that the vessel *Forrest* was moored alongside the jetty below them, and Jack Sollis had lowered a Gemini inflatable boat that might provide the means of escape. The men decided to make a dash for it; as they did they could hear the first Amtrac approaching.

In full kit they ran to the jetty, clambered over *Forrest*'s deck, dropped into the Gemini – and found that the engine would not start. Marine Marcus Bennet pulled at the starter like a man possessed, but it was hopeless. And then an Argentinian helicopter appeared immediately over them and Wilcox thought, thank God for a faulty engine because he was sure if it had started they would have been blown out of the water. Corporal Carr ordered his men on to *Forrest* but Jack Sollis refused to set sail. The marines went below to await their fate.

Meanwhile at Navy Point, Corporal York similarly decided it was time for his section to disappear. He had planned to wait for nightfall, but having watched the Argentinians land at Orange beach and at the airport he decided he did not have that long.

His men booby-trapped their heavy weapons by putting armed phosphorus grenades down the barrels, and then York told Government House they were 'going covert', before smashing the radio on a rock. (He actually said, 'Gone fishing', a small joke based on something Norman had said back in England when his marines asked what would happen if the Argentinians invaded: 'We'll go fishing,' said Norman.)

As the men ran down from Navy Point to where their Gemini was hidden someone opened fire on them with the result that when they reached the boat, York said later: 'You've never seen guys paddle like it in your life.' Once free of the kelp they started the engine and headed north – to find themselves pursued by an enemy destroyer. They could only prevent the destroyer from ramming them by heading straight for a Polish factory ship which happened to be moored in the bay. York briefly considered asking the Poles for political ayslum, but thought better of it. They reached the northern shore, hid the Gemini in the rocks and made their escape on foot.

Hunt went on the radio and conceded that with 30mm cannons ranged against them they did not stand a chance. He would, therefore, talk to the enemy he said, but 'I'm not surrendering to the bloody Argies.'

But the logic was against him. Norman had told the governor that the Argentinians could simply sit out of his men's range and reduce Government House to rubble with their cannons. (That is not to say Norman was in favour of surrender. He would have preferred an attempt to break through enemy lines, taking the governor along, in the hope of escaping into the Camp, but there was now precious little chance of that scheme succeeding.) So Hunt decided he would at least talk to the enemy, via a suitable intermediary. The most obvious candidate was vice commodore Hector Gilobert, who had lived on the Falklands for two years running LADE – a quasi-civil airline, operated by the Argentinian air force. (It was to the great suspicion of the islanders that Britain had given LADE the right to operate the only air link with the South American mainland.) Gilobert was, by fortuitous accident, one of the Argentinians whom Dick Baker had not had time to arrest.

Through the ever-helpful telephone operator, Hunt found Gilobert, and found him contrite: 'He was really so upset. He was crying. He was so apologetic he could hardly get a word out. He said: "I didn't want this to happen, I assure you, Governor, Your Excellency" – he always got formal. "I assure you, your Excellency, that I did not know anything about it. I did not know anything." I said: come off it, Hector, you must have known. Go and tell your commander I want to talk.'

Guilty or not, Gilobert agreed to go to Government House for discussions on the promise from Hunt that the British marines would hold their fire. In an effort to get the Argentinians to do the same Norman shouted at the ridge: 'Vice Commodore coming, hold your fire.' But it is doubtful if he was understood because when, some ten minutes later, Gilobert arrived at the main door, he was fired upon by his fellow countrymen, and he stumbled into the hallway ashen-faced and trembling.

Not surprisingly then, he was little attracted by the governor's proposition that he should retrace his steps into town and attempt to locate 'whoever is in charge of this lot out here'. To make matters worse, the three *Buzo Tactico* commandos who had got into Government House some three hours before, and who had since been hiding in the maids' quarters, chose that moment to move. It was Major Gary Noott who heard them moving about upstairs. Noott is the antithesis of his friend Norman: shy, balding, and neither very tall nor apparently aggressive. But he is not a major in the Royal Marines by accident and his instant reaction to the noises above was to put a burst of automatic fire through the ceiling. When that produced shouts of alarm, in Spanish, he fired again. Moments later the three Argentinians ran down the stairs, their hands in the air.

That excitement over, Baker offered to accompany Gilobert on his mission and in time the vice commodore was persuaded. Hunt prepared a white flag of truce. He tore down the bullet-riddled lace curtains from his office window and tied them around the umbrella that he invariably carried. Armed with that, Baker and Gilobert gingerly stuck their heads out of the door and, when nothing happened, set off in search of Argentinians. As they walked down the road towards Stanley, someone fired a couple of shots, but Baker decided they were not the targets and they kept going. They saw nobody at all until they got into the centre of Stanley where, from the police station, two policemen emerged to ask them what on earth they thought they were doing. They explained their plan, and the policemen said they were mad and that seemed possible because renewed heavy gunfire could be heard coming from Government House; Baker thought: 'Christ, we're too late, the sods are shooting up the house already.'

Baker decided they should stay where they were, in the middle of the street, in the hope that somebody would show up, but nobody did. So, in the end, at the policemen's suggestion, Baker and Gilobert went and telephoned the radio station and spoke to Patrick Watts who broadcast Gilobert's appeal for someone in authority to come and talk to them. An age seemed to pass, but eventually three men – who looked to Baker like characters from an American war film – emerged from behind the Upland Goose Hotel. One of them turned out to be Admiral Carlos Busser, deputy commander of the invasion force. He greeted Gilobert warmly and then agreed with Baker that they should all go to Government House. As they walked line abreast up the road, steel-helmeted men appeared from their positions on the ridge and began chanting something which sounded to Baker like 'chi-i-king'; he soon realised that their chant was 'Ar-gen-tina'. There was a bad moment when someone opened fire on the group, but Admiral Busser merely stopped and shouted a command of extraordinary volume. The firing immediately ceased. Busser turned to Baker and said: 'Ah, the age of electronic communication.'

The little delegation reached Government House without further incident. By that time the governor had tidied the operations room somewhat and taken up his position behind the desk, not under it. Admiral Busser was shown in and wanted to shake hands but Hunt said he was not going to do that with someone who had invaded his territory; he ordered Busser 'and all your people' to quit the Falklands immediately. Failing that, Hunt said, there should be a truce to allow attention for the wounded. (The three commandos who had been cut down at the beginning of the battle as they tried to break into the house were still lying where they fell. At least one of them was alive because every time the marines attempted to reach him, he threatened to release the armed grenade he held in his hand.)

Busser tried reason. The Argentinians had only come to take back 'what is rightfully ours' he said and, anyway, they had come in such overwhelmingly superior force there was nothing Hunt and his marines could do about it, except die. And if the fighting went on, civilians might also get hurt. The marines had fought with bravery and skill, Busser said. They had killed one of his best captains. Now, they should lay down their arms.

The appeal succeeded in that the governor decided he had no choice but to accept the inevitable. And at 9.25 a.m. – as the radio broadcast *British* martial music – he ordered Norman to surrender. The marines at Government House laid down their arms and Major Noott was sent, under escort, to round up the remaining sections scattered around Stanley, and Corporal Carr's men who were still lying low aboard *Forrest*.

(As for Corporal York and his men, after a couple of miserable days in the Camp, they gave themselves up.) As a result, Norman discovered that his men had not suffered a single casualty: on the other hand, in the course of firing 6,462 rounds, they had killed five (two confirmed), wounded seventeen (two confirmed), taken three prisoners and knocked out an Amtrac. 'We came second', Norman said, 'but at least we won the body count.'

At 10 a.m., or thereabouts, the Union Jack was lowered, to be replaced by the blue and white flag of Argentina.

We will return again to the invasion because there were other heroes and other events of extraordinary drama – and absurdity. We will also return to Major Norman and his marines because that morning the marines vowed to each other that they would see the Union Jack flying over Stanley again – and some of them did.

But first we must look at the decisions and the failures that led to the invasion.

CHAPTER TWO

The Yawning Gap

'Argentina maintains the right to
end the system.'
– Gustavo Figueroa, March 1, 1982

The talks that were destined to decide the future of the Falklands had been planned with diplomatic *savoir faire*. They were also intended to be thoroughly civilised.

The idea was for a two-day conference in New York with each side acting as host on alternate days. The Argentinians would take charge on the first day, Friday, February 26, 1982, in their luxurious offices on the twenty-fifth floor at One UN Plaza. There would be a long break for lunch at Le Perigord, a delightful restaurant at 405 East 52nd Street specialising in gourmet food from the south-west of France. Then, on Saturday, the British would take over in their tenth floor offices at 845 Third Avenue, with lunch at La Côte Basque at 5 East 55th Street, another French restaurant, whose menu offered a distinctively different regional cuisine.

But at the last minute there was a hitch. The British could not get the heating turned on in their building at the weekend, so they asked if the dates could be switched. It was too late to change the restaurant bookings, so the Argentinians conceded that the British could preside on the first day, though *they* would still host the Perigord lunch. The British could pick up the tab at La Côte Basque on the second day.

It was just about the last agreement the two sides managed to reach.

Although the talks were later to be described by Britain's prime minister, Margaret Thatcher, as 'cordial', and by Lord Carrington, her foreign secretary, as producing an 'agreement', neither statement reflects what actually happened. So badly did the discussions go in fact that at one point the head of the British delegation, Richard Luce, feared they would break down altogether.

The problem was reflected in the expectations each side had as they went into the conference. For the British delegation, headed by Luce, a junior minister at the foreign and commonwealth office, accompanied by two officials, the idea, crudely speaking, was to stall. Britain had no concessions of substance to make on the future of the Falklands, so all they could offer was a promise that talks would continue. The Argentinian delegation, headed by the debonair Enrique Ros, deputy foreign minister, saw things in a somewhat different light. For them the talks were to be a watershed: the crucial test of Britain's intentions towards the Falklands (or Malvinas as they knew them). If Britain would agree to a serious programme, with a deadline for a decision on sovereignty, then that would be acceptable. It would involve the setting up of a negotiating commission; a fixed schedule of monthly meetings, with agreed agendas for each; and a target date of the year's end for a decision. Ros had been instructed by his government to return with a substantial commitment to these goals.

Just in case anyone had forgotten whom the talks affected most, there was another party present round the table: the Falkland Islanders themselves. They were represented by John Cheek, a member of the islands' legislative council, and by a Falklands farmer, Tony Blake. 'They were the conscience of the British,' said one of those who took part. 'They were just there to remind us all of what this was about.'

The first day was spent in wary discussion (though lunch at Le Perigord was voted excellent). It saw only one positive decision: the British agreed to the setting up of a negotiating commission empowered to look into sovereignty, among other things. Luce was convinced that this gave the Argentinians the 'substance' of what they were after. But it left out any mention of a fixed timetable.

As to when the commission should meet and how often, all Luce could do was object to the various Argentinian suggestions: once a month was far too often (the Falklanders would be in the air almost permanently); April 1 was a bad date for the first meeting (Luce mentioned April Fools Day); a deadline by the end of the year was quite unacceptable; and finally, anything agreed by him was subject to cabinet approval back in London.

Ros took these rejections hard. Lunch at La Côte Basque was ruined as he stalked to the telephone to ring up Buenos Aires to speak to his boss, Foreign Minister Nicanor Costa Mendez. The call was long and voluble. In the end Ros was instructed not to walk out, but he was to insist on something more positive to bring home. He demanded British cabinet approval of a deal within three weeks, and he said the negotiating commission should meet as soon as possible. The British hedged. Neither side felt that they had achieved much.

Looking back, much later, on those crucial two days which were to determine so much of what followed, one British official was struck by the yawning gap that existed, not only between the two sides, but between the negotiators in New York and their governments at home. It was a failure of communication that was to mark much of what happened over the next few fateful weeks.

'We did not appreciate, I think, the kind of pressure Ros was under from Buenos Aires,' said the official. 'But I think we got some way in explaining to him the realities of political feelings in London.'

Luce, an agreeable politician from a distinguished diplomatic family, spent most of the second afternoon spelling out to Ros, who listened patiently enough, just how strongly the British Tory Party at home felt about the Falklands. He emphasised that the Falklanders themselves were extremely keen to remain British, that the British public were behind them, and that members of parliament considered any concessions unacceptable. The government's freedom of action was limited by these three factors. If they were ever to sell a deal to these three groups, then they needed help from Buenos Aires. But Luce appears to have misjudged one thing: he was convinced that *the negotiating commission* was the key to the talks, whereas in reality what mattered to the Argentinians was *the timetable*. In Buenos Aires they wanted quick action. Patience had run out. Anything less than an agreed deadline would be seen as procrastination.

The final communiqué revealed little of this dislocation of views. Issued jointly on March 1, it spoke of the 'cordial and positive spirit' in which the meeting had taken place; and then it went on: 'The two sides reaffirmed their resolve to find a solution to the sovereignty dispute and considered in detail an Argentine proposal for procedures to make better progress in this sense. They agreed to inform their governments accordingly.'

But Luce did not fool himself that things were going to be easy from now on. That Sunday he flew to Washington and, next day, called on Thomas Enders, assistant secretary of state for Latin American affairs at the state department.

The role played by Tom Enders in the Falklands saga was to be a crucial one. It was also much misunderstood – not least by the British foreign office who suspected him of being too close to the Argentinians for their liking.

An immensely tall (six foot eight inches) and extremely clever foreign service and intelligence officer, Enders was summed up by his admiring boss, the secretary of state Alexander Haig, as a 'can-do personality' who believed in practical action rather than ideology. *The New York Times* described him as 'brilliant, intimidating ... an imposing figure who is no stranger to controversy'.

That controversy had followed him from Yugoslavia, where his assertive nature led to a blinding row with his own ambassador and a request that he should be shipped back to Washington; to Cambodia, where he approved bombing targets for American B-52s; to El Salvador, where he supported US aid for the military authorities.

In each case Enders's motives had been those of the professional diplomatist. He judged what would best serve US interests at the time, then did it. When it came to Argentina, his interest lay in building an economically sound and politically stable ally for the United States.

He was not at all close to the Argentinian leaders – his background was European rather than Latin American. But he was interested in the grand design of a pro-western alliance throughout Latin America. And Argentina, he believed, had a large part to play in this.

When Richard Luce walked through his door at the state department that Monday morning, Tom Enders could hardly pretend to an over-riding interest in the Falkland Islands; indeed, he scarcely knew where they were. But since he was due to travel to Argentina later that week, he listened sympathetically as Luce explained about the New York talks and about the impatience of the Argentinians who were, he said, getting 'more bristly and hawkish' all the time. If Enders could urge them 'at the highest level' to keep on talking, he, Luce, would be most grateful. The message to be delivered essentially was: 'Cool it.'

Enders asked only one question, but it was an important one: were the British, he asked, actually interested in a negotiated solution? Luce said they were. Enders said that in that case he would pass on the message to Buenos Aires.

The significance of the exchange was this: in diplomatic language, Luce's reply meant that Britain was willing to explore the means whereby Argentina might eventually achieve their goal of sovereignty over the islands, and that, if they were patient, they would get it. Coming from an American source, the message would carry some weight. Just in case Luce's pitch was not strong enough, two days later a brief telegram arrived for Enders from Lord Carrington saying simply that he reinforced the view given by his junior minister, Luce.

On March 8, Enders delivered the British message directly to the foreign minister, Costa Mendez, in Buenos Aires, and later that day to Enrique Ros, now returned from New York. Costa Mendez listened, then gave a non-committal reply to the request to keep diplomacy going. 'He did not say yes, and he did not say no,' commented one US official. When Enders met Ros he was given a long lecture on the Malvinas, and told that the Argentinians were waiting for a British response. 'We are not prepared to let things drag on indefinitely,' he concluded. Enders murmured something about the problems of solving the difficult aftermath of empire, but did not reiterate Luce's assurances.

This was the message that Enders transmitted – faithfully, he maintains – back to London. He had not, it is true, done exactly what the British had asked him. He had not transmitted their assurances 'at the highest level' (he had not, for instance, mentioned them to President Galtieri whom he had also seen), and he had not added any American pressure to reinforce the message. But then no one had given him the impression that it was anything like an emergency.

The British, however, were later to make a more damaging accusation. They claimed that Enders had sent a reassuring and optimistic message back to London from the Argentinians, one that said, in effect, there was no need to worry. And they maintained that this helped give a false impression of Argentina's intentions.

That is unfair: Enders's reply was simply a factual report of what he had been told. He had not picked up any overt warning but he had not glossed over what he had been told either. The interpretation of what he sent was entirely a British responsibility.

This was to be only the first of many misunderstandings by Britain which would colour the next few weeks. But even if Enders had gone further and attempted to give the British a deeper insight into the current thinking of the Argentinian government, it is doubtful if a much clearer picture would have emerged. For although the country's leaders had a fixed view about their ultimate goal on the Falklands, there was little certainty at that point about how they should now proceed. The mood in Buenos Aires was angry but imprecise.

The decision to recover the Malvinas Islands, by force if necessary, had been taken secretly in early December by President Leopoldo Galtieri and his naval commander Admiral Jorge Anaya. That decision had been accepted by the air force commander Brigadier Basilio Lami Dozo, and it had been endorsed by Argentina's foreign minister Nicanor Costa Mendez later the same month. It became operative following the break-up of the New York talks in February 1982.

If this sequence of events suggests careful and considered planning, however, it is misleading. The Argentinian leaders were divided and uncertain over nearly everything concerning an invasion, from its timing and consequences, to the more profound question of why it should be carried out in the first place. It is possible to argue that they were as guilty of misjudging the issue as the foreign office in London was naïve in reading the signs that it was coming to a head.

But there is no question that they were determined to have the islands back again.

The task of preparing the Argentinian people for an invasion had begun in late December 1981 when Costa Mendez began briefing a close circle of senior journalists about the government's intentions. Argentina, he said, was determined to regain the Falklands by the end of 1982. By diplomacy if possible, by force if necessary. He went into considerable detail about the type of military invasion which might be necessary.

On January 17, the influential columnist Jesus Iglesias Ruoca, writing in Argentina's leading paper, *La Prensa*, drew a parallel between the Beagle Channel in the far south of Argentina, long disputed with neighbouring Chile, and the Malvinas. Both, he said, were crucial to the defence of the South Atlantic, but taking the Malvinas by force was 'a far less costly option than war with Chile, and one which would enjoy an international consensus'.

27

A week later he went further. On January 24 he wrote: 'The United States ... would support all acts leading to restitution [of the Malvinas], including military ones ... As far as the UK is concerned, there might be a freezing of relations for a while, but in the context of western strategic interests it seems improbable that the situation would be prolonged.' The time, he added, was opportune. There were no more than about eighty armed men on the island.

Perhaps even more significantly, three days later, on January 27, the daily newspaper *Conviccion*, which accurately reflects the thinking of the Argentinian navy, ran a long leading article on the whole subject. It concluded that the taking of the Malvinas would actually help resolve the Beagle Channel issue since it would strengthen Argentina's negotiating hand. 'Right now,' it said, 'conditions are at their best. We have a decisive president and an excellent foreign minister. If, having won the war against terrorism, we recover the Malvinas, history will forgive the economic stupidities ... Argentina will be alive, conscious of its vigour and disposed to take its place in the world.'

By this stage, according to Ruoca, government sources were being open with trusted journalists about the possibility of an invasion soon. 'They talked about it as an accepted fact,' he said. 'The plan was that if negotiations got nowhere there would be an invasion by July.'

On March 1, the joint communiqué, issued by Ros and Luce, was announced to the Argentinian press, to be greeted loudly by them as yet another British prevarication.

That afternoon, even before Ros could return to Buenos Aires to give a detailed briefing on the talks, a press conference was called at the ornate Palacio San Martin, where a statement was read out by Gustavo Figueroa, Costa Mendez's right-hand man. 'If a solution should not be reached,' he told the assembled reporters, 'Argentina maintains the right to end the system and freely choose the procedure it may deem most convenient to its interest.'

To the British – and indeed to Ros who was furious that he had not been consulted – that looked very different from the communiqué they hoped had been agreed upon in New York. In the House of Commons, Richard Luce admitted it was 'disappointing'. But compared to the comments from Argentinian newspapers it was mild. 'If you had seen the reaction of the press to the New York statement, you would have seen why we had to produce something a bit harder,' said a foreign ministry official in Buenos Aires.

That was ingenuous: the press comments he referred to had been busily inspired by the government staff.

Within that government the one man who was undoubtedly most single-minded in his determination to recapture the Malvinas, and who was most disposed to use force to do it, was Admiral Jorge Isaac Anaya, the 55-year-old navy commander. A small, dapper figure with a lifetime's service as a naval officer behind him, Anaya comes from the naval town of Bahia Blanca, and his career in the navy had reinforced his rigid right-wing nationalism. To Anaya the future of the navy and the future of Argentina were inextricably and irrevocably linked.

What worried Anaya most about the future capability of the navy was the rapidly approaching settlement of the Beagle Channel dispute with Argentina's neighbour and traditional enemy, Chile. It seemed likely to confirm Chile as an Atlantic as well as a Pacific power and to deprive Argentina of the chance to dominate the great shipping route around Cape Horn. The importance of the Channel was as much symbolic as strategic. Western strategists had long argued that the Cape was no longer of major importance, but to Argentinians, and especially to the navy, it offered a stage on which to play a truly global role.

For years Argentina had claimed the disputed islands of the Beagle Channel. In 1979, the Pope had agreed to Argentina's request to mediate, and in 1980, had delivered a secret ruling. A long Argentinian silence did not disguise the fact that the Pope had decided in favour of Chile. The navy grew increasingly worried about the lack of operating bases in the south – the only one they could boast was the port of Ushuaia in Tierra del Fuego, and access to that lies directly beneath the shore guns of Chile.

Anaya had turned to the Malvinas as an alternative. His interest in them was of long standing. As head of the navy he had taken part in one of the basic planning exercises the Argentinian navy conducts: the recovery of the islands. Each year the plan had been dusted off and given a run-through, ready for the day when the exercise became a reality.

The attraction of the islands to Anaya was that from there his navy could not only provide a southern base, it could control the Cape Horn route and stay safely clear of Chilean firepower.

This, then, was Anaya's dream when, in July 1981, his close friend Leopoldo Galtieri began to manoeuvre for power under the presidency of Robert Eduardo Viola. As the plotting went on Anaya pledged his support to Galtieri and when, on December 22, Viola stood down and Galtieri succeeded to the presidency, Anaya was there by his side. The new president was heavily in his debt.

The friendship between the two men meant something else: for the first time since the military regime was established in 1976, the rivalry between the army and the navy, with the navy constantly playing the injured underdog, was removed. Between them the two forces could perhaps achieve something remarkable for Argentina.

Galtieri's interest in the Malvinas was of a different nature from Anaya's. He saw them as a short-cut to popularity. The military, after five years in power, was almost completely discredited; the economy was in serious disarray; the beginnings of public unrest could be discerned; there was even dissent in the armed forces. The junta badly needed a success.

Between Anaya and Galtieri, therefore, the objective became firm. 1983 would mark the 150th anniversary of Britain's seizure of the Falklands. What more popular emblem could be offered to the people than the promise that before 150 years of 'colonial rule' were over, the beloved Malvinas would be returned to Argentinian sovereignty?

The third member of the junta, Brigadier Basilio Lami Dozo, was not disposed to disagree, though his approach to the issue, as it later turned out, was to be far less belligerent than theirs. To him, too, the recovery of the Malvinas made sound political sense, and since he was determined that the military should salvage its political reputation, he was content to support the idea. With the objective now firmly in mind, the junta set about picking their team.

In mid-December Galtieri approached Costa Mendez, a man who, since a brief spell as foreign minister in the 1960s, had been closely associated with the problem of the Malvinas. Known and respected as an intellectual, a fervent nationalist, and strongly pro-western, Costa Mendez seemed an ideal choice.

To begin with he was reluctant to become foreign minister again, but when Galtieri put it to him that he now stood on the verge of going down in history as the man who restored the Malvinas to Argentina, the offer proved irresistible. Costa Mendez accepted. As it turned out, the appointment was to be disastrous. For one thing his assessment of how Britain and America would react to the seizing of the islands was fatally misjudged. For another thing he appears to have misunderstood the true objectives of his fellow plotters.

Both Galtieri and Anaya saw the taking of the Malvinas as an end in itself – for the president, a glorious objective, for Anaya a strategic triumph. For Costa Mendez it was an exercise in diplomacy. The landing itself, if carried out with a minimum of violence, would help tip the ultimate sovereignty of the Malvinas irrevocably in Argentina's favour. With the careful preparation of international opinion, and the neutral station of the United States, coupled with a suitable stress on Argentina's willingness to negotiate generous terms, an international row, in Costa Mendez's estimation, could be avoided.

He was wrong. Just how wrong, Costa Mendez was to realise, well before the others, on a warm April day in 1982, as he watched his president on the balcony of the Casa Rosada inciting an ecstatic crowd in the square below as he told them that their moment of triumph had come. Suddenly Costa Mendez would know that Galtieri had something very different in mind than an act of diplomacy. In that moment of realisation Costa Mendez would offer his resignation in anger and despair. But by then it would be too late.

For now Costa Mendez offered his assessment of the likely reactions throughout the world to an armed invasion. The questions he addressed himself to were: how will Britain react to losing the Falkland Islands by military action? Will the United States approve, stay neutral, or intervene? And how will Latin America react?

The answers he provided were almost entirely wrong. They were to be as misleading in the end as Britain's own assessment of Argentina's intentions. They were to lead directly to a war. And they would result in great suffering and loss of life. Just why both countries miscalculated so badly is the key to the entire Falklands crisis. In order to understand what happened, it is necessary to know something of the Falkland Islands themselves, and the troubled role they have played in the history of both Britain and Argentina.

CHAPTER THREE

The Rights and Wrongs of History

'Fortune often delights to dignify
what nature has neglected, and that
renown which cannot be claimed by
intrinsick excellence or greatness,
is sometimes derived from unexpected
accidents. The Rubicon was ennobled
by the passage of Caesar, and the
time is now come when Falkland's
Islands demand their historian.'
– Dr Samuel Johnson, 1771

On April 1, only hours before the invasion of the Falklands, the United
Nations' security council assembled in New York to listen to the grave
concern of Sir Anthony Parsons, Britain's ambassador to the UN. 'We
have evidence,' he said, 'that the Argentine navy is about to launch an
invasion, possibly as early as tomorrow morning . . . we ask the council
to call upon the government of Argentina to exercise the utmost
restraint and to refrain from the use of threat or force in the South
Atlantic.'

Then came the speech of the Argentinian ambassador, Senor
Eduardo Roca, who also managed to sound injured and in the right.
Only in Senor Roca's case, the hurt derived not from that week's
events in the South Atlantic – or from last month's or last year's or
those of the year before. Senor Roca rumbled in Spanish through a list
of dates that were roughly contemporaneous with George Stephen-
son's early attempts at steam locomotion; 1820, 1823, 1826, 1828, June
10, 1829. He mentioned sail-driven warships by name. He referred to
Viscount Palmerston. And then he reached the climactic month –
January 1833 – when 'in yet another episode of British violence'
Britain seized and 'brutally occupied' the Falkland Islands.

Sir Anthony replied with the bland aloofness of Lord Palmerston
himself. 'My Argentine colleague and I could debate endlessly the
rights and wrongs of history,' he said, 'and I doubt whether we would
agree.'

The British themselves seemed confident about the rights.
According to Francis Pym, Britain's new foreign secretary, Her

Majesty's Government was 'not in any doubt about our title to the Falkland Islands and we never have been.' But Pym was being less than frank – as, over the centuries, have been many of his predecessors. For, as we shall see, Britain has not been slow to fudge or omit the historical facts which might hamper the British claim to sovereignty. Neither has Argentina. The Falklands, despite their remoteness, have in their time unsettled some of the great and famous names of European history: the elder Pitt as well as the young Palmerston, George III and Louis XV, Madame du Barry and Dr Samuel Johnson.

The 200 islands in the Falkland group lie about 480 miles north-east of Cape Horn, straddling the line of 52 degrees latitude and comprising about 4,700 square miles of land, an area roughly two-thirds the size of Wales. Rock formations and fossil finds suggest that in prehistory the islands might have formed part of the same land mass as southern Africa; the remains of ancient tree stumps, on the other hand, suggest close connections to South America. There is no evidence that, before the European settlements of the eighteenth century, the islands were ever inhabited other than by multitudes of seals and sea birds. The only indigenous quadruped, the Falkland Fox (Charles Darwin named it *canis antarctica*), became extinct in the 1870s.

The arguments begin with their discovery. The British view – held by the British foreign office and repeated without question in almost every British history of the subject – is that the British navigator, John Davis (of Davis Straits and North-West Passage fame), first sighted the islands in 1592 when his ship was 'driven among certain isles never before discovered by any known relation, lying fifty leagues (150 nautical miles) or better from the shoare east and northerly from the Streights (the Straits of Magellan)'. Several non-British historians, however, believe that the islands may have first been sighted by Amerigo Vespucci almost a century earlier, in April 1502, when gales drove his ship so far down the Atlantic that 'the southern pole stood quite fifty-two degrees above our horizon'. Vespucci goes on to record that, soon after, his ship ran along the coast of some unknown land for twenty leagues: 'wholly a rough coast, seen fitfully'.

But it is the next sighting, allegedly by Sir Richard Hawkins, which is the more contentious claim. A pamphlet produced by Britain's Central Office of Information shortly after the Argentinian invasion – in late April 1982 – once again credits this feat to Hawkins in 1594. But did Hawkins ever see the Falklands at all? According to his account, written twenty-five years after the event, he sailed along 'threescore leagues of coast . . . the land is goodly champion country and peopled; we saw many fires but could not come to speake with the people. This I have sorrowed for many times since, for that it had likelihood to be an excellent country. It hath great rivers of fresh water, for the outshoot of them colours the sea in many places . . . it is not mountaynous, but much of the disposition of England and as temperate.'

This does not sound anything like the Falklands; they are not, as Hawkins also describes them, 'a goodly low countrie'; they have no great rivers; and when Hawkins sailed, the Falklands had still to wait another 160 years for their first human settlement. It is much more likely that Hawkins had simply sailed along a piece of the Patagonian coast and spotted the fires of the Patagonian Indians.

It was a Dutchman, in fact, who first plotted the position of the islands with any precision. In 1600, Sebald de Wert sighted a group of three islands which later proved out-liers of the then uncharted West Falkland. De Wert christened them the Sebalds (they are now the Jasons) and they soon made their appearance on Dutch maps of the early seventeenth century.

But it was Spain which held (or imagined it held) the legal title to all land discovered or undiscovered in the region. The Treaty of Tordesillas, signed in 1494 between Spain and Portugal and promoted by Pope Alexander VI, had conveniently divided the New World into Spanish and Portuguese spheres of discovery. The demarcation line ran from pole to pole through a point about 1,200 miles west of the Cape Verde islands: Spain held the title of the territory to the west, Portugal of the land to the east. True, Spanish resolve to defend this entitlement had been weakened by the rise of English sea-power, but Spain was still sensitive to evidence of foreign encroachment – a fact which Britain recognised until well into the eighteenth century.

In 1690 an English sea captain, Captain John Strong from Plymouth, became known as the first recorded man (certainly the first recorded Englishman) to step ashore on the Falklands. Captain Strong, who was bound for the South Seas where he was to conduct 'general reprisals against the French King', sailed down the sound which separates East and West Falkland. He called it 'Falkland's Sound' after Lord Falkland, commissioner of the admiralty, and on January 27, 1690, put ashore to inspect the immense amounts of kelp, geese and 'pengwins'. In Strong's wake came increasing numbers of Frenchmen. By the early eighteenth century the British were calling the islands 'the Falklands'. But the French stuck to their own name. They called them after their home port of St Malo, the Iles Malouines, which later became in Spanish Las Malvinas. Between 1698 and 1712, French captains had charted enough of their north coast for the islands to be rendered, fairly accurately, in the first map known to show the Falklands as well as the Sebalds, published by the French cartographer Frezier in St Malo in 1716.

Discovery was one thing; occupation quite another. For more than seventy years after Strong landed, no European country seems to have considered either encouraging or forcing people to go and live there. The islands were cold, treeless, remote, and thought likely to be economically unproductive. But, as the eighteenth century wore on, three nations began to see their potential significance. Successive wars stripped France of most of her colonies and threatened Spain's grip on South America. Some Frenchmen saw the Malouines as offering them a fresh colonial start. Spain determined to possess them as an example of her will to resist further encroachment. And Britain, rapidly emerging as the most powerful nation in Europe (thanks largely to the wars that Spain and France had lost), reckoned that they might be a useful, strategic tool of expansion, a base from which to protect Britain's growing trade routes.

In 1745, Lord Anson returned to Britain from a successful war against Spanish shipping in the South Atlantic, carrying with him £500,000 in Spanish booty. He urged the admiralty to investigate the potential of the Falklands. Four years later the Duke of Bedford, one of the king's ministers, wrote to the British ambassador in Madrid and asked him to sound out the views of the Spanish court on a British expedition which was already being prepared on the Thames. Britain, wrote the duke, intended to send sloops to undertake 'a full discovery of the Falkland Islands [but] there is no intention of making a settlement in either of these islands.' When this was put before the Spanish minister, Carvajal, he is said to have replied: 'Then what do you want to discover them for?' Spanish disfavour led Britain to cancel the expedition, and it was not until 1764 that Captain John Byron, the grandfather of the poet, left England with a frigate and a sloop and a royal commission. This time Britain kept the expedition's purpose secret; when the ships left they were alleged to be bound for the China Seas.

Byron entered the bay at Saunders Island, off West Falkland, on January 15, 1765, and named it Port Egmont after the first lord of the admiralty. Byron was an optimist by nature, with some of his grandson's gift for poetic licence. At Port Egmont, he wrote, 'the whole navy of England might ride in perfect security from the winds'. The climate and the soil were also good (according to Byron) and a surgeon from the sloop *Tamar* fenced off a plot of ground and planted it with vegetables. And then the British ships sailed off, with Byron naming a few rocks and headlands in East Falkland before setting course for the Straits of Magellan.

Had Byron made a more thorough investigation he might have discovered an alarming fact: the French already had a settlement – rather more than a vegetable plot – on East Falkland. There a young French nobleman called Antoine de Bougainville had raised the flag on February 3, 1764, and on April 5, 1764, he and his colonists held a 'ceremony of possession' at their new fort and settlement of Port (or Fort) Louis.

Britain remained ignorant of the French colony, or at least pretended to be so, and in September 1765 dispatched a further expedition to 'immediately complete the settlement begun last year at Port Egmont ... and if any lawless persons should happen to be found seated on any part of the said islands, they are to be compelled either to quit ... or to take oaths, acknowledge and submit themselves to His Majesty's Government as subjects of the Crown of Great Britain.'

Captain John McBride was the man charged with these instructions and he found he had soon to use them. In December 1766, he stumbled upon the French colony during a voyage to East Falkland and was amazed by the sight of houses, fortifications and people, who by now numbered 250. The French were at first baffled and then angered by McBride's peremptory notes – issued from the safety of his ship – which ordered them to quit or swear allegiance to George III. They did neither. Early in 1767, after British marines had erected a wooden blockhouse at Port Egmont, McBride set sail for England with the bad news. Captain Anthony Hunt and a small British force were left behind in the Falklands.

As it happened, McBride need not have felt so sore at the French, for the Port Louis colony (though its colonists did not yet know it) had been sold to Spain in October 1766. De Bougainville had come under pressure to sell from the French court, which was anxious to placate Spain as France's ally. He had gone to Madrid and negotiated a price of 618,108 livres (about £250,000). In March 1767, he and two Spanish ships reached Port Louis with the news and on April 1 the colony was formally handed over to Spain.

It was not considered an ideal place on which to settle. 'I tarry in this unhappy desert, suffering everything for love of God,' wrote a Spanish priest dispatched to Port Louis in 1767. And Thomas Coleman, a lieutenant in the marines, wrote from Port Egmont: 'The most detestable place I was ever at in my life ... one wild heath wherever you turn your eye.'

For the next two years these twin bands of miserable colonists soldiered on independently in their colonies, separated by eighty miles of rough country and the Falklands Sound. They did not sight one another until Captain Hunt's sloop met a Spanish schooner in November 1769. Each side asked the other to quit the Falklands; each behaved as though legal right was on its side. The exchanges went on for several months, and the impasse was solved only when the Spanish governor of Buenos Aires, Francisco Bucarelli, sent down a fleet of five frigates to expel the British from Port Egmont.

It did not require bloodshed. Captain Hunt had already left for England and the garrison of thirteen marines capitulated after a few shots and a warning from the Spanish commodore that the fire of his guns and muskets 'would be the cause of their own ruin'. On June 10, 1770, the Spanish came ashore to hoist their flag and lay claim to such valuable booty as a cabbage garden (well-stocked) and 422 bushels of coal.

Neither George III of England nor Lord North, his prime minister, was keen to embark on a new war against Spain, but parliament grew loud in its clamour to have national honour and the Falklands restored to Britain. And Lord North was up against a formidable leader of the opposition in the shape of the Earl of Chatham who soon emerged as the leader of the pro-war faction. Raging from the opposition benches, he described Lord North's government as 'the greatest criminals ... who have done everything that they ought not to have done, and hardly anything that they ought to have done.'

By December 1770, war seemed inevitable. Britain withdrew its ambassador from Madrid (fortunately he travelled only as far as a nearby village, lovesick for his Spanish mistress) and instructed British shipping to be ready to leave Spanish ports. And then came one of those small human accidents of history which illumine the pages of children's history books. Louis XV, under the influence of his court favourite, Madame du Barry, sacked his leading minister, the Duc de Choiseul, the French court's leading hawk. Without him, Louis XV felt free to tell Charles III that the time for war with Britain was not yet ripe. Spain would not fight without French support. The Spanish king instructed his ministers to talk to the British again. The British restored their ambassador to Madrid, and the arms of his mistress.

On January 22, 1770, Spain and Britain signed a peace declaration, though Spain reserved her position on 'the question of prior right of sovereignty of the Malouine Islands, otherwise called Falkland Islands'. The British copy of the declaration simply omitted the latter clause, but even so there was uproar in parliament. Spain had not climbed down enough. Chatham said the declaration offered 'no satisfaction, no reparation ... even the restitution was incomplete; Port Egmont alone was restored not Falkland's Island'. Worse, a strong rumour grew that Britain had secretly agreed to abandon its settlement at Port Egmont, and its claims to the islands.

Proof of this agreement has always been difficult to establish – it was after all a *secret* agreement. But there is no doubt that Spain – and later Argentina – firmly believed that it existed and Lord Chatham's party certainly suspected so.

The babble against the government grew so strong that Lord North called in Dr Samuel Johnson to quiet the row. The lexicographer and wit – then aged sixty-two and enjoying a government pension of £300 a year – obliged with a pamphlet which lashed the pro-war lobby. Johnson called his work 'Thoughts on the Late Transactions respecting Falkland's Islands', but the mildness of the title is deceptive. According to Johnson, the speeches of Lord Chatham were 'a feudal gabble'; the war-party 'sat like vultures waiting for the day of carnage'.

But it was the Falklands themselves that drew the real fire in Johnson's polemic. He wrote: 'We have maintained the honour of the crown and the superiority of our influence. Beyond this what have we acquired? What, but a bleak and gloomy solitude, an island thrown aside from human use, stormy in winter and barren in summer; an island which not even the southern savages have dignified with habitation; where a garrison must be kept in a state that contemplates with envy the exiles of Siberia; of which the expense will be perpetual and the use only occasional; and which, if fortune smiles upon our labours, may become a nest of smugglers in peace, and in war the refuge of future buccaneers.'

Johnson's view prevailed, for although Spain did formally restore Port Egmont to the British – on September 16, 1771 – Britain made no attempt to consolidate its occupation. Three years later, in May 1774, the British pulled out completely. 'It is neither more nor less than a small part of an economical naval regulation,' said Lord Rochford, though others suspected it was the result of a secret treaty with Spain. Either way – so it seemed at the time – it hardly mattered. The British did not return for another sixty years, by which time the Spanish Empire had crumbled.

The British did, however, leave a token of their ownership behind. The last act of Port Egmont's governor before he embarked for home was to nail a lead plaque to the blockhouse door. It read: 'Be it known to all nations, that Falkland's Island, with this fort, storehouses, wharf, harbour, bays, and creeks thereunto belonging, are the sole right and property of His Most Sacred Majesty George III ... in witness whereof this plaque is set up.'

In 1816, a patchwork of independent republics in South America, which included the United Provinces of Rio de la Plata, declared independence from Spain and later became Argentina. The fledgling state immediately laid claim to all territory previously governed by the Spanish vice-royalty of Buenos Aires. This stretched south to Tierra del Fuego, west to the Andes – and south-east to the Falklands. In 1820, an Argentinian frigate took formal possession of the islands; in 1823, the first governor was appointed; and in 1826, ninety colonists landed under the leadership of Louis Vernet to found what their leader termed 'a great national fishery'. Vernet, a Hamburg merchant of French origin, was very much in the mould of de Bougainville. He imported books and even a piano to Port Louis (now Puerto de la Soledad), as well as skilled tradesmen and a variety of live-stock. In 1828 he was appointed governor and installed to the sound of artillery. Above all, he took his duties seriously; he wanted to prove that the colony could work.

It was Vernet's zeal that led to his downfall and allowed the British to retake the Falklands. In 1831, he arrested two American schooners for poaching seals in Argentinian waters and sailed back aboard one of them to Buenos Aires, where its captain was to stand trial. Alas for Vernet, some American sea-power was on hand in the shape of the corvette *Lexington*, which took reprisal by sailing to the Falklands, razing the fortifications at Port Louis, taking prisoners and declaring the islands free of all government.

Argentina objected furiously to the American president, but the United States did nothing and a year of chaos ensued on the Falklands. Argentina dispatched a new governor – Vernet never saw the Falklands again – and charged him with the job of setting up a penal colony. His prisoners promptly murdered him. Argentina then dispatched a schooner and troops to arrest the murderers. They were in the act of pursuit when His Britannic Majesty's sloop *Clio* suddenly hove round the headlands and into the view of the Port Louis settlers; a sight, according to the Falklands historian, W. F. Boyson, which constituted 'the embodiment of dazzling order, discipline and restraint'. The *Clio* had come to claim the islands for Britain.

The *Clio*'s captain, James Onslow, acted quickly. He weighed anchor on January 2, 1833, and the next day went ashore to strike the Argentinian flag and raise the Union Jack. There were naturally angry scenes, but the Argentinian force was outmanned and in no mood to fight. They opted to leave and when they reached Buenos Aires, the news of the British capture cut deep into the psyche of the new nation. Boyson records: 'The young republic was ablaze with indignation at the insult to her dignity and the resentment lasted for long.'

The government in Buenos Aires instructed its ambassador in London to protest to Lord Palmerston, the British foreign secretary. Arguments over sovereignty flew back and forth – arguments which are worth examining now because they still comprise the Argentinian case: Britain, as we shall see, has shifted its position.

Argentina argued that it owned the islands:

1. because it had succeeded Spain in the territories formerly ruled from Buenos Aires;
2. because Spain, by purchasing the islands from France, had acquired the right of prior occupation;
3. because Britain had abandoned its claims to the Falklands in the secret, unwritten clause of the 1771 declaration;
4. because Britain had abandoned its settlement in West Falkland in 1774.

Palmerston replied that Britain had, during its negotiations with Spain, 'unequivocally asserted and maintained' its rights to sovereignty, and that Argentina could not expect Britain to 'permit any other state to exercise a right derived from Spain which Great Britain had deprived to Spain itself.'

Argentina found no redress through protest, though it went on protesting for most of the next 150 years. In 1982 the public posture of the two sides looked much as it had done in 1833. Privately, however, Britain began to have doubts about its position more than seventy years ago.

These doubts first arose in 1910, after the British foreign secretary, Sir Edward Grey, received a telegram from the British ambassador in Buenos Aires. It was a small request for advice. What, the ambassador asked, should he do about a new Argentinian map which showed the Falklands as part of Argentina? The telegram passed down the civil service's line of command and the opinion appeared unanimous: Argentina had no valid claim and the best thing was to follow the practice of the previous seventy years and do nothing. Nonetheless the head of the foreign office's American department, Sidney Spicer, decided to commission a memorandum on the Falklands, from a member of the foreign office's research department, Gaston de Bernhardt. Spicer was surprised by the result. 'From a perusal of the memo,' he wrote, 'it is difficult to avoid the conclusion that the Argentine government's attitude is not altogether unjustified and that our action has been somewhat high-handed.'

De Bernhardt's memo was devastating for the British posture, for it concluded that Palmerston's argument was riddled with holes. For example, the question of sovereignty was specifically excluded from the agreement of 1771; Britain started to claim sovereignty over East Falkland only in 1829; and Palmerston had examined only the *official correspondence* (de Bernhardt's italics) when seeking evidence of the secret treaty, whereas other evidence clearly pointed to such a deal. In other words, the Argentinian argument contained a good deal of truth.

Soon the word spread. Writing to the colonial office in the next year (1911), another foreign office official said: 'We cannot easily make out a good claim, and we have wisely done everything to avoid discussing the subject with Argentina.'

The British case remained in this dubious state for more than two decades – until, with the development of international law, after the First World War, a new type of argument was possible. It rested on the doctrine of 'prescription', which says, in effect, that uninterrupted peaceful occupation over a period of time can establish sovereignty, whatever the rights and wrongs of the initial occupations; 'squatters's rights', as it were, on an international scale.

The prescription argument soon became entrenched in British policy, but some foreign office men had doubts about making it public. They included the head of the American department, now John Troutbeck, who wrote in 1936: 'The difficulty of the position is that our seizure of the Falkland Islands in 1833 was so arbitrary a procedure as judged by the ideology of the present day. It is therefore not easy to explain our possession without showing ourselves up as international bandits.'

Britain's reluctance to put the dispute before an international court was therefore understandable. Much less so, however, was a similar reluctance on the part of Argentina. The answer here seems to be – surprisingly – that many Argentinian officials believed their case to be as shaky as Britain privately suspected its own to be. In 1927, for example, Argentina's foreign minister, Dr Angel Gallardo, told the British foreign secretary, Sir Austen Chamberlain, that he had recently examined the British case and concluded that it was 'exceedingly strong'. Nevertheless Argentina enlarged its claim to include the Falkland Islands Dependencies – South Georgia and the South Sandwich Islands – and the British Antarctic Territory.

Beneath the public confrontation, however, lay a remarkable degree of agreement between the two foreign ministries. The 'leaseback' solution, by which Argentina would be given sovereignty in return for a long British lease on the islands, was certainly talked about by both sides before the Second World War; and during the war, with Britain anxious to make an ally of Argentina, it seems to have got as far as a written document (the index of foreign office files at London's public record office shows a file for 1940 entitled: 'Proposed offer by HMG to *reunite* (our italics) Falkland Islands with Argentina and acceptance of lease.' The file is closed to the public.)

Britain's private attitude after the war is not easy to ascertain because the appropriate foreign office documents are still secret, but from the slender evidence available it seems likely that Britain still based its case on 'prescription'. A paper produced by the foreign office's research department in 1946 reveals a strong preference for this argument and describes the occupation of 1833 as 'an act of unjustifiable aggression'.

Argentina's case began to gain momentum, however, when it reached the United Nations. In 1965, Argentinian lobbying paid off when the United Nations passed Resolution 2065, which specified the Malvinas as a colonial problem and reminded the general assembly that under a previous resolution (number 1514 of 1960) the UN was pledged 'to bring to an end everywhere colonialism in all its forms'. The 1965 resolution went on to press Britain and Argentina to find a quick and peaceful solution to the problem, bearing in mind the UN charter and 'the interests of the population of the said islands'.

The last phrase passed without much comment at the time because both sides had a rather sketchy idea of who the population were, far less of what they wanted. In fact, the British government had played a negligible (some would say negligent) part in the development of its colony. The islanders owed the shape of their lives not to an office in Whitehall, but to a British private company.

At the post-invasion session of the security council on April 3, 1982, the Argentinian foreign minister, Nicanor Costa Mendez, had harsh words for the Falkland Islands Company. It was 'a typical colonial firm – a complete anachronism; a colonial corporation of the kind which had letters patent from the eighteenth century; the trade branch of colonialism and imperialism'.

Costa Mendez came close to the truth in these remarks. The Falkland Islands Company grew out of the early attempts by the British government to settle the islands, which until 1841 were merely a naval staging-post. Then the government sold a large parcel of land on East Falkland (the area now known as Lafonia) to an entrepreneur based in Montevideo called Samuel Fisher Lafone. He got the land cheap in exchange for a promise that he would settle and develop the islands, but the promise was never fulfilled. Soon Lafone – a financial incompetent as well as a rogue – was heavily in debt. He decided to launch a public company in London, the grandly named 'Royal Falkland Land, Cattle, Seal and Whale Fishery Company', which would raise capital from shareholders and thus pay off his debts. The scheme worked.

Queen Victoria granted the company a royal charter in 1852 (which in theory put it on a par with the monopolistic East India Company) and shareholders were not disillusioned until reports came back from the Falklands from the company's first manager, who found the company's assets to consist mainly of peat bog and herds of wild cattle. The remoteness of the islands, he wrote sadly, had concealed 'the true character of the concern'.

Sheep were the company's eventual salvation, and their wool the source of the settlement's income. In 1851, there were only 1,000 sheep on the islands; by 1880, there were 435,700. With the sheep came the settlers, shepherds from Scotland, Wales and the West Country, who arrived in a landscape which bore a remarkably bleak similarity to the one they had left behind. The British government had intended that each settler should have his own plot of land – allotments of 160 acres each – but it later raised this ceiling to 6,000 acres and the Falkland Islands Company contrived to buy most of the available land through its placemen, agents and managers. Emigrants who came as independent smallholders soon found themselves as company employees. There were complaints and protests but the Falkland Islands Company went on buying land. Today it owns nearly half the total land area, about 1.3 million acres, while a few other large land-holders share the rest. Over the past 100 years it has also been the islands' strongest social influence.

Ian Jack, who visited the islands for *The Sunday Times Colour Magazine* in 1978, wrote: 'The men of the Camp – the country outside the town of Stanley – live in tied company houses on company land. They shop in the company store for goods delivered by company ship, and have bills deducted from company wages. Many of them use the company as a bank, the wool they shear from the company sheep goes to Tilbury, again by company ship, where it is unloaded at the company wharf, stored in the company warehouse and sold on the company wool exchange in Bradford. By means of directorships and shareholdings, and by owning the only means of transport and marketing the Falklands Island Company extends its influence over the islands' few other landlords. For better or worse, the Falklands are company islands.'

Lord Shackleton, commissioned by the British foreign office in 1975 to investigate the islands' economic future, thought it was decidedly for the worse. His report decided that the company had bled the islands of badly-needed investment; profits had gone to shareholders or investment programmes in Britain rather than the Falklands. He also pointed out something which many visitors to the islands have noticed – that while the islanders were 'honest, versatile and physically hardy' they also lacked confidence and enterprise and had 'a degree of acceptance of their situation which verges on apathy'.

Lord Shackleton told Ian Jack: 'If these people had been black, Britain would never have got away with it.' His remark echoed those of a Falklands governor in his farewell speech: 'If you want London to do something for you, I suggest you blacken your faces with boot polish and go and burn down Government House. Then London won't be able to do enough.'

Nevertheless, by the 1960s the islanders were displaying a stubborn and very unapathetic resolve to stay British, while in London, parliament was demonstrating an indignation and concern over the islands that it had not shown since the speeches of Lord Chatham. Argentina's struggle for the islands was only just beginning.

CHAPTER FOUR

The Long Road to War

'I suggested that we tell the Argentinians that
whereas rape would be totally unacceptable, seduction could be
positively encouraged'
– Sir David Scott, June 1982

On November 24, 1968, *HMS Endurance*, the Royal Navy's venerable
ice-patrol ship, eased into Port Stanley. It was one of the more
auspicious occasions in the life of the 3,600-ton vessel, which had been
purchased from the Danish merchant fleet and refitted for her
Antarctic duties just eighteen months before. For on board was Lord
Chalfont, minister of state at the foreign office, paying the first-ever
visit by a British government minister to the Falkland Islands.

Chalfont – formerly Lt-Col. Alun Gwynne Jones, defence
correspondent of *The Times* – had been plucked from journalism,
ennobled, and placed in the foreign office by Harold Wilson when
Labour came to power in 1964. As well as disarmament and the
common market, his foreign office brief included Latin America, in
which guise he had just accompanied the Queen on an official visit to
Chile and Brazil. That he should detach himself from the royal party at
Santiago, and join the *Endurance* for the 400-mile crossing from
Patagonia to the Falklands, was an indication that the government was
at least aware that it had a problem on its hands. As the *Endurance*
dropped anchor and Chalfont waited for the tender that would carry
him ashore, the passions it could arouse were only too clear. Ranged on
the quayside, it seemed to Chalfont, was the entire population of
Stanley, brandishing banners proclaiming: 'We are loyal to you – stay
loyal to us' and 'Don't sell us to Argentina for tins of bully beef.' They
also confirmed Chalfont's worst fears: his bid to find a solution to the
government's problem was already doomed.

In the recent history of the Falklands there are patterns and themes
that have the frightful inevitability of a recurring nightmare. Chalfont
was one of three British government ministers to make the 8,000-mile
journey to the islands in just over ten years. Each departed with fine
intentions, if varying degrees of hope. Each returned with intentions
bruised and hopes dimmed, and each experienced parliamentary
grillings to rank with the most harrowing they were to know. Each left

the foreign office with the ominous feeling that disaster and bloodshed lay somewhere ahead. At the start of that period it had seemed that the aspirations of Argentina and the desires of the Falkland islanders could both be satisfied. When it became clear that they could not, the foreign office attempted instead to prevent the contradictions between them from coming to a head. Eventually delay for its own sake became first the implicit, then the explicit aim of the foreign office, until time finally ran out in March 1982.

The process began with beguiling calm. Early in 1966, following the United Nations' intervention, Britain's foreign secretary Michael Stewart visited Argentina, one of three South American countries targeted for a British export drive. The Argentinian government did raise the issue of the Falklands, but with no great force – an impression confirmed by Britain's ambassador to Buenos Aires at that time, Sir Michael Creswell, who found that Argentinian corned beef was a matter of far greater moment. When Creswell had to inform the Argentinian government that an outbreak of foot-and-mouth disease in Britain had been traced to Argentina, it aroused, in his recollection, far greater outrage than the Falklands ever did.

It was in this pacific atmosphere that Britain and Argentina began negotiations in New York in September 1967. Britain's foreign secretary was now the volatile George Brown; his Argentinian counterpart was Nicanor Costa Mendez, one of the few constant characters in the narrative of the ensuing fifteen years. Britain promised that sovereignty was negotiable, and there was considerable satisfaction in London when the opening talks progressed well, for a solution would not only assist diplomatic and commercial relations with Argentina, but was also required for more substantial strategic reasons. Parallel with its largely honourable policy of divesting itself of its former colonies, Britain had also been reducing its overseas defence forces; and the last thing it wanted was a costly defence commitment to some remote imperial outpost.

But this seemingly smooth path to a solution was about to encounter a substantial obstruction. In chambers at Lincoln's Inn, London, was a barrister named William Hunter Christie, a former diplomat who had spent three years at the British Embassy in Buenos Aires, and who had continued to take a close interest in the South Atlantic. When he left the foreign office in 1948 he had written a book on the complex legal problems of the Antarctic, and was still occasionally consulted by his former colleagues on such matters. Early in 1968 Christie met a friend at the ministry of defence who asked the melodramatic – if exaggerated – question: 'Did you know that George Brown wants to sell the Falklands to Argentina?'

Christie promptly visited a solicitor named Patrick Ainslie, who also happened to be chairman of the Falkland Islands Company and married to the grand-daughter of its founder, Samuel Lafone, and proposed a campaign against the government's plans. Christie pointed out that for the company to do so would appear as a self-interested defence of commercial interests; but if members of parliament could be enlisted to take up the cause, that would be quite different. A campaign committee should be set up; the company would assist with funds and secretarial help.

In this curiously nonchalant manner, what was to become known as the 'Falklands lobby' was born. Outside Britain, lobbies operate through trade-offs, deals, and grafts; in Britain, the Falkland Islands Emergency Committee (the word Emergency was dropped in 1973, presumably because by then the emergency was deemed to have passed) dispensed invitations to the occasional lunch and to a grandiose annual ceremony, serenaded by the band of the Royal Marines. MPs are fond of black-and-white issues on which to expend their rhetoric, and the Falklands presented them with just that. Those on the right could cling to this last relic of the days of empire; the left could denounce a series of authoritarian Argentinian regimes, with the bonus at first of being able to frustrate a scheme advanced by the much unloved George Brown.

The early gatherings were scarcely auspicious. Christie recalls one meeting attended by a handful of people including himself, two directors of the company, and the naturalist Peter Scott who had been invited, Christie frankly admits, because he was 'a name'. But by late March 1968, the committee had been formally established, with a mixture of MPs, islanders, and officials of the Falkland Islands Company; Christie and a Falklands landowner named Norman Keith Cameron began talking to MPs. Within days, a flurry of activity culminated in their first parliamentary triumph.

On March 12, 1968, *The Times* published a letter from four Falkland Islanders which had also been sent to a number of MPs. The islanders, headed by Mr A. G. Barton, who was the company's retired manager at Stanley and one of the committee's founding members, claimed that Britain was about to hand over the Falklands to Argentina, and protested that they did not 'wish to submit to a foreign language, law, customs, and culture'. A right-wing MP, Michael Clark Hutchison, who became one of the most fervent members of the lobby, put down a parliamentary question about the talks with Argentina, which was fielded somewhat uneasily in the Lords by Chalfont. A flurry of stories inspired by the exchange appeared in the British press: 'The Islands That Britain May Give Away' proclaimed *The Daily Telegraph*, while the *Daily Express* hailed the islands' emblem as 'the shield of freedom' (it depicts a rather smug sheep).

The government briefly hoped that it had ridden out the storm, but on March 26 the attacks were renewed. In the Lords, Chalfont was subjected to further rigorous questioning by Lord Carrington, who can scarcely have guessed that the Falklands were to blight his own political career fifteen years later. In the Commons, Michael Stewart, back as foreign secretary once more, faced an even greater onslaught from MPs, several of them future committee members. It left him in considerable discomfort, for he was attempting to defend a position which – unknown to his questioners – had been carefully agreed with Argentina.

During talks, Argentina had cleverly raised the awkward question of whom it was actually negotiating with: the islanders? or the British government? Was Britain – 'a sovereign power' – really going to have its policy decided by 2,000 of its subjects? That would be 'an insult to Argentina'. In response, Stewart had decided that sovereignty could be ceded to Argentina if the government concluded it was in the islanders' *interests* – thus preserving the final say for the British government. In the Commons on March 26, in the face of intense questioning, he cited the islanders' 'interests' four times. But a day or so later Labour's leaders decided that the issue was no longer worth the parliamentary damage it was causing, and on April 1 Stewart rose in the Commons again. This time he told the MPs what they wanted to hear. For any settlement, he assured them, 'the wishes of the islanders are an absolute condition'.

Stewart made one more attempt that summer to keep his negotiating lines open. In August he presented a paper to cabinet which spoke of trying to satisfy Argentina while still promising to respect the islanders' wishes. But the government had been so intimidated by the parliamentary rows of March that it refused to endorse even that modest proposition, and the paper was shelved. When Stewart broke the news to the Argentinian ambassador, his response according to one observer, was merely 'doleful'.

It was thus in the knowledge that there was little his visit could achieve that Chalfont stepped ashore at Stanley on November 24. The islanders, who had been briefed by the committee, realised that they now had a veto over negotiations, and their banners showed that they would exercise it if necessary. Chalfont could do little more than go through the motions of consultation, which, at public meetings in Stanley, and over cups of tea and mounds of sandwiches in the outlying farms, he dutifully did. He had one principal argument to deploy: the islands had no economic future without a settlement with Argentina; and Argentina – as Chalfont had found in Buenos Aires, where he had met Costa Mendez – was eager to assist. In response, the islanders were courteous but emphatic: they wanted no alteration in their status, whatever blandishments Argentina offered.

Back in London, Chalfont wrote a formal report on his visit. It had three main conclusions. The first was scarcely surprising: the islanders wanted to preserve their status quo. But the second and third were more alarming. In Argentina Chalfont had found that the issue was both live and pressing; and if no solution was found, there might one day be conflict. But by now the Labour government was no longer in the mood to search for an answer, especially as its ministers had faced further rigorous questioning on Chalfont's return. Stewart had eventually been compelled to cut short a visit to India to assure the Commons that the islanders would have to view any settlement as both satisfactory to their interests *and* in accord with their wishes. From then on the issue was held in abeyance, a course which, for all Chalfont's warning, appeared to present no immediate danger. When Stewart met Costa Mendez once more at the UN general assembly the next autumn, he found the atmosphere 'all sweetness and light'.

In May 1970, a new government in Britain inherited the problem. The Conservatives regained power after six years in opposition, and immediately found themselves in some difficulty. As foreign affairs spokesman, Lord Home had pledged that the Conservatives would 'strike sovereignty from the agenda'; as foreign secretary, he now had to reconcile that pledge with renewed requests from the United Nations to negotiate with Argentina. The man on whom that contradiction devolved was the assistant under-secretary at the foreign office responsible for the Falklands, David Scott.

Scott proposed a resolution that bespoke both decades of diplomatic experience, and a certain literary flair: the Argentinians should be told that while Britain would not countenance the rape of the Falklands, it would actively encourage their seduction. 'Our aim,' Scott later admitted 'was to get the Argentinians to set aside the issue of sovereignty while we discussed other, more practical matters.' The policy worked – although not for as long as Scott hoped.

Scott explained to his Argentinian counterpart in London, Ambassador Juan Carlos Beltramino, that the 'seduction' of the islanders entailed demonstrating that Argentina was not the bogeyman they feared, and that closer ties could only be to their advantage. Why not reverse Argentina's unhelpful policy of isolating the islands, and provide an air service and regular mail deliveries? After nine months hard talking, Beltramino agreed. The junior foreign office minister Joseph Godber made the crucial proviso that the islanders themselves must take part in talks, thus avoiding Labour's mistake of appearing to go behind their backs. The one issue that Scott somehow managed to deflect, since he knew that agreement was impossible, was a timetable. 'We were thinking about a generation, say twenty-five years. If we had asked the Argentinians how long they were prepared to wait they would have said an absolute maximum of ten.'

In June 1971 Scott visited the Falklands. Whereas to the Argentinians he had pointed out the potential long-term benefits, to the islanders he naturally stressed the short-term gains on offer: 'Let's see what advantages we can get for the islands, then wait and see how it works out.' The islanders accepted this pragmatic approach, and a

48

small delegation accompanied Scott to Buenos Aires for negotiations with the Argentinians. Conveniently for Scott, the Falkland Islands Company had announced that it intended to withdraw the supply ship *Darwin*, enabling him to apply some pressure to the islanders to accept the Argentinian offer to start a regular air-service. The suspicious delegates haggled over almost every point, but Scott resolved most in their favour. At the end of the last session, after the two sides had exchanged notes that the arrangements in no way altered their attitudes towards 'a definite solution' of the dispute, the agreements were signed.

The air-service started modestly, with a twice-monthly sea-plane that carried just six passengers. But sixteen months later the Argentinians had built a temporary landing strip, and Scott and Beltramino – now Argentina's foreign secretary – rode on the first Fokker Friendship to land at Stanley. After a cocktail party at the Argentinian airline office, and a more sumptuous affair at Government House, they returned to Argentina in a mellow mood. Perhaps temporarily seduced by the success of his policy, Scott confided: 'If things go on like this, the islands will be yours in ten years.'

It was a moment of false optimism; for whatever pleased one side in the delicate relationship between Argentina and the islanders invariably dismayed the other. The next politician to encounter that conundrum was James Callaghan, who became foreign secretary when Labour regained power in June 1974. Argentina, still pursuing its seduction of the islanders, had just agreed to supply them with fuel more cheaply than the Falkland Islands Company had been doing. But the islanders did not want to give their suitors the wrong impression, and asked Callaghan to break off all further talks.

It was not long before Argentina made its displeasure clear. In March 1975, a new British ambassador, Derek Ashe, presented his credentials at the presidential palace in Buenos Aires. Isabel Peron, mouthing words whispered into her ear by her foreign secretary, expressed her hope that Ashe's arrival 'would enable progress to be made with the problem of those islands.' Soon afterwards the message was repeated in less diplomatic language. Ashe received demands for the islands inscribed in blood, and a car bomb exploded outside the embassy, killing two of the thirteen guards assigned to his protection. A new instruction was dispatched from the foreign office: the British ambassador could take part in talks, or at least talks about talks; but he was to ensure that they made no progress.

Ashe managed to stall the Argentinian government for a while, but found it increasingly, and understandably, hostile. To break the impasse he suggested that Britain should send an economic mission to consider how the islands' resources might be developed in co-operation with Argentina. He also warned that if Britain did not appear flexible, Argentina would eventually 'try a grab' for the islands.

In London, Callaghan took up the suggestion with alacrity – it was, after all, the best new idea for a long time. But the mission, headed by the Labour peer Lord Shackleton, could have hardly have had a worse start. Argentina suspected that it was a ploy merely to promote the islands' independence, and instructed Ashe to pack his bags and return to London.

When Shackleton presented his report in July 1976, however, Argentina took a different view. It was true that the report said the Falklands' economy should be strengthened and diversified, but that was largely to deal with the Falkland Islands Company. Shackleton pointed out to the Argentinian ambassador that the report also said that the islands' major natural resources, oil and fish, should be developed in cooperation with Argentina. Argentina's response was sufficiently encouraging for Labour to decide that it was time once again to dispatch a minister to the islands to see if the dispute could at last be resolved.

Labour's emissary was Ted Rowlands, a political protegé of Callaghan, who had been appointed to the foreign office in 1975. Far more than any other of the official visitors who went in search of a settlement, Rowlands found that he actually liked not only the islands but also the islanders themselves, whose way of life reminded him of home in the misty valleys of South Wales. ('I'm just a hopeless romantic,' he once confided.) Even that rare advantage was to prove insufficient to achieve a solution.

Rowlands arrived in Stanley in February 1977 imbued with the seriousness of his mission. Callaghan, his mentor, used to warn him that governments were brought down not by major issues, but the minor 'oddball' ones that suddenly escalated. More used to the hustings than his predecessor Chalfont, Rowlands happily drank beer and played darts with the islanders. Yet his political arguments cut little ice. He told the islanders that Shackleton offered a rich economic future; but it could only be secured with Argentinian cooperation, which meant putting sovereignty back on the negotiating table. Only when he promised the islanders that their position was 'totally covered' did they concede that negotiations could take place at all, and even then they refused to send delegates to the talks in Argentina.

For almost two days, Rowlands encountered similar intransigence in Buenos Aires. But then the Argentinian delegation agreed to downplay its demands for sovereignty and to give the 'seduction' policy – described now as 'economic cooperation' – another try. Rowlands faced remorseless questioning in London, but he assured MPs that the islanders' consent to any deal was essential. With new talks due to begin in December, the Falkland Islands committee geared itself for another round of campaigning, and familiar stories soon appeared in the press. 'Falkland Fear Of Sell-Out' proclaimed *The Daily Telegraph*, while the *Daily Express* headlined 'This Island

Larder We Can't Afford To Give Away.' But then an incident occurred which proved a watershed.

In October 1977, the British government received an intelligence report that there was increasing military activity in southern Argentina. It also outlined a forthcoming series of moves which would begin with a landing by a group of Argentinian adventurers on South Georgia. There had been such 'private' initiatives in the past, but this time, if the British government moved to evict the invaders, Argentina might declare itself 'forced to intervene'.

The status of the Argentinian plans proved hard to gauge. But after ten years of fruitless negotiations it was hardly surprising if Argentina's military government, which had taken power in March 1976, was considering other solutions. The cabinet's defence and overseas policy committee took the warning seriously, and decided to send two frigates and a submarine to the South Atlantic, even drawing up rules of engagement and the size of an exclusion zone – twenty-five miles around the Falklands.

There was, of course, no confrontation – but even now one aspect of this highly secret move remains controversial. Was Argentina even told that the task force was on its way? Most of the permanent officials involved believe that it was not. However the politicians insist that it was and that Callaghan, by then prime minister, used an unorthodox channel – a businessman with extensive contacts among Latin American regimes.

Whatever the truth, when negotiations opened in December the atmosphere had been patently soured. The British did not refer to the episode, but they did raise an earlier incident, when they had discovered that the Argentinians had placed scientists on the outer dependency of Southern Thule. The diplomats pressed on valiantly, each side preparing reports reflecting its own priorities, as one participant recalls. 'We used to produce papers on economic cooperation, they used to produce things on how Argentina would administer the islands next year or the year after that.' The gap was as wide as ever. The only difference was that instead of being papered over, it was now formalised. *Two* working groups were set up, one to consider sovereignty, the other to devise forms of economic cooperation. When talks resumed, in Lima, in February, little progress was made.

By now, Rowlands himself had concluded that they were doomed. The British floated the idea of giving Argentina a major share of the islands' oil and fish, if the islanders themselves could stay British. But Argentina was not interested: it wanted the symbol, not the substance, of sovereignty. As for the islanders, they certainly did not want Argentinian officials asserting themselves in Stanley; but they weren't interested in glowing economic futures either. Most wanted to stay just the way they were. In those circumstances, Rowlands concluded like others before him that the only alternative was to 'keep the show on the road' – keep talking, do virtually nothing. In December he met the Argentinians again in Geneva. The latest subject for discussion was a modest project for scientific research on the islands. It was rent by the usual contradictions: for the Argentinians it was the first step to sovereignty; for the British, a substitute for just that. In any case, it was promptly vetoed by the islanders. Too bad, Rowlands thought.

In May 1979, Labour was voted from power and Rowlands' position at the foreign office was inherited by Nicholas Ridley, a somewhat ascetic figure who was favoured by Prime Minister Margaret Thatcher for his firm belief in her stern economic policies. Ridley's attempt to resolve the dispute was in many ways the most determined; it also proved to be Britain's last chance to avoid bloodshed. Whereas Rowlands' main gift in his bid had been his demotic bonhomie, Ridley's was his formidable intellect. It was to take him little further than Rowlands; and it was not to spare him a ruthless and traumatic onslaught in the House of Commons, administered by his supposed friends as well as his traditional foes.

In July, Ridley embarked on a 'familiarisation' tour of his new territory of Latin America, which he had never visited before. He spent some time in both Buenos Aires and Stanley, and returned steeped in the anxieties that had affected his predecessors. He found the ambience of the Falklands almost unreal – 'like an English village in war-time', he is once reputed to have said. He also felt that they posed a threat quite out of proportion to their size. His view squared with information from the ministry of defence, which had now obtained Argentina's plans for a full-scale invasion of the islands, drawn up in 1976. In spring, 1978, a Labour cabinet committee had decided not to station a permanent task force in the South Atlantic, on grounds of cost – £180 million. Instead, the ministry had drawn up plans for a contingency force that could be sent to any remote trouble spot. There was a vital proviso: it would need substantial advance warning if it was to arrive in time.

It was against this disturbing background that Ridley applied his renowned intellect to finding a solution. He settled on a scheme for a 'leaseback', in the style of Hong Kong: Argentina could be given the freehold to the islands, which would then be leased to the islanders for a finite period (Hong Kong was ninety-nine years). From his earlier visits, Ridley believed that this could give both sides what they wanted. Argentina could acquire the symbolic title, while the islanders' cherished way of life would be preserved for several generations at least. Other contacts seemed propitious. In June 1980, Argentina's economy minister met Thatcher and other senior ministers in London, declaring afterwards that there was 'light on the horizon'. Ridley expounded his proposal before the cabinet's overseas defence committee which sanctioned an attempt to sell leaseback to the islanders. But there was one crucial condition: any deal must be acceptable to the House of Commons. Ridley concluded that his only chance lay in winning the islanders' consent first and presenting the Commons with a virtual *fait accompli*.

When Ridley arrived in Stanley in November, 1980, he came quickly to the point. At a series of meetings he told the islanders that a leaseback was their only realistic option. He warned them that the islands could not be defended; and if they rejected the scheme they must 'bear the consequences'. The governor, Rex Hunt, felt that Ridley had 'shocked the islanders into realising that they couldn't carry on for ever as they had been used to carrying on.' But many were unmoved. When Ridley left Stanley airport on November 29, a group of islanders placed a wreath around a map of the Falklands, while a loudspeaker blared out the tunes 'This land is our land', 'We shall not be moved', and 'Land of hope and glory'. While Ridley proceeded to Buenos Aires for talks with the Argentinians, news of his reception was telexed to the Falkland Islands Committee in London; a tape-recording of one of his admonitory speeches was dispatched soon afterwards.

As Ridley flew home, he felt he had a sporting chance of success, reckoning that forty, perhaps fifty, per cent of the islanders were on his side. When pressed on the length of the lease he had suggested ninety-nine years; the Argentinians were thinking of thirty, so perhaps there could be a compromise on fifty. It was in a sanguine, if jet-lagged, frame of mind that Ridley landed at Heathrow at 9 a.m. on December 2, and went almost direct to the Commons to make a brief statement about his trip. He said that the government was searching for a solution 'acceptable to all the parties'; a leaseback was being considered; and 'any eventual settlement would have to be endorsed by the islanders, and by this house'.

In the next ninety minutes no fewer than eighteen MPs, from the left of the Labour party to the right of the Conservatives, including a number with senior government experience, rose to savage this unexceptional statement. Tory Julian Amery – a former foreign officer minister – found it 'profoundly disturbing'. Liberal Russell Johnston talked of 'shameful schemes for getting rid of these islands'. Labour's Tom McNally referred to 'humiliating excursions to the Argentinians'. When Ridley left the chamber he was, according to one MP, 'ashen and shaking'; *The Times* commented: 'Seldom can a minister have had such a drubbing from all sides of the house.' The personal toll it had taken was clear when, at a private meeting of the Conservative foreign affairs committee that evening, Ridley bellowed at a questioner: 'If we don't do something, they will invade. And there is nothing we could do.'

Ridley's ordeal was akin to that suffered by earlier ministers at the hands of MPs. But there was a more puzzling aspect to the debate: the failure of any senior government figure to come to Ridley's aid. He had after all been pursuing a policy which a cabinet committee had endorsed. But the government appeared to have done nothing to enlist backing for Ridley, who was bitter at having received no hint of support from what he was wont to term 'the powers that be'.

The news of the debate soon reached the Falklands, encouraging the islanders to believe that it was not after all necessary to 'focus on the future'. They had asked for time to consider Ridley's proposal, but a meeting of the islands' legislative council soon voted 8–1 for a freeze on all negotiations over sovereignty – although, displaying their usual unabashed self-interest, they asked for talks to continue if any benefits were forthcoming. When talks resumed in New York in February, Argentina still attempted to woo their delegates, offering to make the islands its 'most pampered region'. Their entreaties only confirmed the strength of the islanders' position: they had the final say, and neither Britain nor Argentina could alter that.

It was with the undoubted feeling that time was running out that the foreign office convened a major meeting in London on June 30, 1981. Ridley was there, together with a clutch of senior officials who included Governor Rex Hunt, the permanent under-secretary, Sir Michael Palliser, the head of the South American department, Robin Fearn, and the Buenos Aires ambassador, Anthony Williams, who had been sending cables warning of a possible invasion ever since being posted to Argentina in February 1980. The grim truth that the meeting had to confront was that opinion on the islands in favour of a leaseback, and hence a negotiated settlement, was visibly 'slipping away'. That perception was reinforced by a forthright and undoubtedly well-founded intelligence estimate of what action Argentina was likely to take when negotiations were, once again, stalled.

The action was likely to consist of a series of carefully graduated steps:

1. A return to the United Nations where Britain would be denounced for its 'bad faith'.
2. An air and fuel embargo of the islands.
3. Action against British economic interests in Argentina.
4. Harassment of foreign trawlers using Port Stanley.
5. A landing on South Georgia.
6. 'Pin-prick' incidents such as a freelance landing on the main islands.
7. Occupation of an uninhabited island.
8. A full-scale invasion.

Since the first move presented little to worry about, the meeting spent some time considering how to counter the second, an air and fuel embargo. The bleak conclusion was that it would present 'immense difficulties'. But these paled beside number 8: having to respond to a full-scale invasion would cost 'hundreds of millions of pounds'.

So what options remained? None, save those that had been pursued for fifteen years. Britain should try to persuade the islanders to accept a settlement in the shape of a leaseback. But too much persuasion would create the customary political storm; only 'gentle pressure' therefore should be applied. As usual, the Argentinians should be kept 'in play' for as long as possible. How long did Britain have? Argentina would surely act before the 150th anniversary of British occupation: and that fell due in January, 1983.

The meeting's recommendations were speedily presented to Lord Carrington. It was with some dismay that those who had helped prepare them learned the result. Carrington instructed that not even 'gentle pressure' on the islanders was permissible, and was to be replaced by no pressure at all. An official who heard that news later speculated: 'Carrington found himself under intolerable backbench pressure – or Downing Street pressure. It is not easy to tell which was the stronger.' The stark consequence was that Britain now had no policy left, apart from delay for delay's sake. But this time there was a deadline, at most eighteen months away.

Even that estimate, of course, was to prove hopelessly optimistic, as was the supposition that Argentina would give due warning of its intentions by proceeding step by careful step. The intelligence review could hardly predict that Argentina's leaders would simply change their minds; but it was fallible in another way. It could not take into account how Argentina would react to certain signals which appeared to imply that Britain was less than firm in its resolve to stand by the islands.

The first was an attempt to close the British Antarctic Survey base on South Georgia, through lack of funds. It was reprieved when the Falkland Islands government produced the necessary cash from the sale of its postage stamps, but the Argentinian government had noted the vacillation over its future. The second was more significant, and concerns the steadfast patrol-ship *Endurance*. *Endurance* had featured on defence cut 'hit-lists' for at least five years, but successive foreign secretaries, supported by their prime ministers, had always success-fully resisted. When the *Endurance* appeared in the 1981 defence review, Thatcher sided with her defence minister, John Nott, and the *Endurance* was marked down to be scrapped. At the foreign office, Ridley learned of the decision from his morning newspaper, while Carrington fought valiantly but unsuccessfully to have it reversed. Argentina's interest in the move was clear when a friend from the London embassy telephoned Lord Shackleton to ask if it meant that Britain was losing interest in the region. Shackleton replied that he simply did not know.

In September 1981, Nicholas Ridley was lifted from his bed of nails, to be set down in his true home at the treasury. He was replaced by Richard Luce, a parliamentary under secretary now being awarded his first senior position. Unlike Ridley, he had no time for the luxury of a familiarisation tour, being presented within days of his appointment with the grim mid-summer appraisal and its even grimmer fate. Although Argentina had agreed to await the results of new elections to the Falklands legislative council in October, the foreign office was certain they would show a majority against negotiations. The results were even worse than the foreign office feared. All the candidates elected were decisively against leaseback, and the mere fact that they had even discussed the proposal with Ridley had put several veteran councillors out of office. As one participant said, 'An angst settled over the foreign office. We felt totally boxed in. All we could do was play for time, and the only question was how.'

Talks with Argentina were due to resume at the end of the year. Ten days beforehand, the foreign office felt it had received a long overdue slice of luck. Following machinations inside the Argentinian military junta, General Roberto Viola was replaced as president by army commander General Leopoldo Galtieri, and Argentina asked for the talks to be postponed. The foreign office reckoned it had won a two-month reprieve, at least.

CHAPTER FIVE

A Star in the Casa Rosada

'In any war there are people who disappear.'
– Leopoldo Galtieri, July, 1982

At the age of fifty-five, President Leopoldo Fortunato Galtieri could look back on his progress with a certain satisfaction. From a humble background as the second child of a poor Italian immigrant family living in a dreary suburb of Buenos Aires, he had risen not only to supreme command of the army, but to the highest office in Argentina: *Presidente de la Nacion.*

He had brought to the presidency a certain expansive style which seemed to go well with Argentina's new outward-looking role in the world. Relaxed in shirt sleeves, behind the desk of his office in the Casa Rosada, with a whisky in his hand and, as often as not, his feet on the table, Galtieri exuded a relaxed self-confidence which impressed his many visitors – particularly those from abroad. 'A man who can talk to the people,' pronounced a visiting politician. 'A soldier's soldier,' said a visiting general. Married to a charming wife, Lucia, with three children, Galtieri seemed, as one American congressman put it, 'a regular guy', a welcome contrast to some of his more chilling predecessors.

His rise to power was remarkable, however, because it had been achieved with so little apparent raw material. One contemporary described him bluntly as 'a low grade officer in a generation of low grade officers.' He had been promoted through the engineering corps, the army's least glamorous branch, and had betrayed little sign of brilliance at any point in his career, though his flamboyant charm may have diverted attention from a less than acute mind. His chief weapon in the long fight for personal advancement had been a certain skill in exploiting the divisions of others. In the Argentinian army, riven by factions, such a skill can take a good-looking, ambitious soldier a long way.

By 1976, it had taken Galtieri to the command of the second army corps in Rosario, north of Buenos Aires. There his career might have petered out, eventually ending in a comfortable retirement from a military life undisturbed by the sound of battle. But that year a series of events was set in train which was to shape both the destiny of

Argentina and the political fate of Galtieri. By then the democratic interlude set up by the ageing dictator Juan Peron and, afterwards, his widow Isabel, had deteriorated into corruption and incompetence. The extreme left of the Peronist movement, expelled by Peron himself, had turned to terrorism, infiltrating agents into almost every aspect of Argentinian life.

The terrorists were well organised and determined. By 1976, their campaign of kidnappings and bombing had so alarmed the urban population that General Jorge Videla's military coup, when it came, was greeted by many with relief.

The priorities of the new military rulers were, first, to suppress the terrorists and then to restore sufficient order for an eventual transfer of power back to democratic rule. It was to be a stage-by-stage programme known as the *proceso*. The situation, the military reasoned, was one of war and in war, all methods are permissible. This one became known, rightly, as '*la guerra sucia*' – the 'dirty war'.

Instead of the difficult road of trials, with the burden of evidence and proof of guilt, the military opted for the swifter route of disappearance. Covert operations, conducted by squads of men operating under the aegis of each of the armed forces and the secret police, rapidly became a familiar part of Argentinian urban life. The ubiquitous Ford Falcon cars, old-fashioned family saloons manufactured in Argentina, became symbols of death as, number plates obscured, they cruised the streets looking for victims.

Few of those forced into the Ford Falcons were ever seen again. Occasionally a returning survivor would whisper a story of torture and terror at any one of dozens of locations. In Buenos Aires, the navy's school of mechanics, an elegant neo-classical building with immaculately manicured lawns, became particularly notorious. It was behind that façade that a debonair young naval officer, Captain Alfredo Astiz, who was later to play a significant role in the Falklands saga, operated to deadly effect. In Galtieri's own operational command, the interrogation centre was at nearby Funes, although there is no record of how personal an interest he took in its activities.

As the terror grew, the population largely looked the other way. '*Debe ser por algo*...': 'It must be for something...' the citizens would remark to each other if they were unlucky enough to witness a kidnapping. One old couple tell of how their pregnant daughter and son-in-law vanished in early 1977. One night, some months later, a stranger knocked on the door of their apartment. 'Do you know this person?' he asked, showing them a photograph of their daughter. When they said they did, he thrust an infant into their arms. 'Then this is your grandchild,' he said, and vanished.

Others were also cruelly deceived. A French nun, Sister Alice Dumont, was enduring savage torture after being arrested at a meeting of mothers of the victims in the church of Santa Cruz in Buenos Aires.

She repeatedly asked about the fate of others who had been arrested at the same meeting. Amongst those for whom she showed concern was the 'young blond man', the '*muchachito rubio*', who had organised the meeting. He turned out to be none other than Captain Alfredo Astiz, one of the interrogators. He had been acting as an *agent provocateur*.

In just over two years, according to the estimates of human rights organisations, up to 18,000 Argentinians vanished, including, in Buenos Aires, thousands of high school children. Most of those who disappeared were young, radical and middle class – some, undoubtedly, with sympathies or connections with the *Montoneros*, the guerrilla movement. Others were simply radical idealists and others again cases of mistaken identity. Over 100 journalists and 200 scientists vanished. Even the military have admitted up to a twenty-five per cent error in the two years of bloodletting which followed the coup.

The evidence about Galtieri's personal involvement in the dirty war is unclear. But there is no question that he, like all the leadership, defiantly accept the collective responsibility. 'In any war,' he remarked in an interview in July 1982, 'there are people who disappear.' The operation, he maintained, was justified. The subject is closed.

By 1978, it was almost over. The rest of the world woke up to the enormity of what had happened just as soccer's World Cup contest was launched in Buenos Aires. Argentina's dramatic victory in the finals provided the people with a welcome relief from the trauma of the two previous years. But the dirty war could not be so easily forgotten. The US administration under Jimmy Carter roundly condemned Argentina's human rights record and brought in the Humphrey–Kennedy embargo on arms which formally relegated Argentina to the status of a moral leper.

By 1980, as the country's disastrous economy deteriorated ever further, the military began to sense that the time was approaching for a move away from government, and back to the barracks. Power is only attractive when it works.

President Roberto Eduardo Viola was nominated for the job at the close of 1980; he was conscious of the need to begin a gradual return to civilian democracy, but his period of rule was to prove too brief and ineffective for that. Instead, on March 16, a few days before he assumed the presidency, an event took place which was to prove almost as significant for Argentina. That day, Viola boarded a first class flight to Miami, Florida, and thence to Washington, at the invitation of the president of the United States, to open up a dramatic new era in Argentina's relations with the USA – a friendship which was to have a crucial effect in shaping the Falklands crisis. Ronald Reagan was now president, and Argentina was about to come in from the cold. 'It was like stepping into a warm bath,' recalled one Argentinian diplomat. 'Suddenly everyone who had been freezing you out was giving you bear hugs.' The Humphrey–Kennedy sanctions were lifted. The trickle of US visitors to Buenos Aires became a stream, and then a flood.

One man who was particularly pleased with the new honeymoon was Galtieri. 'It wasn't that sanctions really did us any harm,' he was to confide to a US diplomat, 'it's that we really missed the communion with our brother officers in America.' In the months that followed he was able to make up for lost time. By now commander-in-chief of the army and Viola's right-hand man, he was well-placed to receive the many US military visitors who passed through Buenos Aires.

Galtieri was prominent at all the receptions, even venturing a stilted toast in English at the US embassy in honour of the American army chief-of-staff, General Edward Meyer. Distinguished visitors like former secretary of state Henry Kissinger, and Jeane Kirkpatrick, US ambassador to the United Nations, came to town. 'One star, two stars, three stars – the red carpet was rolled out for all of them,' recalled a US official. 'It was heady stuff for a little country that had spent four years in the wilderness.'

Galtieri, an emotional man, found the reunion especially moving. He had, in 1960, spent six months in engineering training at Fort Belvoir in Virginia. They were, he told Jeane Kirkpatrick, the happiest months of his life. In 1981, he visited the US twice, and on his first trip went to Hollywood and Disneyland. He also discussed with US officials such topics of mutual concern as the march of communism in Central America.

On his second visit Galtieri was treated as a superstar. He was described by one senior US official as 'a majestic figure' and he did not disguise his pleasure at the oft-repeated references to 'Argentina's General Patton'. Indeed, in the months which followed, Galtieri would seem to betray, in occasional gestures or glances, a conscious cultivation of the faint physical resemblance to George C. Scott – who portrayed the Second World War General on film – that his US hosts had pointed out.

The culmination of the visit was a lunch hosted by the Argentinian ambassador Esteban Takacs. The guest list was impressive: Caspar Weinberger (secretary for defence), Richard Allen (White House national security adviser), General Edward Meyer (US army chief of staff) and Thomas Enders (assistant secretary of state for Latin America) were all there. In the keen status-ranking of the Washington scene, anyone who could pull that kind of crowd had clearly arrived.

Galtieri was not slow to form his conclusions. As he told the official Argentinian news agency Telam: 'On the domestic level, Argentina must analyse what this means in the context of the recent past, our present and our future. At the foreign level, Argentina has a leading role to play in the world and must not be satisfied with a secondary role.'

Galtieri clearly felt there were sound reasons for him to believe that Argentina counted for the United States as she had never counted before. The situation in Central America was deteriorating and the US congress – wary after the Vietnam experience – had limited to fifty-seven the number of US 'advisers' permitted in El Salvador. The dirty work America could not do, Argentina was delighted to do for her, and Galtieri agreed to send troops to help out. 'Argentina had 500 army men operating mainly out of Honduras on sabotage raids in Nicaragua,' admitted one American official. 'It was something they believed in – it was an extension of the dirty war.' The renewed warmth of the relationship had revived the possibility – always a popular one in Buenos Aires – of a South Atlantic security pact in which the US and Argentina would join forces against the Soviet menace. As Argentina prepared to step on to the stage of international destiny, he, Galtieri, was convinced he was grooming himself for his own role in history.

By the time of his triumphant visit to the United States, Galtieri was more than just head of the army, he was heir apparent to the president. Viola's good intentions of leading the country back into democracy were being flooded with economic problems. By November 9, it was announced that he was suffering from ill health and for the next few weeks Galtieri, backed by the head of the navy, Admiral Anaya, manoeuvred slowly for power. By December 22, Galtieri had inched his way into the Casa Rosada, and the presidency.

But even as president and commander-in-chief, Galtieri was not an all-powerful dictator, Latin American style. Since 1976, power had rested with the military junta composed of the commander-in-chief of the three armed forces – Galtieri was but one of three members. No major policies or decisions could be made without a consensus from the junta. They, in turn, depended on the approval of a corpus of senior commanders in their respective forces, and these, for their part, relied on retaining the loyalty of their junior officers. Maintaining this complex system intact was a cumbersome business which reinforced vacillation and indecision, since each commander knew that any fatal move might offend his own force.

The most secure member of the junta was Admiral Jorge Anaya, safe at the top of the tightly disciplined and professionally proud navy. The junior member, Brigadier Basilio Lami Dozo, head of the air force, did not, in the public view, count for much: the air force never had.

But the commander most burdened by the knowledge of his own vulnerability was Galtieri himself. The army was the largest and traditionally the most factionally divided force. What is more, although Galtieri's term of office as president ran until 1984, his role as commander-in-chief of the army expired at the end of 1982. At that point, like Viola, he would become a retired general holding a much diminished office. If, therefore, he was to make his mark in politics, perhaps to lead the country through some transition to democracy as a popular president, he had to make his move by then.

Right from the start of his presidency, Galtieri needed a success. He had inherited a disastrous economy, with an inflation rate of 150 per cent, and the signs of political revolt were beginning to surface. Of the military's objectives, only the defeat of terrorism had been achieved. The 'dirty war' was still a potent symbol; there was the fear of an inquest if democracy was restored. Galtieri himself said: 'Let's forget the past, let's face the future instead,' but in order to woo the people away from that past, he needed a spectacular achievement to offer them.

1982 was a key year in other ways. It was the year in which the political process was to be taken a step further with the reconstitution of the political parties and the setting up of a programme for elections. The timetable was subject to notorious slippage, but that, at any rate, was the plan. And yet the year was set to begin badly. The effects of the economic crisis were biting deeper into the pockets of a population which felt little love for the military, and a trade union movement which felt no love at all. This discontent was to culminate on March 30 in the most severe riot in six years in Argentina – a trade union demonstration in the Plaza de Mayo brutally suppressed by the police and resulting in 2,000 detained and several hundred injured.

Meanwhile, all the arguments over the Beagle Channel dispute with Chile were being rehearsed through elaborate leaks in the press. There grew in the minds of all of the key men involved the irresistible attraction of going down in legend as the men who finally won back the Malvinas Islands – the one role in Argentina's brief history which was guaranteed to win universal acclaim. For Galtieri, it might carry him on to greater and more permanent power.

As he contemplated his master-stroke, Galtieri felt a growing confidence. There was, after all, one overriding factor in his favour – the new friendship with America. He was convinced that the United States would favour him in his venture – or at the very least would stand aside as he carried it out. He believed (as we shall see), that his government had dropped earlier hints to various US officials of what was to be done in the Malvinas and that the Americans had tacitly given an assurance of non-intervention. Argentina and the US were blood brothers, Galtieri felt. How could the played-out power of the United Kingdom compete with that superb relationship?

That December, Galtieri finally concluded, in close consultation with Anaya, that the Malvinas should be restored to Argentina within the year. And in that same December, the first weapon to be used for this purpose came to hand.

On the remote island of South Georgia, a small group of scrap metal men was engaged on the survey and reconnaissance of an abandoned whaling station. Their work completed, they returned to Buenos Aires to plan the dismantling of the station. By the time they sailed again for South Georgia, political events had begun to pick up speed.

CHAPTER SIX

My Job is War

'What is the point? This island
of rock and ice belongs to nobody but
the penguins, the albatrosses and the
reindeer.'
– Serge Briez, May 1982

The best witnesses to the start of the Falklands war were there by misadventure. Fortunately for history, one of them was a professional film maker; he filmed what he could, tape-recorded some of what people said and wrote down everything he could remember. That was doubly fortunate because the conflict began not in the Falklands but 800 miles away on a remote island of ice called South Georgia.

How the witnesses – three young Frenchmen named Serge Briez, who was the film maker, Olivier Gouon and Michel Roger – came to be there is a saga in itself. Briefly, they had left Buenos Aires on February 9, aboard their forty-foot sailing yacht *Cinq Gars Pour*, intending to sail to the Antarctic where Briez was to make a film. But on March 5, when they were off Cape Horn at the southern tip of Argentina, the winds gusted to more than ninety miles per hour and raised lunatic seas that rolled the ship over; she righted herself eventually but the wheelhouse had been torn off and the tiller smashed. For the next eleven days *Cinq Gars Pour* and her crew were at the mercy of the wind and, under bare poles, they were swept 1,300 miles due west into the South Atlantic until, mercifully, the gale died. They found themselves in sight of South Georgia and, with the aid of a small sail, steered for the safety of the harbour at Grytviken.

If they had not known better, the Frenchmen might have thought they had made it to Antarctica after all. Roughly crescent-shaped, 105 miles long and eighteen miles across at the widest point, the island is covered by glaciers, ice caps and snow-fields for much of the year. The indigenous population is made up of seals, 2,000 or so reindeer and twenty-nine species of birds including, it is reckoned, some ten million penguins. (Indeed, Captain James Cook who claimed South Georgia for the British Crown in January 1775, thought he *had* reached the Antarctic continent. When he discovered it was only an island – he still had 961 miles to go – he sailed away, naming the last promontory he could see, Cape Disappointment.)

Serge Briez and his two friends found approximately thirty people at Grytviken, all of them members of the British Antarctic Survey – an official body which does what its name implies by operating five permanent research bases, one of them on South Georgia. There, specialists conduct biological, ionospheric and meteorological studies for up to two years at a time. The welcome they gave the Frenchmen was almost as frigid as the climate. There was no offer of help to repair the boat and no offer of food, despite the fact that the Frenchmen had lost almost all of their supplies in the capsize and had survived ever since on a very meagre diet. In the hope of melting the ice, Briez and his friends offered what they did have plenty of, which was cognac, but there were no takers. So, they had to help themselves. They managed some repairs to the yacht and, in an abandoned whaling station, they found canned potatoes and carrots which, the labels said, were twenty years old.

Briez attributed the coldness of the welcome to 'psychological problems' caused by months of isolation in a landscape of – to quote Captain Cook – 'horrible and savage aspect I have not words to describe.' Three days after the Frenchmen arrived, however, there arose a much more pressing reason for tension.

On March 19, four BAS scientists who were on a routine field trip to Leith, some twenty miles up the coast from Grytviken, reported by radio that an Argentinian naval fleet auxiliary, *Bahia Buen Suceso*, had anchored in the harbour; about fifty men, some of them in para-military uniform, were unloading supplies; and an Argentinian flag was fluttering from an abandoned tower. The scientists had approached the captain of the ship and pointed out that all this was illegal since no one could land on South Georgia without British permission; nor could they shoot the reindeer which, by now, some of the intruders were doing. The captain claimed that he had a letter of authority from the British foreign office, but he declined to produce it.

By tradition, legal authority on South Georgia is vested in the BAS commander of the Grytviken base who doubles as postmaster, collector of customs, harbour master, receiver of wrecks, registrar, and, most important, magistrate. But in that last capacity BAS commanders get very little practice: the last criminal hearing on South Georgia took place 25 years ago. So, the current commander-cum-magistrate, Steve Martin, merely reported the invasion to the nearest higher authority, the governor of the Falkland Islands, and asked for advice. (South Georgia is administered from the Falklands for convenience but it is a direct dependency of the United Kingdom and *not* of the islands – an important legal distinction which even the British government did not appreciate until it was pointed out early in the crisis by former foreign secretary David Owen. The point was, even if Argentina's claim to the Falklands had some merit – because of geography or prior settlement – South Georgia was, legally, another world.)

On March 20 Governor Hunt sent instructions that the Argentinians should be told to quit Leith immediately. If they wanted to land on South Georgia they must first sail to Grytviken and observe the formalities of requesting entry, receiving permits and having their passports stamped. The orders were passed on to the captain of the *Bahia Buen Suceso* – and rejected. He would only agree to the temporary lowering of the Argentinian flag.

When this news reached Grytviken the three French yachtsmen decided to sail to Leith in the hope of finding a warmer welcome and the materials they needed to finish repairs to their boat. Steve Martin said he would prefer them not to go but they had completed the landing formalities, so there was nothing to stop them going where they liked. On March 21 they sailed to Leith, and there they received a very different reception.

There were, by Briez's count, thirty-eight Argentinians at Leith and nearly all of them were on the pier to greet the yacht. They immediately offered the Frenchmen lunch and, during it, all the supplies they needed. They also offered to help with repairs. The Argentinians explained that they had come to South Georgia to dismantle four old whaling stations and salvage the scrap metal. It would take them two years, they said, but was worth it because the metal was valued at US $10 million. They said they didn't understand why the British were upset. The flag-raising business apart, and that had been a joke, they had a *bona fide* contract – and the full permission of the British embassy in Buenos Aires.

The man responsible for this bizarre invasion of South Georgia – and, thus, the man who struck the spark – was a snappy, fast-talking Argentinian of Greek extraction, still in his thirties, named Constantino Sergio Davidoff. He liked to be thought of as an Argentinian Onassis of the scrap metal world, though often his grander schemes came to nothing. For instance, he tried for a long time to get a contract to salvage the disused maritime cable between Montevideo in Uruguay and Stanley, but found it impossible to raise the necessary funds. Undaunted, in 1977 he came up with the idea of salvaging the whaling stations on South Georgia. And this time, after two years of fund-raising and hard bargaining he clinched what seemed to be the deal of a lifetime.

The owners of the whaling stations, the Christian Salvesen shipping firm of Edinburgh, had been looking for years for somebody to buy the rusting property. (The stations had been closed in the early 1960s.) So Davidoff was able to strike a keen bargain: on September 30, 1979, a deal was signed in London by which he agreed to pay a mere £115,000, in instalments, for whatever he could carry away of the antique steam-driven whale catchers, floating docks, steam winches and the huge sheds where blubber had once been reduced to oil and bone to meal. Since there was an estimated 35,000 tons of metal there and, since the going price for scrap was then £214 a ton, Davidoff and his backers stood to make well over £7 million before expenses.

All of which suggests that the original motivation for the scrapmen's invasion was purely mercenary. The question is, when did it become something more than that? In fact, from the beginning, the foreign ministry had recognised the potential of Davidoff's project. Oscar Camilion, foreign minister under President Viola in 1981 said: 'I always had my eye on Davidoff. He was clearly going to be useful at some stage to ginger up the negotiations.' Camilion's idea had been to leave a few marines on South Georgia as the Argentinians had done, successfully, on Southern Thule in 1976. But by the time Davidoff's men ran up their flag at Leith, they were playing a role in a much grander scheme, devised by a more aggressive foreign minister backed by a very different president.

This came about in part because the British authorities declined the chance of sharing in Davidoff's good fortune. Faced with the problem of getting his men to South Georgia and, in time, the scrap metal back to Argentina, Davidoff approached the British embassy in Buenos Aires and asked if he might charter *Endurance*. He was politely refused.

Davidoff then approached the Argentinian navy for the services of one of its ships. Soon afterwards, in December 1981, he was taken to Leith by the newly-commissioned ice-breaker *Almirante Irizar*, and he went ashore, by his account, to 'make an inventory and take some photographs.' One of the landing party chalked a slogan on a wall proclaiming that the Malvinas belonged to Argentina, and under it the date, December 20.

It is possible that Davidoff did not realise he had landed illegally, and that he should have sailed first to Grytviken to seek permission from the magistrate. But the next month, when he went to the British embassy in Buenos Aires to report his intention to begin work in March, he was told firmly about the rules. Or that at least is the British version of events. Davidoff remembers only the cordiality of his reception: 'They asked me if I would take medical supplies for the British Antarctic Survey on my next trip, and I agreed.'

But there is the fact that by this time the price of scrap metal had slumped so badly that profit from the venture was now likely to be less than one sixth of the original estimate. And if Davidoff was a totally innocent party to any military conspiracy, as he insists, other people were preparing to take advantage of his enterprise. On January 21, the *Caiman*, a forty-ton yacht flying the Panamanian flag, left Mar del Plata for South Georgia. On board were an Italian crew of three and an

Argentinian bank employee named Adrion Marchessi. They were discovered by chance at Leith on February 15 and taken to Grytviken for questioning. Marchessi claimed that his bank was funding Davidoff's enterprise, and said he was there to conduct reconnaissance – claims emphatically denied by Davidoff when he was contacted by the embassy. Confronted with this news, Marchessi shrugged. He also had nothing to say about the three very sophisticated radios found on board *Caiman*.

Then on March 11, and for the third time that year, an Argentinian air force Hercules C130 flew low over South Georgia from Bird Island on the north west tip right along the coast to Calf Head, where scientists were busy weighing albatrosses.

By then the *Bahia Buen Suceso* was well on her way to South Georgia with Davidoff's scrapmen on board. Also on board were a contingent of Argentinian marines, arms, ammunition, radio equipment, field surgical kits and enough supplies for a year. To the scrapmen's surprise, the *Bahia Buen Suceso* had maintained strict radio silence from the moment she left port.

Serge Briez and his friends had been enjoying the scrapmen's company for a little under a week. Late on the night of March 25, as he was going to bed, Briez saw in the beam of his flashlight the super-structure of a large ship sitting in the bay. The *Bahia Buen Suceso*, and her contingent of marines, had departed two days before and there had been no warning of any new arrival. But the cold overcame Briez's curiosity and he went below.

He had scarcely climbed into his bunk when a shuddering jolt sent him racing back on deck. He emerged to find himself face to face with a group of men in camouflaged uniforms, faces blackened, their belts festooned with grenades, automatic rifles on their shoulders. Briez just had time to see more men leaping from the landing craft that had bumped the yacht before a strong light dazzled him, and a voice asked in bad English if he had a radio on board.

Briez was told he was in no danger so long as he did not use the radio or attempt to take any photographs. Despite that warning, once daylight came, he lay in the bottom of a Zodiac dinghy and filmed the disembarkation of troops and equipment from Argentina's newest fleet auxiliary, *Bahia Paraiso*; it took most of the day to get all the men and supplies ashore.

That evening the Frenchmen were again invited to dine with the scrapmen in what used to be the whaling station's hospital. Also there were the troops, more than a hundred of them, now all dressed in civilian clothes. Briez found himself sitting opposite their obvious leader, a slim, boyish-looking man whose shock of fair hair had earned him the nickname 'el Rubio'. He introduced himself as Captain Alfredo Astiz.

It eventually emerged of course, that 'el Rubio' was also once known as 'the Blond Angel', or 'the Hawk', or 'the Butcher of Cordoba', who is alleged to have played a demonic role in the junta's 'dirty war' against internal opponents in 1976 and 1977. The crimes laid at his door by Amnesty International and by the Argentinian commission on human rights, based in Madrid, include kidnapping, torture and suspicion of murder. The French government wished to talk to him about the disappearance of two French nuns – Sister Alice Dumont and Sister Leonie Duquet – who were arrested in December 1977 and taken to the Naval School of Mechanics, where Astiz was a lieutenant, and never seen again. The Swedish government also wished to talk to Astiz, in its case about fifteen-year-old Dagmar Hagelin, whom he kidnapped from a house in Buenos Aires in January 1977, and whom he shot in the back when she tried to escape.

But none of this side of Astiz's nature was apparent to Briez as the two men talked for hours on that first evening. Briez thought him a liberal-thinking man, 'more like a liberal lawyer than a soldier'. Astiz talked longingly about his two favourite cities, London and Paris, and of the small flat he once had in the rue Lecourbe. 'I led a very fashionable life,' Astiz said. 'Cocktails, private viewings, night clubs and concerts – my favourite memory is of a Calder exhibition at Beaubourg. What I liked best about Paris was that all the cultures were represented. Unfortunately I had to leave France in a hurry as some friends were causing me a lot of bother.' (That was in 1979. The 'friends' were a group of Argentinian exiles whom Astiz was sent to infiltrate. He had to flee when his true identity was discovered.) He then became Argentina's naval attaché to South Africa, where almost exactly the same thing happened.

Astiz did not talk much about his current plans but the next day, when his men began laying mines, he explained they were for insurance 'against a possible English assault'. He said there was no possibility of the Frenchmen being allowed to leave until the conflict was resolved. Briez noted in his diary: 'It is like being in a western: the glacial landscape, the isolation, and this abandoned village contribute even more to the unreality of the situation.'

The fact that Argentina had thus mounted an undisguised *military* invasion of British territory was known to the British government almost immediately. An observation post had been set up on a bluff overlooking Leith harbour, and the arrival of the *Bahia Paraiso* and her troops on March 26 was reported by radio to London via a satellite link. But this alarming news was kept a closely-guarded secret. So far as the British public and parliament knew, the only 'invaders' were the scrapmen and there were, the House of Commons was told, only six to ten of them, the rest having departed with the *Bahia Buen Suceso*.

As a result, parliament adjourned for the weekend on March 26, more angered by the insult of the flag-raising episode than alarmed by the military developments of which it knew nothing. Richard Luce, the minister of state for foreign and commonwealth affairs, promised that the scrapmen would 'not be there for very much longer'. And the ministry of defence let it be known that *Endurance* was on her way to South Georgia, or even already in the area, with a party of marines and the authority to use force if necessary.

In fact *Endurance* had sailed from the Falklands for South Georgia almost a week beforehand. On March 19, the day the scrapmen landed, Lieutenant Keith Mills of the Royal Marines was having dinner in Stanley when he was told to round up his men and get them on board *Endurance*. The order came as a surprise because Mills had only just disembarked his twelve-man detachment after months of idle duty on the ship; he and his men had been looking forward to some land-based training as a change.

After four hours sleep the men grabbed what they could from Moody Brook barracks – including, as a contingency, some plastic explosive – while Mills went to see Major Gary Noott, then commander of the Falklands garrison, to ask for more men. Noott agreed to let him have nine additional marines, and the skipper of the *Endurance* agreed to offload ten of his sailors to make way for them.

The skipper, Nick Barker, must have regarded this sudden call to action with wry satisfaction. Ever since the decision to scrap *Endurance* had been announced, he had made a nuisance of himself by telling anyone who would listen that the Argentinians would regard it as a lack of British interest in the future of the Falklands. Eventually, after Barker had gone to the foreign office – in November 1981 – to pursue his campaign, he had been told by his superiors in no uncertain terms that he was causing displeasure 'in high places', and that he was to desist.

Endurance sailed from Stanley at 8.30 a.m. on March 20. But if Barker and Lt. Mills expected to engage in some positive action they were disappointed. On March 23, when *Endurance* was only four hours sailing time from Leith, they were ordered by London to put into Grytviken and await further instructions. Mills decided that he would at least go on and look at the opposition, and he and Sergeant Major Peter Leach were airlifted by one of *Endurance*'s two Wasp helicopters to within eight miles of Leith. After resting overnight, they climbed and scrambled over the impossible terrain to within 500 yards of the Argentinian encampment. They arrived in time to see the *Bahia Paraiso* unloading her men and equipment.

Mills had it in mind to mount a 'police operation' against the ship – the Wasp helicopters were armed with rockets and the *Endurance* herself had two 20mm cannons – but the ministry of defence and the foreign office in London said no. Instead, when the *Bahia Paraiso* sailed from Leith on March 27, *Endurance* was ordered to make daily patrols up the coast to make sure she did not return. On the very first patrol, *Endurance* discovered that the Argentinian ship had gone no further than the edge of international waters, three miles offshore, and was sailing a parallel course.

Meanwhile, London put its faith in diplomacy. The British ambassador Anthony Williams was dispatched to negotiate with the Argentinian foreign ministry. He went armed with a concession: if the scrapmen wanted to remain on South Georgia they would have to complete the landing formalities, but, to save them the trouble of going to Grytviken, the magistrate would go to Leith. When the offer was declined, Williams complained to Foreign Minister Costa Mendez. Costa Mendez replied by complaining of an 'outrage' that had occurred at the Stanley offices of the airline LADE: on March 22 someone had got into the place, removed the somewhat tatty Argentinian flag that hung there, and left a message written in toothpaste which said, 'Tit for tat you buggers.' After consulting with London, Williams, in his turn, demanded that the LADE office should be closed down.

On March 27 Costa Mendez announced that the *Bahia Paraiso* was being sent to South Georgia, which was disingenuous since she was already there. More ominous were reports in the Argentinian press that two corvettes, two destroyers and a submarine had sailed 'in readiness for operations in the South Atlantic', and that all navy leave had been cancelled. On March 29, the aircraft carrier *Veintecinco de Mayo* sailed from Puerto Belgrano.

Yet it was not until about 8 p.m. on March 31 that Lt. Mills was summoned by Captain Barker and told that London now believed full-scale invasions of the Falklands *and* South Georgia were 'probable'. The orders were for the *Endurance* to sail for the Falklands within the hour, and for the marines to remain on South Georgia.

Barker told Mills that the marines were expected to put up 'enough of a show' to make the Argentinians use force, but not enough to get themselves killed. 'In three weeks time this place is going to be surrounded by tall grey ships but we are not going to be able to help you if you're dead,' said Barker. He thought that half an hour's resistance would be sufficient.

But as Mills went down the gangplank he was heard to say: 'Fuck half an hour; I'm going to make their eyes water.'

Twenty miles up the coast, where the Argentinian marines were obviously preparing for something, Serge Briez asked Astiz whether 'this island of rock and ice' was worth fighting for. Astiz's reply was sharp: 'Your job is to make adventure films. Mine is to make war. I don't like war but I have chosen to be a soldier, and I'm ready to give my life for my country.'

CHAPTER SEVEN

A Case to Answer

'No one likes an unpleasant surprise. The immediate reaction of all
of us when we have an unpleasant surprise is to say, first, "Why
was I not warned?" and secondly, "Could not something have
been done to stop it happening?"'
– Humphrey Atkins, former minister of state, foreign and
commonwealth office, July 1982.

Inquests can be dangerous: not only for those who are being
investigated, but often for those who carry them out. Political inquests
are the most lethal of them all. They tend to backfire.

Nevertheless, the events that led up to the invasion of the Falklands
warrant the closest scrutiny, not just because no country should go to
war without knowing precisely why it has done so, but because the
Falklands war was a peculiarly unnecessary one. The misjudgments
made, both in London and Buenos Aires, in the weeks that preceded it,
reflect not just on the leadership of both countries but on the
institutions set up to prevent just such a thing occurring.

Lord Carrington accepted that when he resigned as foreign
secretary. And Mrs Thatcher accepted it when, within six days of the
Argentinian invasion, she announced the setting up of an inquiry
whose terms of reference were published later: 'To review the way in
which the responsibilities of government in relation to the Falkland
Islands and their dependencies were discharged in the period leading
up to the Argentine invasion of the Falkland Islands on April 2, 1982,
taking account of all such factors in previous years as are relevant.' She
appointed one of Britain's most distinguished diplomats, Lord
Franks, to head it.

The analysis that follows is not an attempt to pre-empt that inquiry.
It could not possibly do so without the access to civil servants,
intelligence agents, diplomats and classified papers that Lord Franks
has. What it aims to do is to pose some of the hard questions that will
have to be answered if the inquiry is to do its job.

We can go some way, of course, to filling one gap which Humphrey
Atkins identified in the House of Commons on July 8: 'It takes two to
make a bargain,' he said, 'and it takes two to make a quarrel.' The
inquiry will not be able to hear at first hand the junta's version of

events, and without that, it will inevitably be a one-sided affair. We have been able to talk to many of those in Buenos Aires who had an intimate knowledge of the Argentinian leadership and its intentions towards the Falklands. That evidence is crucial.

The most fundamental thing to decide is also the hardest: what were President Galtieri's plans at any one point? The line put out by the foreign office in London is that until March 29, the eve of the invasion, there was no intention by the junta to invade, and so no intelligence could have discovered anything to report.

That explanation is inadequate: 'You don't set up an invasion in forty-eight hours,' observed one Pentagon official. 'There's more to it than putting a few guys on a few boats.'

There is, however, a more subtle line of defence: the Argentinian invasion plans were made up as events moved along. It was an ad hoc affair, the seizing of chances as and when they occurred. This version implies that the junta made no collective decision until very late on. So again, intelligence could not possibly have picked up the *intent* to invade.

Again, this is hard to believe. For one thing, intelligence *did* pick up intent – far earlier than has been admitted. But the signals were either misread or ignored.

In early July 1981, as we have seen, the foreign office handed Lord Carrington its assessment of what was likely to happen over the Falklands, prepared at the all-day conference of June 30. It predicted that with the 150th anniversary of British rule looming, Argentina would try and force the issue before the end of 1982. But invasion, it said, would be Argentina's last card, to be played when all else failed. Before then, Argentina was likely to build up pressure with a series of carefully calculated moves, from a protest at the United Nations to the occupation of one of the uninhabited islands. The assessment concluded that the purpose of any such moves would be to speed negotiations rather than pre-empt them. Meanwhile, a little 'gentle pressure' should be applied to the islanders.

It is interesting to note that this assessment was a fairly accurate view of the possibilities then perceived by the foreign ministry in Buenos Aires. But it failed to take any account of the *junta*'s view – which turned out to be very different.

In fact, Carrington rejected the recommendation that 'gentle pressure' should be applied, since he was aware of the intransigence of the Falkland Islands lobby in the House of Commons. But the notion of a gradual build-up of pressure by Argentina rather than an invasion was now a central part of foreign office thinking.

Over Christmas and New Year the foreign office took stock of Argentina's new president, Galtieri, and his foreign minister, Costa

Mendez, and concluded that there was little to concern them. To them, Galtieri seemed a strong but moderate figure, more interested in improving relations with the Americans than in any aggressive adventure. His Oxford-educated foreign minister was seen as distinctly pro-western. Although Galtieri would be likely to press the Malvinas question more strongly than his predecessor Viola, there seemed no reason to alter the view that nothing drastic would happen before the end of 1982.

But why did this judgment persist in London? British embassy officials in Buenos Aires insist that they warned the foreign office in London that the junta was likely to take a hard line, and that Anaya in particular had long nursed ambitions to seize the Falkland Islands back – ambitions which he would like to put into effect. There were several cables along these lines to Robin Fearn, head of the South American department. These warnings, say the officials, were discounted.

The reason is seemingly that there was some scepticism when messages of this kind arrived at the foreign office. The Buenos Aires embassy had been sending back similar warnings ever since Anthony Williams had arrived there in 1980, and it had, in consequence, acquired in London the reputation of being alarmist.

Costa Mendez's private briefings to journalists in Buenos Aires at the end of 1981 about the possibility of Argentina using force, do not seem to have caused any reaction, if indeed word of them got back to London at all. But the now famous article in *La Prensa* on January 24, with its overt discussion of the invasion option, was certainly transmitted back, as were other articles along the same lines.

Three days later the foreign office received a *bout de papier* from Buenos Aires setting out what the junta expected from the forthcoming talks in New York. The main demand was for an agreed programme leading to a transfer of sovereignty.

Since the foreign office's policy amounted to little more than spinning things out, this demand was a blow. Richard Luce replied that he could agree nothing in advance of the talks. Any outcome would have to be endorsed by the British cabinet. But, to show seriousness, he proposed to bring along two representatives of the Falkland Islands executive council.

This response clearly upset the junta. It is noticeable that from this moment on they began to harden their attitude considerably. Costa Mendez had been given twenty days by Galtieri and Anaya to produce a plan of campaign for the Malvinas, and in late January he did so – the *Prensa* article was a reflection of it.

What Costa Mendez envisaged was a plan to have the Malvinas back by the end of 1982. To do it he would step up the diplomatic pressure. If this did not work, there would be some form of military action, possibly a commando landing, which would be used as a powerful diplomatic weapon. Meanwhile, they would offer considerable inducements to persuade the British to accept the inevitable, like joint plans for oil exploration, and generous terms for any islanders who wanted to leave.

Many of these ideas, including the threat of force, were reflected in the Argentinian press as the New York talks approached. Indeed, Luce complained about their tone when he met Ros on February 26. But on the more substantial issues – such as Argentina's renewed insistence on an agreed timetable for talks – he could only stall, as usual. The failure to produce a time table went down very badly with the junta, who had anyway been responsible for encouraging the hard-line press reports, and it was reflected in the statement issued on March 1 in Buenos Aires.

On March 8, Tom Enders made his visit to Buenos Aires and transmitted to Costa Mendez the British assurance that they were keen to continue talking. The reply, as we have seen, was non-committal.

At this point, the difference in perception between the two sides is enormous. The British have, in their possession, all the information that points towards an Argentinian disposition to use force – the press comment, the hard-line junta, the relative failure of the New York talks, and the tough statement issued in Buenos Aires which flies in the face of the joint communiqué. All this should indicate that the foreign ministry is no longer a reliable indicator of the junta's opinion.

Yet, paradoxically, the British foreign office appears to interpret all these signs as being predictable actions giving no cause for concern. The view that the Argentinian approach will be a gradual one is still well entrenched. It is also compounded by the miscalculation that in New York the Argentinians had basically got what they wanted. There is, therefore, little apprehension. Indeed there now occurs a crucial decision by Carrington that is evidence of this.

On March 2, Costa Mendez had sent Carrington a tough letter threatening to break off talks unless the British were prepared to make concessions. Carrington drafted an equally tough letter and sent a copy to the Falkland Islands executive council for their approval. So strong was Carrington's tone that the islanders not only approved his letter without change, they cabled back their delight.

But *the letter was never sent*. Carrington was later to say that he had not had time to send it. In fact it had been decided not to send the letter at that stage because it was judged better to do nothing precipitate and to wait instead for the outcome to the Enders mission. Great importance was attached to this – far more than Enders himself ever realised. And when he came back with a strictly neutral response the foreign office seems to have read it in an over-optimistic light. 'It's OK, you've got nothing to worry about,' was how one foreign office official characterised it. This was reinforced by a reassuring interview that Williams had in Buenos Aires with Costa Mendez.

Carrington's failure to respond to Costa Mendez in any vigorous manner was influenced by the thought that the Argentinians were probably trying to pick a quarrel. The best response, therefore, was not to rise to the bait. But ironically this had the opposite effect in Buenos Aires where it confirmed the Argentinian view that the British were not disposed to take strong action over the Falklands. It undoubtedly acted as a spur to what was already being mapped out.

There was, however, another tack to the British approach. In the week between March 3 and 9, the foreign office and the ministry of defence looked at various contingency plans – 'in case the Argentines do something silly.' This mainly involved assessing how Britain should respond if Argentina cut the supply line to the Falklands. But the Defence Operational Planners in the MoD did also pull out a standard plan for sending a small naval task force to distant oceans.

It would be interesting to know how far these plans were taken. What *might* have happened at this point, had there been genuine concern, was that Carrington might have raised the matter at the cabinet's overseas and defence committee where all the evidence would have been given a thorough airing. It certainly needed some political muscle at that point to raise it beyond mere civil service theorising. But no moves were made.

The next two weeks mark a new phase in the run-up to the invasion, and here the questions become more insistent. On March 11, an Argentinian military plane made what was apparently an emergency landing at Stanley airport. Governor Hunt reported it as suspicious. Then, on March 20, the landing of the scrap metal men and the running up of the Argentinian flag at Leith on South Georgia were reported back to London.

The foreign office reaction showed that their original assessment of what the Argentinians were likely to try, still held. Davidoff, the scrap dealer, was well known in London. It was considered possible, though by no means definite, that he was being used by the Argentinian government to spark an incident. But that in itself was not seen as particularly threatening. Indeed it positively confirmed the original judgment: that the junta would begin to apply a series of pin-pricks. A provocative landing on South Georgia was just the kind of thing that had been predicted.

This view was reflected in the way the British now became a little tougher – but not too tough. They insisted that Davidoff had to apply properly for a visa to Grytviken. But at the same time they took care not to make too great a fuss and above all to do nothing to give the junta any excuse for further action. *Endurance* was dispatched to South Georgia with a party of marines. But on arrival they were instructed not to do anything. The British Antarctic Survey base commander was required to get the scrap metal men to take down their flag, and in

Buenos Aires a protest was lodged at the foreign ministry. But no warning of British retaliation was made. The remonstrations were extremely well-mannered. The foreign office line at this stage was: 'not an important problem, though one that has to be dealt with'.

On March 21, word got back to London (inaccurately, as it turned out) that the Argentinian navy had responded to the requests to remove the scrap metal men, and that most of them had gone. Although Humphrey Atkins was to tell the House of Commons that it had happened, the party remained in place. It was on the same date that the LADE airline office in Stanley was mildly vandalised in retaliation for the South Georgia flag-raising incident, and this incident was used in Buenos Aires to raise the temperature considerably. Ambassador Williams found himself summoned no fewer than three times to the foreign ministry to hear of Argentina's outrage.

Plainly by now the junta was deliberately stepping up the pressure. But had they decided to invade? It is here that a more sophisticated interpretation of Argentinian politics might have helped, for its government was far from united on the issue. As far as Costa Mendez and the foreign ministry were concerned the answer was: not yet. The screw was being tightened, but there had not yet been time for it to have an effect on the British, and this combination of threat and promise was still at a relatively early stage. But Costa Mendez *was not the junta*. As was to become increasingly clear, he was already out of step with events: the pace had begun to accelerate.

Anaya and Galtieri had undoubtedly by now embarked on a plan which would result in invasion. That is not to say it was irrevocable: if the British suddenly caved in on negotiations, or indeed reacted with overwhelming force, then the plan could still be called off or altered.

The evidence to back up this assertion comes from several sources, but the main one, surprisingly, is Galtieri himself. In an interview with the Italian journalist Oriana Fallaci, he pin-pointed the British decision to remove the scrap metal men from South Georgia as the spark that led to invasion. That may be judged inconclusive evidence, but there are other clues.

On March 22, Jeane Kirkpatrick, lunching in Washington with the Argentinian ambassador, was given what she now recognises as 'an elliptical warning' that the invasion was at hand. She was told that the Argentinians viewed the Falklands just as seriously as the Beagle Channel and would not hesitate to take steps to retrieve them.

The same warning was given to Tom Enders. But the wording was too opaque for both of them, seasoned operators though they are. Both now confess that they simply failed to read the signs.

More explicitly, however, British intelligence sources in Buenos Aires, on March 24, picked up definite information that an invasion was in train. Not only was that information passed back to London. It was partly confirmed by further intelligence possibly gathered by

Sigint, the signals intelligence headquarters at Cheltenham in the West of England.

Since this evidence is so crucial, it is worth giving in some detail. The British secret intelligence service, or MI6, has a base in Buenos Aires. Every Wednesday a meeting is held after lunchtime to assess current information and this meeting is attended by, amongst others, the naval and military attachés at the British embassy.

That Wednesday, March 24, the subject for assessment was the growing feeling that something was up, and specifically that the Argentinian naval manoeuvres currently taking place were a prelude to invasion in the Falklands. Evidence from various naval ports suggested that these were more than just ordinary exercises. The explanation that they were routine and were being carried out jointly with the Uruguayan navy did not conform to first-hand intelligence from naval bases. Through sources in the US embassy, checks were carried out which convinced the British that invasion plans were indeed underway.

After comparing notes with their opposite numbers at the American embassy, the British concluded that it was all for real. They even predicted the exact date of an invasion. *And they were right.*

All this was apparently passed back to London. Two days later, March 26, Captain Astiz and his marines arrived in South Georgia, fully armed and equipped. They had obviously been preparing for several days in advance, if not weeks. And again the information was sent back to London because they were spotted on the day they arrived by Lieutenant Mills who had by now landed on South Georgia himself.

The same day news was transmitted to London that the Argentinian guided missile corvettes, *Drummond* and *Granville* were heading for South Georgia (the news was published in Argentina next day). Mike Norman's contingent of marines, who left that day to take over duties in the Falklands and had been briefed at the foreign office a week earlier, were told that there would be 'sabre-rattling', no more.

That evening in Buenos Aires the junta met late into the night at their military headquarters. Costa Mendez addressed them, then left. There was no word of what they had been discussing. The British ambassador, Anthony Williams, requested the US ambassador, Harry Schlaudemann, to invoke American assistance in resolving the South Georgia incident, and Schaludemann agreed to do what he could.

The question that has to be posed at this stage is: why, if all this information was floating about, was it not correctly channelled and assessed in London?

That can only be answered by Lord Franks's committee. But the questions revolve around the function of a body called the Joint Intelligence Committee, which assesses all incoming intelligence from abroad, from whatever source. The JIC is a department of the cabinet office, reporting directly to one of the most senior officials there. He in turn answers directly to the prime minister. The virtue of the system is that it is intended to perform independently of the foreign office and thus to bring a different view to bear on the information flowing in. The disadvantage appears to be twofold: it relies heavily on the foreign office for much of the information it receives. And it has far too much to cope with. The fact that the JIC is part of the cabinet office means it has no direct line to any politician except the prime minister, and she is far too busy to give its reports the attention they need.

Just as the foreign office tended to put a low priority on information from its embassy in Buenos Aires, so the JIC does not appear to have been geared to process the raw intelligence it was receiving from South America. It may be relevant to point out that the assessments sub-committee of the JIC is always chaired by a foreign office representative.

On Monday, March 29, four days before the invasion, the JIC did report. Its assessment of the SIS intelligence reports from Buenos Aires was given to Thatcher and Carrington as they flew to Brussels for an EEC meeting. At last, light began to dawn, for it was almost certainly at this point that a decision was finally taken to send a nuclear-powered submarine to the South Atlantic. Travelling-time: approximately ten days from Gibraltar. That day, reports that five Argentinian warships had left port were confirmed. British intelligence also picked up the movements of an Argentinian submarine operating off the Falklands and passed the message to Hunt in Stanley. And an Argentinian Hercules flew low over Mike Norman's marines.

In America, the state department had also begun to take the South Georgia issue seriously, but they were only reacting to the British mood. Carrington had promised to send Haig a message explaining the background, but it did not arrive until the weekend of March 27/28. Both the British ambassador, Sir Nicholas Henderson, and his Argentinian counterpart Esteban Takacs were summoned to the state department and offered the mediating help of the US – on an even-handed basis, much to Henderson's fury. It was not until Schlaude-mann in Buenos Aires was told directly by Costa Mendez next day that the so-called South Georgia problem was far bigger than that – involving as it did the future of the Falklands – that the scale of the crisis emerged.

On March 30, for the second time in a week, Costa Mendez snubbed Williams in Buenos Aires by failing to turn up for a dinner engagement. The assessments were growing more precise, and were judged sufficiently serious for Carrington to alter his travel plans, although not serious enough for him to cancel them altogether. He was due to proceed directly from the EEC meeting at Brussels to Israel; instead he returned briefly to London to make a statement in the Lords before continuing his journey.

It has often been said since that by this stage not only was there nothing Britain could do – a task force would have taken at least ten days to reach the area – but that the best approach was to stand back, partly to avoid provocation, but also so that in the event of an invasion Britain could go to the United Nations 'with clean hands' as the innocent party. Carrington's departure for Israel, early on March 31, however, suggests that even at this stage he did not appreciate the political magnitude of the threat.

But even if this was the game-plan, one thing is still baffling: throughout the whole period of diplomatic exchanges between the two capitals, not once does Britain appear to have said to Argentina: 'If you invade, we will take action.' It is possible, of course, that the message would not have been believed. But it should at least have been sent. Perhaps, however, the British decision to resort to force was not taken until the eve of the invasion – when Mrs Thatcher finally appreciated the seriousness of the problem, and decided to act. In which case there is a nice irony: could it have been Argentina which was consistent – and the British who played it by ear?

On March 31, the penny finally dropped. That afternoon defence secretary Nott was handed a piece of intelligence which almost certainly came from Sigint, and included news that the *Veintecinco de Mayo* had changed direction, and that an Argentinian submarine was checking landing-sites around Stanley. He hurried straight to Number Ten Downing Street. That evening Mrs Thatcher and her advisers began refining the plans that were to lead to the sending of the task force.

The final attempt to prevent a war took place that evening, March 31, when a cable arrived late in the evening at the White House from Mrs Thatcher asking President Reagan if he would intervene personally with President Galtieri. Next day several attempts were made to contact Galtieri at the Casa Rosada. For a long time the message came back that the president was not available.

Finally at approximately 8 p.m. on April 1, the connection was made. Speaking slowly and precisely in English, Reagan spelled out to Galtieri the consequences of an invasion. American public opinion, he said, would not stand for it. An invasion would be a grave set-back to good relations between Argentina and the United States. It must be called off.

Galtieri began by speaking in his broken English. But Reagan could not understand him. So a state department interpreter took over and began to translate Galtieri's long explanation of his country's inalienable right to the Malvinas. Fifty minutes later, Reagan, having made one final appeal to Galtieri 'to avoid tragedy and bloodshed' hung up the phone. 'I guess I spelled it out,' he said. 'But it didn't sound as if the message got through.'

Reagan can hardly be blamed. The message had not been getting through for a long, long time.

CHAPTER EIGHT

A Most Ungentlemanly Act

'It looks as if the silly buggers mean it'
– Governor Rex Hunt, April 1982

Sometime after breakfast on Wednesday, March 31, Governor Rex Hunt learned from London that the Argentinian submarine was on its way. At 10.30 a.m., Hunt summoned the two marine majors, Mike Norman and Gary Noott, to discuss what their meagre garrison might do. Nothing indicates better just how badly Britain was still miscalculating the looming crisis than the plan that emerged from that meeting.

That afternoon, Corporal David Carr was dispatched with two marines to the lighthouse overlooking Cape Pembroke, armed with binoculars and night sights. Lance Corporal Steve Black meanwhile volunteered to mount a lone vigil on Sapper Hill. Between them they were supposed to spot the submarine and, when they did, call out the Reaction Squad. Ready to react were Corporal Steve Johnson, five marines and two Land Rovers. They would, in theory, race to whichever beach the submarine had chosen to reconnoitre, and arrest the landing party. And that, Britain firmly believed, would be that.

As Norman later explained: 'We believed that the Argentinians were simply in the niggling game and the submarine wasn't anything for us to worry about.' Or, as the governor put it: 'We thought there would be a bit of a scrap on the beach and then we would all have a glass of sherry and I'd tell them to go away, and jolly well not come back.'

The blame for that gross delusion can scarcely be laid with Hunt or the marines. Their reading of the situation inevitably depended on such intelligence as the foreign office chose to pass on; and on London's interpretation of that information. And though we do not know the precise content of the cables sent to Hunt in the final days, it is apparent from what happened that they did not even contemplate the immediate possibility of a full-scale Argentinian invasion. Rather, London clung to the belief – formulated in the 1981 intelligence review – that invasion would be the very last step in a march of steady and predictable escalation; and though the pace was undoubtedly mounting, there were still several steps to go.

So when, on that Wednesday night, Norman and Noott dined on roast beef and pork with a local doctor and the first secretary, Dick

Baker, the talk was reassuring: the mission of the submarine was, like the landing on South Georgia, just another example of Argentina raising the stakes.

As if to confirm that, the submarine did not even show up – or if it did, it stayed well away from the best landing beaches. For all that night the motor vessel *Forrest*, with its skipper Jack Sollis and six marines on board, sat anchored in York Bay keeping watch. The radar saw nothing and neither did the marines. At dawn on Thursday they gave up and sailed back to Stanley, tired and a little downcast.

It was not until the middle of that Thursday afternoon – just thirteen hours before the first Argentinian troops would land – that the foreign office finally told Hunt what was in store for the islands. London said that a considerable invasion fleet was on its way and unless it changed course it would be off Cape Pembroke by first light.

Norman and Noott were out at the airport, doing a little spying on the LADE offices, when they were summoned by radio to Government House. Hunt showed them the latest cable. 'It looks,' he said, 'as if the silly buggers mean it.'

Very few people on the islands were aware of the mounting evidence that invasion was imminent. The marines had kept watch for the submarine with deliberate stealth. And Hunt had kept the secret from almost everyone, including his wife.

So, as usual, Mavis Hunt went shopping that Thursday afternoon. It was a ritual she thoroughly enjoyed: being driven to the West Store supermarket in the governor's official car – a maroon-coloured London diesel taxi – and touring the shelves with her husband's chauffeur, Don Bonner, in tow, carrying the basket. Bonner had a very acute nose and insisted that something was 'going on at GH' but Mrs Hunt, in all innocence, reassured him.

Clues to the crisis were, however, beginning to emerge. Claudette Moseley, who worked at the local radio station, met a girl friend from the cable and wireless office who had finished her stint of duty at 2 p.m. but who had now been urgently recalled. 'What's up?' asked Claudette. 'I don't know,' said the girl, 'but it's bad, very bad.' At the offices of the government secretariat, sixteen-year-old Natalie McPhee was told to pull out the file containing the telephone numbers and home addresses of all the island's officials; they were wanted for a meeting at Government House at 4.30 p.m.

At about the same time, a piece of very solid evidence fell into the hands of Simon Winchester, a senior foreign correspondent from *The Sunday Times*. Along with three other British reporters, he had flown to Stanley, via Buenos Aires, to write about the scrapmen's invasion of South Georgia, and in the harbour the ever-resourceful Winchester had found a Czech round-the-world yachtsman willing to take him to Leith. ('There's no problem at all,' said the Czech. 'It'll take us four days – if there's a good storm.') That Thursday afternoon, in preparation for the voyage, they went sailing in York Bay to check the alignment of the compass and, on the way back through the narrows, Winchester saw a group of marines setting up something on Navy Point; he was sure it was either a machine-gun or a mortar.

When Winchester got back to the Upland Goose Hotel, where the journalists were staying, he found another clue: Ken Clark of *The Daily Telegraph* had been due to interview the first secretary, Dick Baker, but at the last moment Baker had cancelled the appointment, pleading an urgent meeting at Government House.

That meeting had just begun when Mavis Hunt returned from her shopping expedition. She was alarmed to hear voices coming from the drawing room and, thinking there might be intruders, she burst into the room. 'We are busy, darling,' said her husband. 'We'll see you later.'

They were indeed busy. Hunt and the dozen or so of his officials gathered in the drawing room had just received more and quite devastating news from London. The latest signal interceptions showed that the Argentinians had somehow gathered the most detailed intelligence about the dispositions and habits of the British marines: how many of them there were; where they slept and when; and precisely how they spent their days. John Fowler, the superintendent of education, remembers being quite staggered by the extent and the accuracy of the espionage. Hunt, in similar disbelief, held his head in his hands.

The speculation as to how the Argentinians knew was more or less unanimous. The seventeen Argentinian 'gas workers' almost certainly included spies, and the LADE airline office possessed a radio transmitter powerful enough to send the information back to Buenos Aires. But, as Hunt said, for the moment that was irrelevant. There was work to be done.

The first thing was to ensure that nothing important fell into enemy hands. John Fowler went off to the treasury to lock up the accounts and administrative records. Meanwhile, Brian Wells – a foreign office man who, though officially described as the governor's archivist, was essentially in charge of communications – set to work on destroying all classified documents. His wife, Christine, who was Hunt's private secretary, had the necessary security clearance to operate the shredder but the sheer weight of paper meant she could not cope alone. Wells therefore asked the governor to give four of the navy men, left behind by the *Endurance*, immediate clearance. He did, and at 5 p.m. the wholesale destruction began; one of the sailors helping Christine to shred, two more burning papers in disused oil drums, the fourth setting to work on wrecking a cypher machine.

To Mavis Hunt the oil drum bonfires were ominously reminiscent of the last days in Vietnam, and she remembered the awful scene she had made when her husband tried to persuade her to leave Saigon. This time, she resolved, she would not insist on staying with him because if she went to the Bakers' house for the night it would give him one less thing to worry about. She pottered around in the garden for a while and then went indoors to drink some brandy. Don Bonner, the chauffeur, took her a customary bucket of ice. She said she couldn't tell him what was going on because 'H.E.' – as she invariably called her husband – wanted to tell everyone himself, in an official announcement. But Bonner guessed. He used to be in the navy and when the ship's papers were thrown over the side it was always a sign of trouble. 'It's grim, isn't it?' he said.

At 7.30 p.m. Falkland Islands radio opened up for its evening transmission by broadcasting, as always, 'The Thunderer', a stirring march played by the band of the Irish Guards. There were very few islanders who would not have been listening because the radio was one of their most important life-lines, not only with the outside world but also between Stanley and the scattered communities at Darwin, Goose Green, San Carlos, Teal Inlet, Fox Bay, Pebble Island, and elsewhere. It re-broadcast important items from the BBC World Service but its main fare was news about the essential trivia of daily life: the schedule of mail drops and pick-ups to be flown by the internal airline, Government Air Services; the names of passengers booked on the various flights; when and where medical supplies would be available. That would be followed by the 'smallads' – the houses, the farms, the cars and the carpets that were for sale. And then would come seemingly endless record request programmes that would only occasionally allow the intrusion of 'disco sounds' for the youngsters; the main diet was the comfortable beat of country and western, and rollicking Scottish tunes from the likes of Jimmy Shand and his Band.

But that Thursday evening the pattern was changed. After 'The Thunderer' came the news that at 8.15 p.m. the governor would broadcast an important announcement.

All over the islands, people speculated. Ian White, one of the inter-islands pilots, had already guessed that something was up because the governor's plane, a Britten-Norman Islander, had been moved from the airport and parked, near White's house, on Stanley Racecourse – the title grandly given to the neat stretch of turf where race meetings were occasionally held. Angela, his wife, hurried to get their two sons to bed so they could listen to the announcement in peace. The thought of invasion never entered their heads. But, fortunately, White still decided to tape-record the broadcast. He was thus able to preserve for posterity what must surely be a unique piece of radio – the first invasion 'phone-in'.

It began, at precisely 8.15 p.m., with a somewhat irreverent introduction from the station's chirpy Canadian announcer, Mike

Smallwood: 'Get your ears tuned in for the governor, folks.'

Good evening. I have an important announcement to make about the state of affairs between the British and Argentine governments over the Falkland Islands dispute. We have now sought an immediate emergency meeting of the (United Nations) security council on the grounds that there could be a situation which threatens international peace and security. I don't yet know whether it has been possible to arrange a meeting today but our spokesman has been asked to make the following specific points.

Hunt then went on to spell them out: the refusal of the Argentinians to negotiate over 'the illegal presence of Argentinian nationals on South Georgia'; and the 'mounting evidence that the Argentine armed forces are preparing to invade the Falkland Islands.' In those circumstances, Hunt said, he thought it necessary to take certain precautions.

I have alerted the Royal Marines and I now ask for all serving members or active members of the Falkland Islands defence force to report to the drill hall as soon as possible. They will be on guard tonight at key points in the town. Schools will be closed tomorrow. The radio station will stay open until further notice. If the security council's urging to keep the peace is not heeded by the Argentine government I expect to have to declare a state of emergency, perhaps before dawn tomorrow. I shall come on the air again as soon as I have anything to report. But in the meantime I would urge you all to remain calm and keep off the streets. In particular do not go along the airport road, stay indoors and please do not add to the troubles of the security forces by making demonstrations or damaging Argentinian property. This would play into their hands and simply provide them with the excuse they need to invade us. So please do not take the law into your own hands. Let us show our visitors that we are responsible, law abiding, resolute citizens. I shall let you know as soon as I have anything further to report.

There was a pregnant pause before Patrick Watts, the station chief, came on the air to say that as 'the situation here is rather serious' they would keep broadcasting through the night, but:

Please don't expect that every five minutes or every half an hour we are going to be able to give you an information bulletin because this may not happen. As His Excellency said, as soon as he has news he will broadcast with us. Please don't become impatient and expect us to bring you hot news every five minutes. Thank you very much and just keep listening to the FIBS. If there is news we will certainly tell you about it.

Mike Smallwood, who then took over the microphone, had lost none of his bounce:

Well, as it says in those large famously friendly letters on The Hitch-

Hiker's Guide to the Galaxy, *DON'T PANIC. It's now time for requests ... and we begin with 'You are my Best Friend' by Don Williams. This is for Fred, Joyce, Pop, Maggie, Eileen, Jim and Cyril ... from Dolly.*

As the music faded in, Smallwood interrupted to say that after the record, and 'by popular request', there would be a repeat of the governor's announcement.

Ian White switched off his tape-recorder. He and Angela looked silently at each other for a moment. Was it really true? They both decided it could not be; it was some kind of bad taste joke. The Argentinians were just using scare tactics to try and frighten the islanders into giving them what they wanted.

At the Upland Goose Hotel, Simon Winchester and his fellow newsmen were incredulous. They were expecting something extraordinary because the governor, before going on the air, had telephoned Winchester to alert him: 'When you've heard my announcement I would like you to come to my office immediately so that I can tell you other matters,' Hunt had said. But talk of armed guards, a state of emergency, and the rest of it smacked of panic. Winchester raced to Government House while his colleagues went to the cable and wireless office to set up the circuits to London.

Hunt was alone in his study. Winchester found him outwardly calm but looking very pale. He showed Winchester the handwritten script of his speech and asked if he had been right to omit a passage which would have announced the internment of all Argentinian nationals on the islands. Winchester said yes: that might have given the Argentinians an excuse to invade. 'They don't need one,' said Hunt. 'They're on their way.' Then he showed Winchester the cable from London which warned that invasion was now inevitable.

While the journalists filed their copy, Hunt went back on the air to confess the news to the islanders. He said the invasion force consisted of one aircraft carrier, four destroyers and four landing craft. Nevertheless, he declared, 'We will resist this illegal entry into this colony.' So the public works department was organising emergency food supplies, the runway at Stanley airport was being blocked – and doctors were getting the hospital ready.

Of course, people responded to the news in very individual ways. At Government House, Tony Hunt, the governor's 17-year-old son, watched a trusted retainer named Mary Fullerton prepare to leave with what valued possessions she could carry; a portrait of the Queen in one hand, two bottles of gin in the other. Tony thought she had got her priorities about right.

Owen and Marjorie McPhee and their daughter, Natalie – the clerk at the government secretariat – decided they might as well go to bed. But Marjorie could not sleep and kept going downstairs to the sitting room where they had left the radio on, just in case there was any more news. Natalie had a transistor radio in her bedroom, and lay in the dark listening to it. She was very frightened and she cried bitterly.

Claudette Moseley and her boyfriend, Philip Rozee, decided to spend the night on the porch of Claudette's house. It was a perfect night. They had a stock of beer, packets of cigarettes, and an unimpeded view of Stanley Harbour where they expected to see the Argentinians arrive.

True to the promise to herself, Mavis Hunt left Government House with Tony, for the Bakers' house where their two young daughters, Helen and Karen, had gone to bed with the warning that things might not be quite the same when they woke up. Connie Baker had tried to explain what an invasion was but the children had not really understood; they just went to sleep. Connie decided to do the same but she kept her clothes on, in case. Mavis Hunt stayed downstairs, with her son, Dick Baker and the radio.

The four journalists, naturally enough, went in search of more copy. They first tried the drill hall, where the defence force volunteers were assembling, but they were smartly ejected by a burly sergeant; not before seeing, however, that the volunteers were receiving some fairly basic instruction on how to load and fire their weapons. Next, they went to the radio station where Patrick Watts suggested he should drive them to the splendid Swiss-style chalet that was home to the Stanley manager of LADE airlines. There Roberto Gamen, the current manager, and Hector Gilobert, his immediate predecessor – who had unexpectedly returned from Argentina two days before – denied they had any knowledge of any invasion but the journalists did not believe them, and said so.

Back at the Upland Goose Hotel, they tuned into Argentina's *Radio Nacional* in time to hear a triumphant voice announce: 'The Malvinas will be ours by dawn.' A few minutes later, sometime after midnight, the Falklands' station broadcast news from the BBC World Service that the UN security council had called on Britain and Argentina not to use force, but then the governor came on the air to say the invasion fleet had still not altered course. There was a short silence, followed by an orchestral arrangement of 'How Green is my Valley'.

So it went on. Music and more music, interrupted by occasional announcements from Patrick Watts, who had now taken over the microphone – but there was not very much for him to say. Until, that is, 4.15 a.m., when he once more introduced the governor, and Hunt declared his state of emergency.

As it happened, the journalists at the Upland Goose already knew, because Winchester had opened the hotel door to allow Dick Baker and his naval escort to arrest the Argentinian 'gas workers'. Now that action was obviously imminent, the journalists decided to move to a cottage within the grounds of Government House. It turned out not to be a very good vantage point because it was in the line of fire, and bullets kept flying through the windows. Winchester, for one, was to spend most of his time lying on the floor, unaware of what was really going on.

The same was true for most people. Connie Baker had just woken up when the first explosions occurred at the Moody Brook barracks. Her two young daughters began to cry but she and Tony Hunt calmed them down by making a game of carefully peering out through the windows to see what was happening; all they could see was tracer bullets lighting up the sky. Connie huddled everyone in an upstairs bedroom which seemed the safest spot, and asked Tony to fetch the radio from downstairs. As he did so, a bullet smashed through a ground floor window.

The governor was on the air once more:

Those of you who are living in Stanley will have heard some shots, some confused shooting. We do not yet know what it is all about. But we have had sightings of an aircraft carrier and a destroyer . . . It appears that the first vessel is attempting to come through the narrows into the harbour and is probably heading for . . . trying to get to Government House. Ah, we will keep you . . . we will keep you up to date for as long as we can here . . . If we go off the air, the radio station will carry on. That's all for now.

From her window, Connie Baker could see the flashes in the direction of the airport and tracers around Sapper Hill, and then, to her horror, Argentinian soldiers coming over the top of it.

The Governor reported:

They are passing behind us. They got very close to us, but now they have withdrawn. It is only a matter of time before they regroup and come again. They have not done much damage and I think they have been shooting . . . not to get . . . not to shoot the men but to get the vehicles. They have flattened the tyres of the vehicles outside and they have got three . . . five armoured personnel vehicles on the way from those landed in York Bay. It is just a matter of time before they . . . er . . . overrun us but we'll . . . we'll see how long we can hang on anyway.

Patricia Watts asked him if he was going to surrender.

We'll see . . . No we're not surrendering. I am resisting . . . If someone is prepared to come into me and talk to me I'll have them in but . . . I'm not going out to talk to them . . . Or to surrender to them . . . We're staying put here. But we are pinned down . . . We can't move.

Hunt told Watts that as yet no one had been injured at Government House, 'thank goodness', but he estimated there were now 200 Argentinian troops surrounding the place and they were using grenades and 'maybe mortars'.

Watts: *Right, sir. Well obviously you are having a very harassing time there and I'll leave you, sir, for now.*
Hunt: *It's getting light. They've got a much more commanding position. We can't move from here without being shot at because they are above us . . . behind us . . . So I'm afraid it is just a matter of time . . . But we'll do what we can.*

Of course, not all the action was going on around Government House and, taking a leaf from the governor's book, other people began ringing the radio station with reports of what they could see and hear. Watts broadcast their calls, too.

Alistair Grieves: *There have been some really heavy bangs and some machine-gun fire and some fairly small arms fire as well. I had a quick look out through the curtains and all I could see was smoke, so honestly I haven't a clue to what's happening. But every time something big goes bang, we feel it.*
Watts: *Where are you phoning this report from, Ali? Are you standing up or sitting down?*
Grieves: *I am lying on the floor, boy.*

The rest of their conversation was punctuated by the sound of loud explosions going off near Grieves' house. Watts asked him if this was cannon fire from the armoured personnel carriers which the governor had warned were on their way. Grieves said he did not know because he was not prepared to look out of the window.

Watts: *Right, I don't blame you. Keep your head down, Ali. If you see them passing perhaps you'd give us a call . . . Cheers.*

Next on the line was John Peatfield who ran the school hostel in Stanley where children from the Camp stayed during term time; he said the children were very calm, and about to have breakfast, and there was no need for their parents to worry.
Then the governor called in to report more shooting at Government House, but also his resolve not to surrender 'to the bloody Argies'.

Watts: *Fantastic . . . well done, sir. Thank you, bye bye. Well, you heard those brave words from the governor. We all echo those . . . I never thought they would do a thing like this, I can tell you. I told everyone they wouldn't. Anyway, that's not the problem at the moment. The problem is that they're here . . . There's another call . . . Hello, Alistair.*
Grieves: *There is a chopper outside as well.*
Watts: *A chopper?*
Grieves: *Yup, coming up the harbour . . . It seems to have disappeared . . . but the armoured cars seem to be moving up the road . . . difficult to say but it could be five or six.*

After more conversation Grieves rang off but Watts had barely had time to say 'We'll go back to the music' before he telephoned again to report that 'a very big' white helicopter had now landed at the airport.

Watts: *Well, that's it . . . It looks as if they are coming in a big way now, I'm afraid ladies and gentlemen. So we'll just have to carry on and do the best we can . . . what the governor said. He's not going to give up that easily.*

But very soon Malcolm Ashworth, who worked at Stanley dairy, was on the line to say that two Argentinian flags were now flying at the airport.

Watts: *Well, let's be fair, Malcolm, it looks as if they have got control of the airport.*
Ashworth: *Well, they are still fighting it out . . . I think. There is a lot of smoke flying around now down there.*

There was only an exhausted sigh from Watts before he put on another record. But moments later:

Watts: *We'll switch off the music because we understand there is a message coming through from the Argentines . . . We want to hear what it is.*

There was the sound of considerable atmospheric interference and then, faintly:

British colonial government . . . (The voice is drowned by static) *. . . for the purpose of avoiding bloodshed . . .*
Watts: *I have been instructed by the governor of the Falkland Islands to call you, the person who relayed that message . . . I don't know if you are hearing us or not, I have been instructed to call you and ask you to repeat the message that you have just read to us.*
(Interference) *. . . our concern is for the welfare and safety of the people of the Malvinas . . .*

The message never did come through clearly but a caller did – to say he could see an aircraft carrier and a corvette just outside the entrance to the narrows.

Watts: *And I'm afraid there is some more bad news. The Argentinian flag is now flying at Moody Brook . . . Moody Brook has been taken . . . and some of the Argentine intruders are now visible behind the houses at Racecourse Road.*

By this time, Hector Gilobert of LADE and Dick Baker had walked into Stanley with their improvised flag of truce, and Watts had broadcast Gilobert's appeal to the Argentinian commander for talks. While they waited for results Watts played another record: 'Granada'.
Then Tom Davis, who lived at White City, called in to say that his house had been hit and the water tank had burst and 'I think we could do with a bit of help sometime'.

Davis: *The house is a wreck . . . It's a write-off, I think.*
Watts: *Gee, Tom.*
Davis: *There is a gaping hole about six feet wide in the roof.*
Watts: *Oh my God.*

The conversation was interrupted by the Argentinian response to Gilobert's appeal for talks.

Your message to the officer commanding of the force of disembarkment . . . He is coming on now to the catholic church to see the people there you have suggest. I say again . . . accepting your requirement . . . Please tell me if you have received my last one? Over.
Watts: *Hello, commander of the group. Yes, I have received your message loud and clear. That is great news . . .*
Argentinian voice: *Malvinas . . . Radio Malvinas in Puerto Stanley, this is the Argentine armed forces . . . It is correct . . . it is correct . . . We are waiting.*

While everybody was waiting, Watts reported some more news:

I've just had a call . . . There are many camp stations, Fitzroy, Green Park . . . are reporting planes. They are flying in . . . But at this moment we are awaiting the outcome of the conference.

Watts replayed 'Granada', then more music, and then the listeners heard him say this:

Just a minute. Just wait there . . . No, I won't do anything until you take that gun out of my back . . . We have been taken over as expected by the Argentine invasion. They have just given me some tapes they want to broadcast. One thing I want to clarify: some people have been phoning me and they are not happy with the way I have been presenting this information to you over the last two hours, or three hours, or ten hours . . . whatever. Well, I am very sorry for those people that think I have not given the information as you wanted. I don't know what you wanted me to say but I tried to give an unbiased and fair report on what's happening. And when I say that I think it is good news that a truce has been agreed, I think it is good news because I hope that a truce has been agreed. I think it is good news because I hope that none of our boys are going to get shot . . . That's what I mean . . . So long as nobody gets shot.

And with that, the exhausted Patrick Watts went off the air.

Having ordered the marines to lay down their arms, Hunt went on a final tour of his official residence. There was water everywhere. Bullets had punctured the tanks, the radiators and the pipes; in the kitchen the water was dripping on to live electrical wires that had been laid bare by the shrapnel from a grenade. The upper floor was riddled by bullets. Hunt went to his daughter's bedroom (she was away in Venice) to

91

rescue a print of a Picasso nude. There was a bullet hole drilled in its bottom. 'Spot on,' said Hunt.

By now he had met one of Argentina's more sinister representatives, an intelligence officer of Irish descent named Major Patricio Dowling. For two hours Hunt refused Dowling's order to go to the town hall but then Hector Gilobert arrived and said, 'They will send the army to get you and it would be very undignified for you to be taken like that.' So Hunt went.

There he came face to face with General Manuel Osvaldo Jorge Garcia, the just-installed military governor of the Malvinas, who smiled and wanted to shake hands with Hunt for the benefit of a posse of Argentinian photographers. Hunt said 'No' and put his hands behind his back. Garcia said that was very 'ungentlemanly'. Hunt said it was very ungentlemanly 'to invade my country'. Garcia stopped smiling and said that Hunt, his family and the marines would have to leave the island at four o'clock that afternoon.

Hunt went to the Bakers' house where he was reunited with his family and where everyone sat down to the most extravagant lunch Connie Baker could provide: caviar and casserole and a great deal of wine. Patrick Watts arrived, still shattered by his broadcasting marathon and resolute that he would not work for the Argentinians. Dick Baker sensed he was close to breaking down and took him into the kitchen. Watts began to sob. 'The bastards have got me,' he said. 'I'm going to have to carry on running the station because everybody depends on it, and if I do that I am going to have to do it under Argentine supervision. They've got me. I can't win.' Baker told him he was right, it was his duty to carry on – but he thought to himself 'poor sod'. Baker decided he, too, would carry on with his job.

The Hunts were allowed to return to Government House to pack and Tony, seeing the damage, realised for the first time how dangerous it had been. He found his father shaving and said: 'Why don't you wear your official uniform, dad?' Hunt put it on, plumed hat and all.

'Don't be so bloody stupid, darling,' said his wife. 'That'll annoy them and cause all sorts of trouble.' Hunt said he did not care: 'It was Tony's idea and I think it's a jolly good one.' And by the time they were ready to leave for the airport, Mavis thought so, too; as she sat by his side in the London taxi, she felt quite proud.

At the airport, Major Dowling was as unpleasant as he could be. He confiscated the governor's official pennant from the bonnet of the taxi and some Falkland Islands flags which he found hidden in Tony's luggage. (He did not find a dispatch from Simon Winchester which Tony had hidden in his shoe.) Since Dowling also insisted on going through their clothes item by item, Hunt took the opportunity to change out of his uniform into something more comfortable for the journey.

His Excellency the Governor was evicted from his colony at a little after 6.00 p.m. on April 2. He was quite sure he would be back.

Over 800 miles away at Leith Harbour, the French yachtsmen were woken early that day by one of the scrapmen they knew as Tito. He was very excited. He told Serge Briez that the Malvinas had been taken, and now South Georgia was to be taken too. There was to be a flag-raising ceremony and Captain Astiz had given permission for Briez to film it, to provide 'a historical document of this great day'.

Two flags were duly raised at Leith. Forty-mile-an-hour winds tugged at the blue and white emblems as Astiz's marines in battledress – and the scrapmen – stood to attention and sang the national anthem. Then, while Briez continued filming, they applauded and shouted *'Viva la Patria'*. Afterwards, Astiz asked everyone to sign the text of his declaration: 'On 2nd April 1982, South Georgia became *Isla San Pedro* and is now under Argentine authority. A double flag-raising has been performed to commemorate this event.'

All of which was a little premature since Lieutenant Keith Mills and his British marines, along with the British Antarctic Survey scientists, were still in control of Grytviken; Argentina had intended to invade there and Stanley simultaneously but foul weather over South Georgia had wrecked that ambition. So, late that night, a suprisingly subdued Astiz and his men sailed from Leith for Grytviken aboard the *Bahia Paraiso* to turn the declaration into reality. If they expected it to be easy, they were wrong.

The resistance that the twenty-three British marines offered was truly extraordinary. Afterwards one Argentinian officer was driven to tell Mills: 'You took on two ships, 500 marines and three helicopters! There are no kamikazes left in Japan – they're all here.' The lieutenant, who was only twenty-two, was subsequently awarded the Distinguished Service Cross for gallantry, and one of his men, Sergeant-Major Peter Leach, was also decorated. But the fact that they resisted at all was no thanks to London. In the hours before the battle, *Endurance* – which had abandoned the voyage to Stanley and was steaming back to South Georgia – relayed three sets of orders which amounted to: 1. only shoot in self-defence; 2. don't surrender; 3. don't endanger life. Mills had no idea how to reconcile the contradictions, so he just got on with building his defences.

At 10.30 a.m. on April 3, the *Bahia Paraiso* sent a radio message to Grytviken: 'Following our successful operation in the Malvinas your ex-governor has unconditionally surrendered the Falklands and its dependencies. We suggest you gather in a group on the beach and we will send a party of marines ashore to accept your surrender.' Mills and the BAS commander, Steve Martin, tried to play for time. They asked for two hours to think about it – and, against Argentinian orders, they broadcast their reply on high frequency radio in the hope that *Endurance*, and everyone else in the Antarctic, would hear what was happening. The angry response was: 'You've got five minutes.'

When their time was up, two Alouette helicopters came clattering overhead and a small warship, the corvette *Guerrico*, sailed towards the harbour. Steve Martin went to take refuge with the other scientists in a church while Mills walked towards the jetty to tell the first officer ashore that South Georgia would be defended.

He never got the chance. One of the Alouettes landed and began unloading troops. As Mills raced back to the trenches where his men were dug in, the Argentinians opened fire and the British marines returned it – aiming primarily at a large Puma helicopter that was hovering over the water about 150 yards from their position. They hit it, they think, with about 600 rounds of rifle and machine-gun fire, and missed it with a rocket by only a matter of feet. The Puma belched smoke and flew away, apparently out of control; if the twenty or so Argentinians on board survived, it was only because of superb piloting skill.

Encouraged by that, the British marines turned their attention to the corvette. They waited until it had sailed right into the harbour, and then hit it with everything they had. One rocket exploded against her side, another in her Exocet launcher, a third on her gun turret; and, according to the Argentinian count, 1,275 rounds of rifle and machine-gun fire made their mark. The *Guerrico* beat a very hasty retreat.

But it could not go on. About fifty troops had been landed by the Alouette and now surrounded the British position, and the *Guerrico*, once safely back to sea, began to lay down a bombardment of 100 mm shells that deafened and demoralised the marines. To make things worse, a corporal had taken two bullets in his left arm and was in considerable pain. After an hour or so, and having done a great deal more than 'make their eyes water', Mills surrendered.

When Astiz returned to Leith later that night he told Serge Briez that four of his men had died in the battle and a fifth had been seriously injured. He seemed to think it was worthwhile.

But his mood had drastically changed. To the Frenchmen, he no longer seemed like a liberal-minded lawyer; more 'like a barrel of dynamite waiting to explode.' They decided they would leave South Georgia, and take their chance with the storms. Astiz insisted on writing a dedication in their log: 'We were lucky to meet each other although we were all in the wrong place at the wrong time.' He signed it 'Alfredo Astiz, At the end of the world.'

PART 2

CHAPTER NINE

Task Force South

'Let us hear no more about logistics, and how difficult it is to travel long distances. I do not remember the Duke of Wellington whining about Torres Vedras. We have nothing to lose except our honour.
– Edward du Cann MP, April 1982

'This is going to be a sad and bloody business.'
– Admiral Sir John Fieldhouse, April 1982

The way the British public learned that its sovereign territory had been invaded did little to reassure it that its government was in control of events. By mid-morning on Friday, April 2, Fleet Street was receiving news agency messages from Buenos Aires that Argentinian forces had just landed at Stanley. In the House of Commons, Humphrey Atkins, second in the foreign office hierarchy of ministers, was insisting that this could not be so. The reports, he said at 11.00 a.m., had come from 'an Argentinian newspaper. We were in touch with the governor half an hour ago and he said that no landing had taken place at that time.'

At 10.30 a.m. London time, in fact, Governor Rex Hunt was crouching beneath his table in Government House, steeling himself to shoot the first Argentinian soldier who came through the door. That Atkins was so embarrassingly wrong was further indication of the extent to which the crisis had caught the British government unawares. Atkins himself had had virtually nothing to do with the Falklands until a week before, when he had been obliged to make a statement to the Commons about the landing on South Georgia, purely and simply because Britain's foreign secretary was a member of the House of Lords. Then Carrington had departed abroad, to Brussels and Israel, returning only the previous day. Shortly before he was due to speak, Atkins had asked his staff if there was any untoward news from the Falklands. He was handed a piece of paper which indeed implied that at 10.30 a.m. all seemed calm. The timing was a basic error: an official had been confused by the time difference between London and Stanley. Nor had anyone actually spoken to the governor, as Atkins had claimed: London had merely sent a telegram which had been formally acknowledged. But the damage to the government's image was done. And it was not until just before 6.00 p.m. – when Hunt was packing to leave the Falklands – that Carrington and defence secretary John Nott appeared before a hastily convened press conference to confirm that the islands were under foreign occupation.

It was in a tense and excitable mood that MPs packed into the Commons the following morning. It was the first Saturday session of parliament since Suez in 1956, which was also the last occasion that Britain had been at war – or rather, in a state of armed conflict, for then as now the British government remained coy about making that final, irreversible declaration. The morning press added to the air of expectancy, with even the government's supporters talking of its 'humiliation' (*The Daily Telegraph*) and 'shame' (*Daily Mail*.) When the session opened there was a brief apology from Atkins for having 'inadvertently misled' the Commons the day before. Then Margaret Thatcher rose, uncharacteristically nervous. Here was the Iron Lady – the epithet mockingly awarded her by the Soviet Union, in which she took such personal delight – having to answer for the first enforced loss of British territory since the Second World War. There was only one way she could respond: by promising to get the islands back.

The three-hour debate took an unexpected turn. Although Thatcher was firm, she was far from clear. She began by attempting to dispel rumours with the best account available of what had happened, where and when. Yet she did little to anticipate the imminent attacks on the government's lack of foresight and preparation. She announced that a task force would begin to sail for the South Atlantic on Monday; the Falklanders were British and the government would do 'everything we can' to protect their allegiance to the crown. Just what this meant remained an open question, for she eschewed statements of naked belligerence and emphasised the diplomatic efforts then in train.

As speaker after speaker rose, Thatcher, astonishingly, seemed in danger of being outflanked on the right. Labour's leader Michael Foot, veteran of peace marches through the decades, employed unprecedented warrior rhetoric, including an apparent declaration that Labour would meet 'foul and brutal aggression' wherever it occurred. He did lay down several markers about the government's culpability: what had happened to intelligence and diplomacy? Why had Britain not acted sooner, as Labour had when it dispatched its secret task-force in 1977? Otherwise hardly a word of caution crossed his lips.

Of course, no opposition leader could appear to betray the nation's fighting men, with the task force departing in two days' time; and the Labour party's anti-war group clearly decided this was no time to break cover. There were attacks on the Argentinian junta and its appalling record on human rights from both left and right; and several

Falkland Islands committee veterans, on familiar ground now, offered their contributions. Sir Nigel Fisher wanted Argentina excluded from the soccer World Cup; and when Ray Whitney, a young Conservative MP who had once been a diplomat at the British embassy in Buenos Aires, had the temerity to argue a case for the foreign office, Sir John Biggs-Davison interrupted to ask: 'If defeatism of this kind is to be spoken, should it not be done in secret session?'

The foreign office, predictably, ranked only a short distance behind the Argentinian government as the villain of the piece; and several MPs wanted Lord Carrington brought before them to answer for its derelictions. But Carrington remained safely in the Lords, where the questioning was of a more emollient kind. ('I think the House will wish to treat the foreign secretary with kindness,' Lord Shackleton generously proposed.) To answer its critics, the government had nominated defence secretary John Nott.

A balding, bespectacled 49-year-old, Nott could be mistaken for a maths teacher of the kind given to sarcastic jokes, flashes of irritation, and penetrating questions to arouse the duffers at the back of the class. Although he was a merchant banker before becoming an MP for a Cornish constituency in 1966, the comparison is not entirely unjust. He is a clever but erratic figure, a man of ups and downs; moody when things go badly, sometimes threatening to give up politics altogether – a threat he finally carried out in September 1982, when he announced he would not stand in the next election. Even during the Falklands war he would escape for a few hours to his farm in Cornwall and to the company of his beautiful Yugoslav wife Milovska, who does not care for politics at all. At other times he displays unmitigated political ambition – he made no secret of his desire to be chancellor after the 1979 election. He is also a skilled political operator, and when the Falkland crisis broke and recriminations were flying, he believed that in departmental terms he was secure. The problem had been created by Britain's foreign policy; his ministry's role was to lay out options for others to act upon. But even though he was usually a good parliamentary performer, he felt apprehensive when he rose to speak; he knew that in Carrington's absence, the Commons would be lusting for a scapegoat.

Nott's performance betrayed his anxieties: he stumbled and blustered, and gave lame answers to interventions by Michael Foot and David Owen, the former Labour foreign secretary who had defected to the SDP. He deferred little to the Commons' sense of outrage, and at the end of his speech he made a major tactical error in trying to turn the attack on to the Labour party, 'with its well-known and well-advertised anti-defence bias and lack of commitment to defence spending.' The rest of his words were drowned in jeers and calls of 'resign'. The ordeal was as bad as he had feared: 'mob rule prevailed,' it was observed afterwards on his behalf. Yet he was reasonably satisfied when he read his speech through in Hansard later;

and when he appeared in the prime minister's room at the Commons ten minutes after the debate ended, he seemed quite composed.

But for the government, the reverberations of that parliamentary episode had not ended. *The Sunday Telegraph* called it 'the worst day in the life of this government'; and the following morning the crisis deepened. By the traditions of British political life, ministers whose policies are held to have brought failure and ignominy are expected to resign from office; and although there has been no lack of brazen exceptions to the rule, on this occasion four ministers stepped forward to do the decent thing. Three were the foreign office trio seen to have presided over the debacle; the fourth was Nott.

Of them all, the position of Lord Carrington was the most intriguing. As foreign secretary and a senior party figure, he had been one of the few ministers to whom Thatcher would defer in her views. She relied on his judgment and respected the standing he had enjoyed in world affairs – to lose him would be a personal blow. Yet Carrington had forfeited much of his credit with the party's increasingly dominant right wing through the settlement in Rhodesia, which bequeathed the new nation of Zimbabwe to the militant Robert Mugabe instead of the compliant Bishop Muzorewa. For some observers, that helped to explain why he had allowed Nicholas Ridley to pursue such a lonely course in attempting to sell leaseback in 1980; and why he had refused to permit even 'gentle pressure' to be exerted on the islanders to accept it in the summer of 1981. To outsiders, the foreign office had displayed manifest culpability in misreading Argentinian intentions before the invasion; but since Thatcher had transferred oversight of Britain's senior intelligence body, the Joint Intelligence Committee, from the foreign office to the cabinet office, it was an open question where ultimate responsibility lay. Certainly Carrington let it be known later that he had no fear of the inquiry that would pursue those matters. His followers also put it about that the trigger for his resignation was the Commons debate itself. Whereas Nott might say that he was accustomed to the extremes of rhetoric that MPs like to employ, for Carrington the experience was something new. In the words of his friends, the near-universal loathing expressed for his department convinced him that Tory MPs were what he had always suspected, a bunch of treacherous opportunists who had shown him not a jot of loyalty.

When Carrington tendered his resignation, Home Secretary William Whitelaw, an ally from the old patrician wing of the party, tried hard to dissuade him from his course. Thatcher dutifully resisted too. But it was clear he had to go. There had been a colossal blunder; and if Carrington did not step down, then the prime minister herself might well be in the firing line. Alongside Carrington fell Humphrey Atkins, the foreign office number two, whose involvement in the Falklands had lasted precisely nine days; and the number three,

Richard Luce, who had watched mesmerised as the catastrophe unfolded from the moment he took office in September 1981. Although Atkins told Luce he did not need to sacrifice himself, Luce responded that if his chiefs were going, he could hardly stay.

The one survivor was Nott, who now displayed considerable political ingenuity. He considered resigning when reflecting on the onslaught he had received from his own party in the Commons, and formally offered to do so when he heard that Carrington was going. When Thatcher resisted his offer he agreed to stay, provided she supplied a letter laying out her reasons for asking him to do so. She obliged, inserting a veiled barb at the foreign office – 'the ministry of defence is not the department responsible for policy towards the Falkland Islands.' (When Carrington later read this sentence, he was heard to observe that it was a pity this had not applied when the ministry of defence insisted on scrapping the *Endurance*.) When Nott spoke again in the Commons on April 7, he seemed to have acquired renewed confidence. This time he stole the opposition's colours by acknowledging the government's errors in allowing the crisis to arise: 'Clearly we were wrong. I am not disputing that.' The question of the costs of retaking the islands was brushed aside. 'We have made no estimate,' he declared with Churchillian bravado. 'We are concerned with the success of the operation.'

Despite Nott's survival, with three victims parliament felt satisfied. Retribution had been exacted, and the guilty men had gone; the foreign office had met its moment of truth. But there was another, greater truth to confront: Britain was about to go to war. Of course, some MPs welcomed that too, and would exult in the victories to come. But the MPs' moment had passed; the focus was about to shift to the men-at-arms, fighting for the principles the politicians had so easily enunciated, dying for the mistakes they had made.

'The government have now decided that a large task force will sail as soon as all preparations are complete. *HMS Invincible* will be in the lead and will leave port on Monday.' With those prosaic words, Thatcher announced to the Commons what Britain's military response to the Argentinian invasion would be. The process, in fact, had begun the previous Wednesday, March 31, three days before the Commons debate, and the day when the British government had finally concluded that Argentina was about to invade. With Carrington in Israel, Nott was the first senior minister to receive the clinching information from Sigint, and he hurried to see Thatcher at Number Ten. From then on, two parallel courses were pursued. One was the last-ditch diplomatic effort to dissuade the Argentinians from going ahead, finally aborted with Galtieri's decisive rejection of President Reagan's telephoned personal appeal. The other was the preparation of the task force which, not uniquely in this story, began with a moment of low comedy. Britain's First Sea Lord Admiral Sir Henry Leach returned from a naval function to Whitehall to learn that preliminary arrangements were already being made. Still wearing his naval uniform he hurried to the Commons in search of his defence secretary, John Nott. As he waited in the central lobby, several MPs who knew him passed by, greeting him with banter and mock surprise.

Propriety was soon restored; and it was not long before the due chains of communication and command were established. The committee of the chiefs of staff of each of the armed services met each morning, usually at 9.30 a.m. It was followed by – and subordinate to – the South Atlantic sub-committee of the cabinet's overseas defence committee, which became known as the war cabinet. The main link between the two was Sir Terence Lewin, the chief of defence staff, who attended both meetings. Although he was a navy man – 'dark blue' in the trade – he was trusted by the other services. Nott had appointed him his chief military adviser, and he was accustomed to delivering his views with confidence and force. In Whitehall there was no doubt of his influence, and he became closer than anyone in the crisis to Thatcher herself. One civil servant termed him: 'the most powerful man in Britain.'

The decisions that emanated from these bodies were directed to the operational headquarters at the north-west London suburb of Northwood, a giant granite and glass structure presided over by Admiral Sir John Fieldhouse; it was from there that all communications were dispatched to the task force itself. Many of the day-to-day logistic decisions, that nonetheless had political overtones, were made in the defence situational centre at the ministry of defence. A series of interlocking rooms with a staff of close to a hundred, it was particularly active in the early days of the crisis. Should seventeen-year-olds be allowed to go? What to do about Chinese crews on the royal fleet auxiliaries? How to cope with the anomalies that were bound to arise in calculating merchant navy compensation? A flood of paperwork emanated from the situation centre to land at Nott's office, for endorsement or arbitration. But even if some decisions were finely balanced, and gave rise to charges of injustice – such as the decision to cut the war-pay allowance for some troops in order to raise it for others – all paled beside the overriding political aim: the islands must be repossessed.

The enormous effort of dispatching a fleet that was to number some hundred vessels got underway. But there was one terrible irony involved. Thatcher was visibly impressed when First Sea Lord Leach assured her on the evening of Wednesday, March 31, that its core, the two aircraft carriers *Invincible* and *Hermes*, could sail from Portsmouth on the morning tide of Monday, April 5. Yet these were the two most celebrated ships in the notorious document, 'Command 8288' –

Whitehall shorthand for the 1981 defence review – which listed forthcoming cuts in Britain's surface fleet. Although the two carriers would not be phased out until their replacements had arrived, the navy was outraged: one fuming admiral termed it 'the con trick of the century.' In fact, Nott was merely continuing the process of shrinking Britain's overseas forces that had gone on since the war, parallel with the shedding of the British colonies; the fact that the navy was now being called upon to defend one of those colonies after all, made the irony more painful to bear. But the navy's anger also reflected the skill with which Nott had outflanked them in Whitehall, using a handful of trusted civil servants to bypass the labyrinth of committees that habitually obstruct change. When Leach protested at the cuts proposed, he would be reassured that it was only an 'exercise'; until it was suddenly too late.

When the Falklands war was over, these Whitehall battles were to be refought, with the navy regaining some of its lost ground. But for the moment politicians and admirals sank their differences in the common cause. When *Invincible* and *Hermes* sailed, they would link with a large segment of the navy that was fortuitously already at sea, off Gibraltar. The assembly and departure of the fleet would go on for several weeks, encompassing not only the Royal Navy's warships but also the vessels of the Royal Fleet Auxiliary, providing vital logistic support, and ships from the British merchant fleet. The privy council order requisitioning these was approved by the Queen at Windsor Castle on the evening of Sunday, April 4, with Nott – who had just made a flying visit to the *Hermes* at Portsmouth – in attendance.

The Royal Air Force was alerted with equal dispatch. The first Hercules transport planes took off from their base at Lyneham in Wiltshire on Thursday, April 1, touching down at Gibraltar shortly after dark that evening. Seven arrived in all: some unloaded supplies for the naval ships then in port, which included the frigates *Broadsword* and *Yarmouth*; but others merely refuelled, to head a further 3,000 miles south to the British island of Ascension, a tiny dot in the Atlantic, midway between Britain and the Falkland Islands. It had been chosen as the logical forward task-force base after the alternatives of Simonstown (South Africa), Montevideo (Uruguay), Punta Arenas (Chile) and Freetown (Sierra Leone), had been briefly considered but then ruled out as politically impossible. Despite its location midway between Britain and the Falklands, Ascension was far from ideal. In the first place it was not even a British base, but an American one leased from the British, who now had to apply to use it. Second, it was simply not equipped to service the mass of flights to come. Thus the first personnel to arrive there were technicians and engineers, equipped with radar and traffic-control apparatus, to handle the thousands of flights that would pour through.

In Britain meanwhile, the fact that the armed services were readying for war was all too clear. Convoys of trucks crowded down the roads to the south-west Channel coast, ferrying men, ammunition, and supplies. In some quarters the preparations were tinged with chagrin, for several dockyards, now busy day and night, had only recently learned that the latest round of defence cuts meant heavy redundancies. But there was no stinting of effort; and when messages were posted at London railway termini summoning soldiers to their regiments, *The Times* was moved to reflect that these were 'scenes reminiscent of the last world war'.

The comparison, however attractive, was also dangerous. There is always a tendency when reflecting on the victories of war to assume – even if painful losses have occurred – they have somehow been inevitable, as the logical outcome of superior resources and the pitting of irresistible national effort. The assumption is misleading, for it conceals the enormous potential for success or failure that rests on the decisions and actions of individual soldiers confronted with the confusion and unpredictability of war. It was like that from day one of the Falklands campaign for the men who were to recapture the islands, the 3 Commando Brigade, composed initially of three battalions of the Royal Marines. The first active officer to be alerted was their 47-year-old brigadier, Julian Thompson, who on the evening of Wednesday, March 31, was at home in his cottage on the edge of Dartmoor. Thompson, the brigade's senior fighting officer, occupying third rank in its command hierarchy, had returned briefly from preparations for a NATO exercise in Denmark, where most of his senior staff had remained. The telephone rang, and a major on Thompson's staff said, with studied understatement: 'I think you should know there is a problem on the Falkland Islands.'

Since Thompson had been reading in the newspapers of the activities of the scrap-dealers on South Georgia he was not especially surprised. What concerned him most was that at that precise moment his units were widely dispersed. Of the three fighting battalions in the third brigade, one was undertaking rifle practice in north-west England; one had only just returned from arduous yet highly appropriate arctic warfare training in Norway, and had virtually all gone on leave; and one was in Scotland, having served recently in Northern Ireland. Thompson decided to alert the battalion in the north-west, 40 Commando, and instructed a colonel at the brigade's Plymouth headquarters to track them down. They were found at a rifle-range on the coast near Liverpool, and their commanding officer, the dapper Lieutenant-Colonel Malcolm Hunt, was told to return to Plymouth as soon as possible.

In the morning, a group of distinctly excited officers gathered at Hamoaze House, the Georgian mansion in Plymouth that housed brigade headquarters, its curious name drawn from the local term for the estuary of the River Tamar. Then came a deflating message from the office of the marines' commandant-general, Sir Steuart Pringle, in London: the cabinet had just met and the whole operation was off.

The message was a good indication of the indecision in London as the government still sought to avert the invasion through diplomatic means. The vacillations were certainly felt in Plymouth. Throughout the day, an ever-changing stream of instructions was received. After the operation had been stood down, it was revived again, but this time with only one company – 110 men – to stand by. That was reduced to a single air defence troop of thirty-five men; and shortly afterwards increased to two such troops, totalling seventy men. When the officers returned home at the end of the day, most were convinced that nothing would come of it all. Thompson consoled himself with a glass of whisky by the fire in his cottage, fantasising about his men passing through Buenos Aires airport en route for the Falklands, with Blowpipe anti-aircraft missiles concealed in their baggage.

At 3.15 a.m. on Friday, April 2, cold reality was restored. Thompson was roused by a phone-call from his immediate superior, Major-General Jeremy Moore, telling him in suitably guarded terms: 'You know those people down south. They are going to be attacked.' Malcolm Hunt, head of 40 Commando, received his call forty-five minutes later. This time Moore announced: 'Malcolm, this is your general speaking. We've got an operation'.

The officers convened once again at Hamoaze House. One man surprised to find himself there was Lt-Col Nick Vaux, the soft-spoken 46-year-old commander of 42 Commando, who had been due to fly that morning to the American NATO headquarters in Norfolk, Virginia, to discuss his battalion's recent exercises in Arctic Norway. When his staff car arrived at 6.00 a.m., he simply diverted to Plymouth. That was one officer safely retrieved. Others were still in Denmark, and Thompson spent a large part of the day rounding them up by phone. His problems paled beside those of Nick Vaux, whose men had departed on leave just two days before – twenty-five of them out of the country. Unluckiest of all was the battalion's intelligence officer Lieutenant Henk de Jaeger, who had flown to New York to get married. He was found that afternoon and handed a recall telegram just as his reception was getting underway. Although he was safely married, consummation was postponed.

By Saturday morning, April 3, soldiers were streaming into Plymouth, while their baggage and equipment was being tracked down. Some of it was still at sea, en route from Norway; as it arrived it was simply re-routed to Southampton, from where most of the brigade would depart. By now it comprised 3,400 men: the marines' own three battalions, plus two of paratroopers (2 Para and 3 Para). The composite was still to be called 3 Commando. Three of those battalions would embark on the commandeered passenger cruise-liner *Canberra*, which had been secretly surveyed for its task by naval experts in Gibraltar as it neared the end of a world cruise. The *Canberra* was due to sail on Thursday, April 8, and although it finally sailed on April 9 – Good Friday – the delay of just one day was impressive enough. A fourth battalion was carried in the North Sea ferry *Norland*; and the fifth eventually reached Ascension by air.

The senior officers of the Royal Marines were scheduled to depart on Tuesday, April 6. A helicopter would carry them from Plymouth and deposit them on the land forces' command ship *Fearless* as it steamed down the English Channel from Portsmouth. The final days were hectic in the extreme. On Sunday, April 4, the officers met once again at Hamoaze House. They had been joined now by the key figure of Major Ewen Southby-Tailyour, one of those genuinely eccentric yet valued people whom fighting units always seem to attract, and whose idiosyncracies they tolerate. Southby-Tailyour was a renowned yachtsman who just happened, while serving in the Falklands as part of its marine guard detachment in 1978, to have mapped every major bay on its complex 10,000-mile coastline and to have filled a 126-page notebook with a plethora of useless – now invaluable – details. Strictly speaking, as the officer commanding the marines' landing craft section at Poole in Dorset, Southby-Tailyour had no place on the operation. But when Thompson asked him to yield his notebook for the operation, Southby-Tailyour replied that he would only do so if he could come too. Thompson appointed Southby-Tailyour 'staff officer without portfolio' and that morning he gave his fellow officers a briefing at which he ringed a number of possible landing sites, including one at a place called San Carlos.

In the afternoon, the group flew to operational headquarters at Northwood, where Southby-Tailyour repeated his performance before an assembly of admirals. As well as detailing the islands' problems of wind and temperature, he gave a warning against the 'Caribbean effect', whereby the clear air would mislead observers into underestimating distances. The meeting concluded that no landing could take place before sea and air battles had been won; the best course of action would be a naval battle followed by an unopposed landing, coupled with a blockade and raids on the islands to demoralise the Argentinian troops. Afterwards, the Northwood commander, Sir John Fieldhouse, took Thompson and Southby-Tailyour aside. 'This is going to be a sad and bloody business,' he told them. 'I only wish I could offer you more ships.'

On the Monday, Moore, Thompson, and Southby-Tailyour, together with Commodore Michael Clapp, the navy's head of amphibious warfare, flew to the RAF base at Brize Norton. Rex Hunt had just arrived and the marine officers questioned him closely. But even now, some of them found it hard to credit that it was all for real. Back in Plymouth that evening they told each other it would be a very long time before they reached the Falklands – if ever.

106

On Tuesday morning, they made their final preparations to depart. Southby-Tailyour had a new brain-wave: during his spell on the islands in 1978 he had come to know a woman named Leif Barton, now married and living in Edinburgh. He telephoned her and asked her to compile a series of lists. They included the names of all the islands' radio hams, and all known Argentinian sympathisers. She willingly agreed, and the information was later sent to the task force from Northwood.

The helicopter that would carry the officers away to the *Fearless* was due to collect them from the soccer pitch behind the Plymouth barracks at 5.00 p.m. With twenty minutes to go, Thompson received a disconcerting piece of news. Major-General Moore told him that Northwood wanted one company – 110 men – to stay in Britain for a 'special operation': a top-secret plan, still barely formed, to repossess South Georgia separately from the main task force. 45 Commando had one company then on jungle training in Borneo: could they be brought back to perform this task? Thompson thought that idea absurd: it would be far more sensible to hold back a company from 42 Commando, since they had just spent several weeks doing arctic training in Norway – rather more suitable for South Georgia, he pointed out. But nothing appeared decided, and Thompson departed for *Fearless* not knowing what the outcome would be.

Once on board, Thompson and his team met the *Fearless* captain, Jeremy Larken, and the commander of the SAS troops assigned to the operation. That evening, they enthusiastically held a planning meeting to see what ideas everyone had for an assault. But for the next two days, the weather forced them to temper their enthusiasm. There was a heavy sea running and they were copiously sick.

CHAPTER TEN

The Battle for Peace

'Britain is a Morris Minor country,
but with Rolls Royce diplomacy.'
– UN delegate, April, 1982

'The British people expect the government to be able to defend our people wherever they are in the world,' thundered one Tory knight at the height of the Commons debate. 'We must pursue every diplomatic measure that we can first of all, but after that there is only one possible action.'

Diplomacy, in fact, was to prove almost as important to the British government as the ships and planes of the task force. By the time those words were spoken, on the afternoon of Saturday April 3, Britain's diplomatic offensive had already begun. It was to be a campaign waged with subtlety and persistence in the corridors of the United Nations, the Common Market, NATO and the Commonwealth. Few ministers doubted that unless world opinion could be swiftly and convincingly aroused to condemn the invasion, the initiative would slip away from Britain, leaving the Argentinian claim to the Falklands to go by default.

Even if diplomacy failed – 'and it will probably do so,' admitted a gloomy John Nott in the same debate – it would still have an essential part to play in demonstrating to the world that the use of British force was justified. It was, however, no easy task, and the fact that Britain did indeed win almost universal support in the course of that first April week is a tribute to the diplomatic machine now brought into play.

At the United Nations in New York, luck and fine judgment played almost equal parts. The key to Britain's success was the head of its UN delegation, Sir Anthony Parsons, a highly skilled and experienced diplomat. But the fact that Parsons found himself there at all was a stroke of luck to begin with. Just approaching his sixtieth birthday, he was due for retirement. The invitation cards for his farewell party in early June had already gone out, and he had returned to Britain in March to carry out one of his final duties – a round-the-country speaking tour.

Parsons was in Edinburgh on March 25 having lunch with the Lord Provost when he received a telephone call from the foreign office asking him to return to New York for an awkward UN debate on the West Bank issue. He jumped on the afternoon shuttle to London, caught the Concorde flight to New York and was in the UN building by 6.00 p.m.; he was thus on the spot to receive the first of many calls from Downing Street on Friday night as the Falklands crisis grew.

To have Parsons in place was an immense bonus for Britain. He had made just the right number of important friends at the UN in his two and a half years there, and his relaxed manner enhanced his popularity. Parsons described himself nevertheless as 'a government man born and bred' and his family has a long tradition of military and diplomatic service. He graduated from Balliol College, Oxford, with a degree in Arabic and Turkish while already in the army, and went on to a distinguished military career that lasted fourteen years. As a forward artillery officer in Italy during the Second World War he won the Military Cross, Britain's third highest army award for valour; he ended up as an assistant military attaché in Baghdad.

It was, therefore, at the relatively late age of thirty-two that Parsons joined the diplomatic service – which was seen by some colleagues as a distinct advantage. 'All our best people start out as something else,' commented one of his fellow diplomats. 'That way by the time they come to us they're too old to learn to be pompous.' Parsons served in Ankara, Amman, Cairo, Khartoum, Bahrain and Teheran – during the fall of the Shah – before coming to the United Nations. He acquired a reputation for toughness and resilience, but kept a lively sense of humour which was to prove enormously valuable at the UN. He was particularly open and accessible to journalists.

Argentina was not so well placed – it was in the process of changing ambassadors. The new man, Eduardo Roca, had arrived in New York on March 24 and was just coming to grips with the job when the crisis broke. The strain of subsequent events was to prove too much for him. In the middle of the negotiations Roca had to return to Buenos Aires suffering from high blood pressure.

Parsons made the most of his advantages. From the moment he was first alerted to the need for action, he knew that the decisive moves would be made, not at the UN's general assembly, where every nation has an equal vote and where nearly every resolution churned out is destined for oblivion, but in the security council where resolutions actually carry weight: Resolution 242, for instance, is still the key to a solution in the Middle East.

The security council has fifteen members. Five of them – Britain, the US, France, China and Russia – are permanent, the others are elected to a two-year term. That April they were: Uganda, Jordan, Panama, Guyana, Zaire, Togo (the non-aligned states), Japan, Ireland, Spain and Poland. Heavily biased towards third world countries, the line-up was not a promising prospect for Britain which would need to command a minimum of ten votes to win – always provided, of course, that none of the permanent members used its veto. A veto is final. Parsons used to refer to its use as 'zapping' a resolution.

But Britain's ambassador was able to benefit from another stroke of luck. The presidency of the security council, which rotates month by month, had just changed. On March 31 Jeane Kirkpatrick, the United States' UN ambassador, handed over the task to Kamanda wa Kamanda of Zaire – and as subsequent events were to show, this was a critical change for Britain. The president can have a strong influence on the timing and procedure of meetings and Kirkpatrick, who had close links with the Argentinians, would not have helped smooth the way for Britain.

Certainly, the advice which she gave Parsons as the invasion loomed was not, in retrospect, particularly helpful to British interests. She expressed surprise that he should be raising the issue at the security council, and believed it would be better resolved outside. She knew the Argentinians, she said, and if Britain went on to the offensive at the UN they would be even less willing to compromise than they were already. Low-key diplomacy, she argued, would be by far the best approach.

Parsons, however, pressed on. He believed that speed, not delay, was crucial to success.

He took the Falklands question to the security council on the evening of Thursday, April 1. It was a vital meeting because, on the eve of the invasion, it set up the conditions for Resolution 502, which was to be the main plank in Britain's diplomatic platform. 'We call on the security council to take immediate action in order to prevent an invasion,' said Parsons. He was rewarded finally with a statement from Kamanda, the president, authorised by the council members, which called on both governments 'to exercise the utmost restraint at this time and in particular to refrain from the use or threat of force in the region.'

The importance of the wording was that it allowed the non-aligned countries to vote subsequently for Britain: they could argue that, despite the merits of Argentina's case, she was wrong to use force.

On the next day, Friday April 2, Resolution 502 was formally introduced. It had been drafted by the British mission's Yorkshire-born lawyer David Anderson, and approved by London with very few changes. It read:

The Security Council, *Recalling* the statement made by the President of the Security Council at the 2345th meeting of the Security Council on 1 April 1982 calling on the Governments of Argentina and the United Kingdom of Great Britain and Northern Ireland to refrain from the use or threat of force in the region of the Falkland Islands (Islas Malvinas),

Deeply disturbed at reports of an invasion on 2 April 1982 by armed forces of Argentina,
Determining that there exists a breach of the peace in the region of the Falkland Islands (Islas Malvinas),
1. *Demands* an immediate cessation of hostilities;
2. *Demands* an immediate withdrawal of all Argentine forces from the Falkland Islands (Islas Malvinas);
3. *Calls* on the Governments of Argentina and the United Kingdom to seek a diplomatic solution to their differences and to respect fully the purposes and principles of the Charter of the United Nations.

The Argentinians asked for and were granted a twenty-four-hour delay to allow their foreign minister, Nicanor Costa Mendez, to arrive in New York. It was then that the lobbying began in earnest. The key group in the security council was the non-aligned states. Panama led the Argentinians' campaign. Guyana, worried about the claims on her territory made by neighbouring Venezuela, was on the British side. That left Zaire, Togo, Uganda and Jordan. Since Zaire had provided the president of the council, and had issued the appeal for peace, she would be inclined to vote for Britain. The French, who were Britain's staunchest allies on the Falklands issue, spent a considerable amount of time and effort working on the Togo delegation.

The British were deliberately moving fast – and leaving as little room for manoeuvre as possible. The resolution must be voted on as drafted, Parsons said. It would not be modified. Take it or leave it.

At this delicate stage, Costa Mendez arrived at the UN and tilted the balance firmly – *against* Argentina. On April 3 he addressed the non-aligned group, and instead of seeking to persuade them to his side, he delivered a lecture on how they should vote. The Falklands question was a colonial one, he said, and they should automatically vote on an anti-colonial ticket.

This was not considered a helpful attitude to take, and his peremptory tone irritated the meeting. 'He seriously misjudged our mood,' said one ambassador. When, at the end of the speech, one of those present started to ask questions, Costa Mendez said he had no time to listen and left. 'It was a disastrous performance altogether,' concluded the ambassador.

The Panamanian foreign minister, Jorge Illueca, lobbying hard on behalf of the Argentinians, appears to have achieved almost as little, due to his somewhat irritating manner. The sum total of his efforts was the insertion in Resolution 502 of the words Islas Malvinas after every reference to the Falklands.

The British finally swung things their way by winning over Uganda and Jordan. Initially both had looked doubtful. At a critical stage, Parsons asked Ambassador Olara Otunnu of Uganda how things were going and was told that while Otunnu himself was disposed to vote with Britain, he did not know how his government in Kampala would feel. 'Should we get on to Kampala?' asked Parsons delicately. It was a key question but it could have been taken extremely badly. It was, after all, none of Parsons' business, and ambassadors traditionally resent any approach to governments over their heads. But Parsons knew Otunnu well enough to ask the question. 'No, I think it will be all right,' said the ambassador, adding that British pressure might make things more difficult. Parsons accepted the advice, and on the morning of April 3 Otunnu received instructions to vote with Britain.

The Jordanian vote now became decisive. Parsons was also on good terms with the Jordanian ambassador, Hazem Nuseibeh. The two men regularly conversed in Arabic – much to the annoyance, on one occasion, of the Russian ambassador who was attempting to catch the drift of a particularly interesting exchange. The Jordanians were worried about casting their vote against a non-aligned country, but nevertheless Nuseibeh recommended that his country should back Britain, and early in the Saturday debate he announced that Jordan would support Resolution 502.

As the evening wore on, however, distress signals started to come from the Jordanian camp. Parsons dispatched his number two, Hamilton Whyte, to go round the security council table and find out what was wrong. An embarrassed Nuseibeh told Whyte he had just received instructions from his government to vote *against* the British, despite the fact that he had already spoken in favour of the resolution. Could Parsons bail him out?

Parsons instructed Whyte to make contact with Lord Carrington in London. Carrington could not be found quickly enough. Instead Whyte found Mrs Thatcher at Downing Street and she managed to reach King Hussein of Jordan by telephone. She spent half an hour putting the British case to him, and within an hour Ambassador Nuseibeh had received new instructions allowing him to vote the way he had already said he would.

Parsons now knew he had the votes he needed. But would the Russians 'zap' him by using their veto? Usually every member of the security council knows how the others intend to vote before the formal decision is made but in this case the Russians had received their instructions from Moscow extraordinarily late. 'We just didn't know how they were going to vote until the pencils went up,' said a British representative. One of the Americans, watching tensely, was sure it would be a veto. Whyte bet him a bottle of scotch it would be an abstention, and a few minutes later Whyte had won his bet. The Russians abstained, following a Soviet tradition of using their veto only in cases directly affecting their interests.

Poland, Spain and China joined the Soviets by abstaining. Only Panama cast its vote against the resolution. In the end, therefore, Britain mustered one more vote than the ten she needed, and

Resolution 502 was passed. It was to prove, in the next few weeks, a formidable part of her diplomatic armoury.

Success at the United Nations marked the start of an extraordinary British propaganda campaign throughout America. It was master-minded from the Washington embassy, and was aimed at winning over opinion, both public and political, to the view that Britain was entitled to repossess the Falklands, and that Argentina should withdraw. This in its turn was intended to encourage the United States to provide material support for the British military campaign – should it come to that – and to put pressure on the Argentinian junta to pull out.

The embassy reasoned that if opinion in the country at large and in congress in particular could be rallied to the British cause, then that would help ensure that the Reagan administration was continually reminded where its first loyalties lay. 'We always thought the people were with us, but I don't think we took the administration for granted for one moment,' recalled an embassy official.

The campaign occupied the attention of virtually the entire embassy for the next six weeks. 'It was the biggest single operation we had mounted since World War Two,' said one official proudly, and though – like many British campaigns – it was slow to gather momentum, by the second week in April it had become something of a phenomenon on Capitol Hill.

Each morning, in the ambassador's third floor office in the embassy building on Massachusetts Avenue, a special strategy session was held, chaired by the ambassador, Sir Nicholas Henderson, with his minister Derek Thomas, the head of chancery Robin Renwick, the information counsellor Peter Hall, and a scattering of junior colleagues. They analysed the latest reports from Buenos Aires and London, assessed the reaction in Washington, and planned the day's meetings, interviews and private lobbying calls.

Henderson himself became the most conspicuous expression of the British effort, and performed his role to spectacular effect. A tall, sparely-built figure, with a relaxed and confident manner, he combined elegance with a distinct air of dishevelment. His grey hair seemed always in need of attention from the barber; his suits were expensive but sagging; his shirt collars fashionable but perpetually out of control; and his silk ties hung uneasily outside his jacket, usually with the lining on display. He fitted every American's idea of what a British gentleman should be. And he was perfectly capable of exploiting it.

Beneath the surface appearance of the engaging amateur was a tough professional diplomat, whose charm could swiftly turn to ice, and whose urbanity masked a certain air of menace which frequently made his interviews distinctly uncomfortable.

Henderson's career had included most of the glittering prizes of the foreign service, including Warsaw, Bonn and Paris from where he had retired at the age of sixty in 1979. A month later he was called back to take over in Washington, the pinnacle of any diplomat's career. Despite his long experience of diplomacy, he did not always conceal his impatience with the declining international role of the country he represented, and in Paris, to coincide with his retirement, he had composed a long and bitter valedictory dispatch – subsequently leaked to *The Economist* magazine – which attacked most of Britain's economic institutions but in particular the trade unions; condemned the foreign policy of successive governments; and concluded that 'a considerable jolt is going to be needed if a lasting attenuation of civic purpose and courage is to be averted.'

That jolt came with the Falklands crisis. Henderson immediately faced two daunting tasks: to convince the Americans that Britain was serious in its intentions, and to persuade them that good relations between the United Kingdom and the United States were in the end more important than keeping on close terms with Latin America.

He chose to do it publicly by appearing on a seemingly endless succession of television shows, and privately by careful lobbying of senior government officials, senators, congressmen, and newspaper columnists. He was on first-name terms with most of them, and he took care to expand his circle of acquaintances. Soon it seemed that everyone who was anyone was intimately acquainted with 'Nico' and Mary Henderson. Topics like the deviousness of the ambassador's tennis game, or the warmth of the ambassador's hospitality became familiar currency in Washington that April. Henderson himself is in no doubt about the importance of what he was doing. 'I do not say that we could not have won back the Falklands without the Americans,' he told us later, 'but I think it would, and this is my own view, have been more costly and taken longer.'

Once Resolution 502 was passed he felt his responsibility was to steer the action away from the United Nations, and to convince the Americans that they should abandon their neutral stance, and come down on the British side. In private at first, if necessary, but sooner or later in public.

He faced an uphill struggle. Initially the problem was to show that the British were serious. 'People thought it was Gilbert and Sullivan stuff,' said one embassy official. 'They wondered whether it was for real. "How can you pull it off so far from home?" they would ask. "And anyway, there are only 1,800 people involved." We countered that by pointing out how concerned the US had been over fifty-two hostages.'

Far more difficult to combat was an argument central to America's Latin American policy, and dear to the heart of President Reagan's administration – the importance of fighting communism in Central America. Argentina had been an open supporter of this policy, perhaps

114

the most important new ally the United States had won in South America; President Galtieri had gone so far as to back the US line in El Salvador by sending Argentinian troops in support of the right-wing government. To alienate him now seemed to many state department officials an act of madness.

Reagan himself, grateful to Mrs Thatcher for the public support she had always given him, was anxious to maintain an even-handed stance. 'We're friends of both sides,' he announced, and he stressed that America was only interested in finding a peaceful settlement between two countries he regarded as allies. Any reference to material support was to be played down. This even-handedness was anathema to Henderson. 'I continually contested the American view that by being even-handed – by being pally with the Argentinians – they would succeed in persuading them,' he recalls.

In this endeavour Henderson found a natural ally in the US secretary of state, Alexander Haig, whose instincts from the start were to support Britain but who needed to perform a delicate balancing act to placate the Latin American faction within the state department. The two men began to see a great deal of each other. Haig would call up at all hours of the day and night to compare notes. They would swap stories of the battles they were waging, with Henderson passing on the gossip from London, and Haig explaining the tensions within the administration. Soon Haig's personal involvement in the Falklands grew to the point where he was to lay his career on the line in search of a solution to the problem.

At least as important as these private contacts, however, was the public defence that Henderson mounted to explain the British position. A natural television performer, he was in constant demand for TV chat shows and discussion programmes. He geared his appearances to those which caught the largest audiences, homing in on the three major network shows, for instance, or catching the radio programmes which car drivers tuned into as they travelled to and from work. For the producers of these shows, Henderson was a star turn. His accent and appearance delighted them: 'The guy was a natural,' enthused one.

American opinion, already swept up by the romance of the Falklands conflict, tended to see it in the relatively simple terms that Mrs Thatcher had been at pains to articulate: aggression had been committed, and it was Britain's duty to ensure that it did not pay. Henderson subtly underlined this by suggesting that it was a crisis shared by both countries: the ideals and interests of Britain and America were essentially the same, he argued. It seemed to go down well. By mid-April the polls were showing sixty-six per cent of the public siding with Britain.

But Henderson also enlisted the support of important senators like John Tower of Texas and Charles Percy of Illinois. Both gave pro-

British interviews early on in the conflict, and helped steer a motion of support for Britain through the senate's foreign relations committee.

Somehow the Argentinians were never in the same league. Their ambassador, Esteban Takacs, though a man of considerable charm, never seemed to win the same ratings as Henderson. Early efforts to flood newspapers with pro-Argentinian advertisements, and congressmen with telephone calls, petered out. The British seemed to have successfully stormed the heights of Capitol Hill, and from mid-April on they were to consolidate their hold.

The final achievement of persuading the US government to come out openly on the British side was yet to come. But the assault was well and truly mounted. Looking back on it now Henderson concludes: 'I must say it was the hardest work I have ever done by a long way. It was too tense to be agreeable. I never thought we would lose. There was too much at stake.'

The same pattern of intensive diplomatic activity marked the British effort in Brussels – at the headquarters of the European Economic Community and at NATO. In both places news of the invasion prompted immediate motions condemning the Argentinian invasion, and British officials built on this mood of outrage to secure something more.

At NATO the need was to convince Britain's partners that the detachment of a substantial force to sail to the South Atlantic, with the inevitable weakening of NATO's defences in Europe, was nevertheless an essential reaction to aggression. The argument was accepted early on, and, despite some private alarm as the size of the task force grew, NATO never wavered publicly in its backing for the British military campaign. There was another, more cynical, reason for this enthusiasm: the South Atlantic was to prove the best testing-ground ever devised for the ships, planes and missiles on which NATO forces rely.

The EEC was a far less certain proposition. The Falklands crisis came in the middle of yet another testy argument over the size of Britain's contribution to the EEC budget, and on April 3 Lord Carrington had been due to attend a meeting in Luxembourg which promised to be extremely hard going. There was therefore no great residue of goodwill for Britain to draw on as the campaign to win whole-hearted and unstinting support from her partners began that weekend.

There was, however, once again, a diplomatic hero to rise to the occasion. It was not, this time, the ambassador, since Britain's man at the EEC, Sir Michael Butler, was on a ski-ing holiday. That was, perhaps, just as well since Butler, though immensely able, was nevertheless inclined to brusqueness. He had once, as a junior diplomat in Paris, actually been expelled by the French as *persona non grata*, and his stubbornness was well-known in Brussels. Instead, his deputy, Bill Nicholl, took over, and Nicholl, a softly-spoken Scot from Dundee with a long record of successful trade negotiation behind him, turned out to be ideally suited to the delicate task ahead.

The initial reactions of most of the member countries had been to condemn Argentina's aggression, but to leave it at that. President Francois Mitterrand of France had rung Thatcher on Saturday, April 3 to express his solidarity, and the ten foreign ministers, communicating through their special telex network known as Coreu, issued a joint declaration condemning the invasion and appealing to the Argentinians to withdraw.

But by Sunday, the foreign office was asking for something more tangible, like recalling ambassadors from Buenos Aires, blocking arms sales, and restricting export credits. Next day a message from Whitehall to Brussels asked for a special meeting of the Committee of Permanent Representatives (Coreper), pointing out that the Falkland Islands and dependencies were actually written into Article 131 of the Treaty of Rome as territories associated with the Community, so there could be no doubt that the whole Community, not just Britain, was called upon to react. Britain intended to impose an embargo on all imports from Argentina. 'Early and effective action' in support of this move would be appreciated.

Bill Nicholl noted that the foreign office was suggesting a selective ban on imports. This, he knew, would be endlessly complicated, so he drew a deep breath and decided to go for a total ban instead. On Tuesday morning he talked over the technical problems with a high-powered group of EEC commissioners at the Commission's giant Berlaymont headquarters, and won their support. Then he joined his colleagues in Coreper, next door in the Charlemagne building. Here there was more uncertainty, with questions, worries and objections from the Germans, the Italians, and the French, amongst others. Nicholl sensed the mood and informed the foreign office.

On Tuesday, Mrs Thatcher sent off a personal letter to all the heads of government in good time to catch the regular German and French cabinet meetings. The first effect of this was a stream of decisions by all the member-states banning arms exports to Argentina. Then Greece stepped forward to announce a comprehensive ban on imports which helped move Nicholl's arguments significantly on.

As Easter weekend loomed, Nicholl spent Thursday lobbying his way all round Brussels desperately trying to get trade measures agreed before everyone went on holiday and the British naval blockade went into effect on Easter Monday. But if anything, opinion was moving against the British. 'The fight for this relic of a distant colonial era is not worth the blood of a single British or Argentinian solider,' wrote *Die Zeit*, the Hamburg newspaper. In neutralist Ireland and in Italy, which had close popular links with Argentina (one third of Argentina's population is of Italian stock – Galtieri is one of them – and two million Italian passport-holders live in the country), support was dying away.

Against this uncertain background, Good Friday brought a breakthrough. The EEC's political committee, a sober body set up to issue strong and dynamic joint statements when the occasion arises, did just that. Meeting in the Egmont Palace a mile from the Commission's headquarters, they expressed solidarity with Britain with a warmth that took even the British aback, and then recommended that economic measures should be taken.

'That was the turning-point,' noted one British official. 'It wasn't just the decision itself, it was the enthusiasm with which they backed it up that counted.'

That afternoon the Belgian ambassador, Paul Noterdaeme, chairman of Coreper, decided to propose a total ban, with a decision by that evening. Five countries agreed there and then – Belgium, Denmark, Greece, Luxembourg and Ireland. The Germans, French and Dutch held back. Noterdaeme suggested they should all go away and consider it over the weekend.

At that point there was what one participant described as 'a controlled explosion' from the British bench. Nicholl had finally lost his cool. 'We must have a decision now or it is a waste of time,' he stormed. It had to be now or never. Didn't they know there was a war on?

There was a stunned silence, then a minor hubbub of consultations, telephone calls, and last-minute agonising. Finally, and quite suddenly, the idea took hold that a commitment should be made public right away, with the details left till the following week. Italy was the last to fall into line, but their foreign minister, Emilio Colombo, a staunch European, finally convinced his government on Saturday morning to support the formal declaration that the members would 'take the measures necessary to stop all imports from Argentina.' Noterdaeme poured out the champagne and the exhausted ambassadors shook hands, piled into their cars, and then drove off.

No one actually believed that the ban would have an enormous effect on the Argentinian economy. But the impact on their morale was substantial. The decision was thunderously denounced in the press and a team was immediately dispatched to Europe to lobby against the ban. Meanwhile the boost it gave to European unity was enormous.

For Italy, however, the decision was to be traumatic. A furious political row blew up, fuelled by accusations of treachery from Buenos Aires. Looking back on it, the Christian Democrat leader Guido Bodrato reflected: 'The truth is that in the beginning nobody believed it would come to war. Everybody thought that in a few days a little pressure on Argentina would be sufficient.'

He would never had believed that if he had walked the streets of

Buenos Aires during those early April days, or watched the build-up of troops and equipment that was now taking place on the Falkland Islands. The foreign ministry's response to the UN vote, the EEC sanctions and a world-wide arms ban was, on the surface, phlegmatic: 'There will be much noise,' Costz Mendez had predicted, 'but that is all.'

For the sake of the Malvinas, the people responded with banners and cheers. The politicians and the trade union leaders suspended their complaints and threw their weight behind the great patriotic cause. It was a tide of approval which nobody in Argentina could stand against – or turn back.

Behind the scenes, however, Costa Mendez knew that a key mistake had been committed by Galtieri when he addressed the crowds on the balcony of the Casa Rosada on April 3. 'Up till then,' explained a senior official, 'everything was more or less according to plan. Then Galtieri couldn't resist it – he promised them that not one metre would ever be given back to the invaders.' The promise, with its explicit rejection of any negotiation, caused consternation in the foreign ministry. 'Costa Mendez went to the junta and said "What have you done?"' explained the official. 'He wanted to resign, but Galtieri told him: "Don't worry, we can't lose!"' From that moment, the foreign ministry knew that any concession on the Malvinas would meet with ferocious resistance from a president and a junta who had just given the jubilant people the moon.

At Port Stanley huge armoured vehicles poured off transport vessels and lumbered up the slipway to squat on the streets. Wide-eyed children gazed at the big personnel carriers and amphibious trucks which had taken the place of the battered Land Rovers they were more used to. Everywhere there were soldiers, most of them young conscripts, many of them as bewildered and apprehensive as the children and old people on the islands.

Falkland Islanders, recalling those early days under the Argentinian regime, remember that the weather was for the most part idyllic – blue skies, gentle winds, and still, starlit nights. April marks the onset of winter in the Falklands, and very soon the weather would break. But for the time being it was kind to invaders and invaded alike.

In Government House the British flag had been folded away and the portrait of the Queen removed. The rules which would now govern daily life were broadcast over the radio station. No one was to go outside without a white cloth or flag. Driving must be on the right-hand side of the road instead of the left. Stanley would be referred to from now on as Puerto Argentina. Penalties for breaking the rules were introduced: imprisonment and fines would be used to punish crimes such as defacing the Argentinian flag. 'They told us everything would be normal,' recalled pilot Ian White, 'but right off the bat I knew the military were running the show.'

Owen McPhee, a sixty-three-year-old native-born Stanley resident, who worked at the post office, remembers his wife gingerly venturing out of doors with a white flag to dig peat. 'That was the only reason we had to go out,' he said, 'but everytime you did go, there were Argentines all around us – scores of them.'

It soon became clear that, to begin with at least, many of the conscripts were ill-equipped and often short of food. 'They were a pathetic sight,' says John Smith, a former employee of the Falkland Islands Company. 'Some of them couldn't have been more than sixteen. They were utterly exhausted, some collapsing on the road after the four-mile march up from the airport.'

There are accounts of young soldiers begging for food, and desperately searching for firewood. Betty Rozee, a Falklands housewife, looked out of her window one morning and saw a group of soldiers removing her wooden fence. She chased them off – 'but as soon as your back was turned they were taking the wood again. You couldn't win.'

Angela White, Ian's wife, remembers: 'In the first few days there were guards all the time, and if you were standing at the sink or something you could see they were watching.' She did not feel in danger, but felt the need to keep the children away from them and the guns they carried.

The difficult question of how far the islanders should cooperate with the new regime came to a head early at Stanley post office where an Argentinian officer was put in charge. William Ethridge, who ran the office, decided to read out the Geneva Convention to his little group of post office employees to show them officially that they would not be considered traitors if they carried on working. It was an important issue: stamps are big business on the Falklands and there were about £1 million worth in the safe.

Local teachers were summoned to a meeting and given an outline of the kind of things the Argentinians wished them to tell their pupils. It was fairly mild propaganda, but the teachers refused to contemplate it. The issue was not forced.

In the radio station, Claudette Moseley found the soldiers posted there to keep an eye on things friendly and easy-going. But finally their attentions became a bit too persistent for her liking and she had to insist to the officer in charge that they should be removed from the studio. The request was granted. 'They were perfectly nice,' she said. 'Just a bit too nice, that's all.'

But Claudette saw the other side of the regime as well. Her boyfriend Philip Rozee who worked for the Public Works department, was picked up by Argentinian troops and accused of being a spy. He was hauled off to be questioned by the officer in charge of intelligence, a heavily-built man, wearing dark glasses, a blue blazer and grey trousers, Major Patricio Dowling. Dowling questioned him harshly and then told him he would be shot as a spy. Rozee was searched, manhandled and taunted by Argentinian troops, then suddenly released. He and Claudette decided the time had come to leave the islands.

Dowling was perhaps the most feared character amongst the Argentinian hierarchy on the island. The *Sunday Times* correspondent Simon Winchester recalls him as a man who could be perfectly civil for a time, then suddenly explode with menacing anger. 'I never felt entirely safe when Dowling was around,' he recalls.

But it was landowner Bill Luxton who suffered most directly from Dowling's attentions. Luxton and his wife Pat were in Stanley on invasion night, though the family home was at Chartres on West Falkland. They had gone to the town hall to request permission to travel back to Chartres when they were met by Dowling, dressed in the uniform of an army major. 'We have very bad intelligence on you, Mr Luxton,' said Dowling. 'Don't get into trouble.' He then told them that he had detailed information 'on more than 500 of you.'

Luxton was as forthright to Dowling as the Argentinian was suspicious of him, and relations between the two went from bad to worse. The Luxtons managed to return to Chartres by Land Rover and boat, but just thirty-six hours after they got there – at 10.00 a.m. on Easter Sunday – a Puma helicopter landed on the grass in front of the house, and twelve men armed with machine-guns and grenades leapt out and surrounded the house. Then Dowling himself appeared and told the Luxtons they had to report to Stanley.

Bill Luxton recalls what happened next: 'I said to him, "What happens if I say no?" I got a very real and – how can I say, yes – spine-chilling smile. He said nothing But I got the message from that smile that there was no point in saying no.'

They were flown by helicopter to Government House. 'I had the distinct feeling that I was going to be pushed out of the helicopter as we went over the Sound,' says Luxton. 'I wasn't jumpy, though. You just get numb and fatalistic.' In the end, however, neither Luxton nor anyone else was to join 'the disappeared ones'. They landed safely and were taken to Government House. Three days later, along with a small group of those Falkland Islanders whom the Argentinians considered obstructive, or who had themselves decided they should go, the Luxtons were flown out to Montevideo and back to Britain.

The group included the man who had taken over from Governor Hunt, Dick Baker and his wife Connie. Baker's departure left many Stanley residents feeling particularly isolated. 'One or two of the women broke down and wept,' recalled Connie. 'Once Dick had gone, they did not know who was going to take his place and keep things on an even keel. And we were upset at having to go. We did not want people to think we were leaving them in the lurch. But, with a lump in our throats, we went.'

All of which was perhaps symptomatic of the unease that was beginning to affect the Argentinian garrison. The new governor of the Malvinas, a fifty-two-year-old career soldier named General Mario Benjamin Menendez, had gone to the islands determined to establish good relations with the islanders. A handsome man with a winning smile, he adopted a well-considered genial approach to the locals; for instance, because he spoke no English himself, he chose his cabinet only from those Argentinians who did.

However, the advice he was getting from his staff about the islanders was not encouraging. Written reports, later captured by the British, speak of the 'sabotage' of telephone lines in the Camp, and the existence of a 'resistance movement' which was believed to be using youths on motorcycles to carry messages. Worse, a telegram had been found in the post office which suggested that the British had known the time and date of the invasion; clear evidence, the writer concluded, that someone in the Argentinian army was feeding information to the Falklanders.

Menendez was also told that the morale of the Argentinian troops was being undermined by the 'subversion', the lack of supplies – please could they have more chocolate and cigarettes, said one plaintive note – and, most of all, by the steady approach of the task force.

On that last subject the General had a great deal to read. On April 17 he received from Buenos Aires an intelligence assessment of the British forces and of the options they had. It was a remarkable document. Running to eighty-six pages, it gave an account of the composition of the force – both the ships and the men – which it admitted was based almost entirely on publicly available sources, but which, through astute analysis, provided a surprisingly accurate portrait. It then went on to describe the various ways the British could attack the islands, and what the consequences of each option would be.

It specifically warned that the SAS and the SBS – the Special Boat Squadron of the Royal Marines – would be secretly landed on the islands, 'to begin special operations as of this moment'. (That was a little premature; but they did land on May 1.) Finally it predicted that instead of mounting a frontal assault on Stanley, the British would more probably attempt to establish a bridgehead on one of several sites which it listed. Second on the list: San Carlos.

CHAPTER ELEVEN

Enter Al Haig

'A country's bargaining position has traditionally depended not only on the logic of its proposals, but also on the penalties it could exact for the other side's failure to agree.'
– Henry Kissinger

Everyone recalled afterwards that it had been a thoroughly embarrassing affair. Even the dinner, upstairs in the ambassador's mansion, just off Dupont Circle, had been a disaster. 'A dreadful meal,' pronounced Sonia Adler, editor of the *Washington Dossier*. 'It was very sparse. The main dish was salmon. You had to dig a bit out yourself when the waiter came round. You felt stupid in case you dug out too much, so you just took a little bit and some sauce. We were really hungry at the end of it.'

But it was not the food which was to provoke such a furore in Washington – it was the company. The occasion was a banquet, thrown by the Argentinian ambassador, Esteban Takacs, for the US ambassador to the United Nations, Jeane Kirkpatrick. Among the guests, apart from Mrs Kirkpatrick herself, were Walter Stoessel, deputy to the secretary of state Alexander Haig; Tom Enders, assistant secretary of state with responsibility for Latin American affairs; the US ambassador to the organisation of American states; the secretary of the army; the former secretary of the navy; the US army chief of staff; and the assistant secretary of the department of the interior.

On any other occasion the lineup, though impressive, might have passed without comment. But the date chosen for the dinner was April 2 – invasion night – and to most outsiders the presence of so many members of the Reagan administration in the Argentinian ambassador's house was clear proof of collusion, or at the very least, support by America for Argentina's position.

It was Jeane Kirkpatrick who drew most of the fire. Her presence at the dinner was considered by the British to be a special insult. Sir

Nicholas Henderson said it was as if he had accepted hospitality at the Iranian embassy on the day the American hostages were seized. On television she was accused of 'cosying up to the Argentines.'

There is, however, no evidence that the date was anything but a coincidence. Takacs gave the dinner to mark Kirkpatrick's presidency of the security council, and he offered her six possible dates to choose from. She opted for the last of these because it was the only night she had free. On the day before, as rumours of the invasion hardened, there were some last-minute consultations in the White House over whether she should attend. Finally it was decided to go ahead. If she cancelled, the argument went, then all the other American officials would have to pull out as well, and the result would be a diplomatic slap in the face to Argentina just as Reagan was about to establish his role as even-handed mediator. The result was an evening of some tension. Many of the Americans present felt they had somehow been set up by the Argentinians, and when Mrs Kirkpatrick came to give her speech of thanks she snapped: 'You Argentinians are good at almost everything,' she said, 'except governing yourselves.'

Despite this, in the days that followed, British suspicions about Kirkpatrick's role began to deepen. It was pointed out that she had failed to turn up at the security council to support Britain when Resolution 502 was passed. She was said to be a friend of Argentina, had written a book about the country, had been there several times. Her appointment by Reagan as UN ambassador – an influential post that gave her cabinet status, and a voice in the national security council – had followed the publication of an essay in which she argued that the time had come for America to offer support to right-wing, if repressive, regimes, in order to combat communism.

Her case was not helped in British eyes by a long interview on CBS television some days later when she managed to convey the impression that what Argentina had done did not qualify, technically, as an invasion. 'If the Argentines owned the Falklands,' she commented, 'the moving in of troops is not armed aggression.'

It was not the most diplomatic of remarks, but then Jeane Kirkpatrick has never been famous for tact. Impulsive and direct, she has frequently been accused of speaking first and thinking last, but only by those who have suffered her more controversial judgments. Her targets have included the United Nations itself, for causing more problems than it solves; the Carter administration for undermining pro-American right-wing autocracies; and black African states for pouring out futile resolutions and declarations directed against South Africa. But she is far from a conventional conservative. A lifelong democrat, only recently converted to Reaganism, she considers herself a liberal on human rights, and her arguments in favour of right-wing governments stem less from a conviction that they function well, than from the belief that they are more susceptible to change than left-wing dictatorships. For her the Carter presidency marked a 'period of national withdrawal and passivity' which deprived the United States of the opportunity of influencing events and therefore blocking Soviet expansion. Her views were thus very close to Reagan's own; she argued in addition that while dictatorships of both right and left might be distasteful, in foreign policy one must often choose, not between two goods, but between two evils. 'To say that measles is less frequently fatal than meningitis does not mean you approve of measles,' she said once. Despite the suspicions of the British, she was actually not on particularly friendly terms with the Argentinian junta or its advisers. She undoubtedly knew more about the country's political system than most American politicians; and she had written a thesis on Peronism and its role in Argentinian politics; but she had only visited the country twice, once on a lecture tour, once in her capacity as UN ambassador.

For her critics, however, it was enough that she had always favoured closer links with Argentina. And her critics were not confined to the British. There were others, extremely powerful, within the administration itself. None more so than the secretary of state himself, Alexander M. Haig. For both of them, the Falklands was to mark a crisis in their political careers, and the hostility between them was to have a strong influence on the events of the next few weeks. For though Haig, as secretary of state, rapidly took control of American policy towards the Falklands crisis, Kirkpatrick was able to make her views felt through the national security council; and her conviction that America should not endanger her links with Latin America by tilting too far towards the British side had strong support within the state department. What was rather more important, she was both liked and listened to by President Reagan. Haig was uncomfortably aware of her influence – and her independence.

'Mrs Kirkpatrick works for you, doesn't she?' asked a journalist at one stage.

'Not totally,' replied Haig wrily.

It was, therefore, hardly surprising that in the days following the invasion, as the US secretary of state contemplated what role America should play in the conflict, the one person he did not consult directly was Mrs Kirkpatrick. He accepted her judgment that the crisis had direct consequences for America, but he was certainly not going to take advantage of any special knowledge she might have on the subject.

Haig's decision to involve himself in negotiations between Britain and Argentina, and seek to wrest a peaceful solution from both of them, was a personal one. It won him no glory, and in the end it may well have hastened his resignation as secretary of state. But it was entirely in character for him to accept the challenge. The White House, he once told an aide, is 'a rain barrel of reverberating noise' in which only one official was prepared for action – himself. He had already demonstrated his ability to seize the moment on the night that an attempt was made on the life of President Reagan. Then, with Vice President Bush away from Washington, he strode forward to the microphone to announce: 'As of now I am in charge.' This, it emerged later, was an over-statement. He had misread the constitutional line of succession, and the incident was seized on by his enemies within the White House to demonstrate a serious lack of judgment. 'A man of more ambition than talent, someone whose political scars if they were ribbons, would match the collection already pinned to his tunic,' pronounced the *Washington Post*.

No one doubted his bravery. His war record in Korea and Vietnam shows a string of citations for acts of notable courage. And no one questioned his patriotism. From his middle-class, catholic up-bringing on the outskirts of Philadelphia to West Point where he graduated 214th in a class of 310, and where his 'strong convictions and even stronger ambitions' were noted, his attitudes were moulded by conservative institutions. These included the church as well as the army. Arguing once before a congressional committee that the US should resume arms sales to Argentina, he said that the two countries were entirely compatible. After all, he argued, they shared 'a belief in God'.

Finally, no one doubted his loyalty. From the famous episode – almost certainly apocryphal – when he braved enemy fire in Korea to blow up his commanding officer's bath-tub ('so no stinking Chinese general would get a bath that night'), to the controversial period as chief of staff in the White House when he stood by Richard Nixon during the death throes of the presidency, Haig's career was marked by devoted service to his immediate superiors. The most influential of them all was Nixon's national security adviser, Henry Kissinger, to whom Colonel Haig became senior military adviser in 1969. 'When I met Dr Kissinger,' recalled Haig, 'he explained that he was interested in a military man who was a field soldier and a commander, and not so much a military intellectual.' Haig, the perfect organiser, fitted the bill. 'I don't need an intelligent, sensitive human being for an assistant,' joked Kissinger. 'What I need is a good, smart robot.'

Haig made himself indispensable both to Kissinger and, gradually, to Nixon, winning promotion to four-star general and overtaking 240 other generals in the process. He worked extraordinary hours, often staying behind long after Kissinger had left. 'When you see the lights burning late in Henry's office, it's usually Al Haig,' remarked Nixon. Through the dark years of Vietnam, Cambodia, wire-tapping and Watergate, Haig held the White House fort. To do so he needed more than organisational ability. 'To be sure, nobody survives in the rough and tumble of White House politics ... without a good measure of ruthlessness,' noted Kissinger. The 'robot', he realised, had strong ambitions of his own, and was perfectly capable of manipulating events to suit his own ends.

Following Nixon's resignation, Haig was appointed commander of NATO, and won respect from America's European allies as a military leader. Word got about that he nursed presidential ambitions.

Then, in 1980, Haig underwent triple bypass coronary surgery. He insisted however that his health was unimpaired by the operation, and when Reagan offered him the job of secretary of state he showed no hestitation in accepting. Physically he was as active as ever, 'relaxing' by playing a particulary aggressive game of tennis. There were some who thought that he was more short-tempered than when he had last been in government, more unpredictable perhaps, and he attracted a steady enfilade of leaked attacks from inside the Reagan administration. But there was never any doubt that during his seventeen months in office he was the major force in shaping America's foreign policy. Only hours after taking office he was insisting that it was he who had primacy in all areas of external affairs. He called himself the 'vicar' of US foreign policy, the primary 'formulator, executor and articulator' of the Reagan administration's relations with the world, laying special emphasis on a highly visible US presence and the denouncement of Soviet militarism.

In January 1982, Reagan replaced his national security adviser, Richard Allen, with William P. Clark, Haig's deputy. Clark presented a challenge to Haig's authority, and by March there were signs that the secretary of state was growing distinctly uncomfortable at the way in which his decisions were being questioned. He was particularly incensed by a memo issued by Clark saying that in future he would have to approve all foreign travel by members of the administration, including that of the secretary of state.

Thus, when the Falklands crisis began to erupt at the end of March, Haig was in the mood to re-establish his influence. To begin with, like most US officials, he found it hard to take the issue seriously.

As early as March 25, the day before the Argentinian commandos landed on South Georgia, the state department was alerted to the possibility that the United States might have a role to play in what seemed to be a very minor dispute. On that day the British ambassador in Buenos Aires, Anthony Williams, approached the US ambassador, Harry Schlaudemann, and suggested that the US might involve itself in talks on the South Georgia problem. The same day the British embassy in Washington passed on a message saying that Lord Carrington would shortly be in touch with Haig.

In fact Carrington did not communicate until March 28, and the delay did not suggest to the Americans that there was any great urgency about the matter. On March 29 Haig's deputy, Walter Stoessel, called in both Henderson and Takacs and told them that the 'good services' of the US government were available if necessary, but, as one US official put it, 'Frankly we did not have a massive effort on this.'

The British, however, were extremely unhappy at being treated on the same basis as the Argentinians who were, in their eyes, causing all the trouble. Henderson felt sufficiently strongly about it to go behind the state department's back and see William Clark at the White House to register a strong protest. That same day, March 30, Schlaudemann in Buenos Aires met the Argentinian foreign minister, Costa Mendez, and for the first time the possible dimensions of the crisis became clear. Costa Mendez said brusquely that Argentina was not interested in face-saving measures. If the US wanted to intervene then they should confront the question not just of South Georgia but of the Malvinas as a whole. It was a national issue of the first importance.

Back in Washington messages were sent immediately to London and Buenos Aires offering US assistance. The first cables were even-handed in their tone – the state department did not relish being dragged in on one side or the other. But those that followed were distinctly more critical of the Argentinian position.

Next day, March 31, Henderson and Haig held the first of many meetings together which were to cement a close relationship between the two men and which were to help convince Haig that America would have to become closely involved in the Falklands crisis, and that in the end she would come down on the British side. Henderson's message was simple: 'The evidence that Argentina plans to invade the Falklands is now overwhelming. Something must be done.' The same afternoon a courier from Mrs Thatcher arrived at the White House asking President Reagan to intervene personally.

The meeting held that evening by Haig with his senior advisers showed clearly where the secretary of state's own inclinations lay: the Argentinians, he said, must be told in no uncertain terms to stand off. Armed aggression would neither be sanctioned nor approved of by the United States. Although there were, at that meeting, men who would later disagree violently with the course America was taking, at that stage there was unanimity: everything should be done to persuade Galtieri to desist. One senior official present said: 'We went out that night with a message that said to the Argentines in effect: "If you do this the relationship that we have been trying to build with you will be in jeopardy." It was very strong.'

Thus, even before the junta had launched its invasion of the Falklands, it was being warned by Washington that there was more at risk than just retaliation from Britain. Its links with the United States were also in jeopardy. But in Buenos Aires the message was merely read as yet another act of diplomatic window-dressing by an ally who would ultimately sit back and do nothing. US intelligence confirmed that Argentina was now set on a course which would lead inevitably to invasion. Haig talked twice to Downing Street in the course of the frenzied evening of Thursday, April 1, which set the course of future events. It was he who decided that Reagan should make his abortive telephone call to Galtieri in Buenos Aires. The message proved as ineffective as America's previous warnings. The junta had made its decision.

Over the next week there were almost daily meetings of the national security council's policy group, an informal session of the NSC, at which the extent of America's possible involvement was discussed. At an early stage, Jeane Kirkpatrick pointed out: 'Britain has a stake in this; Argentina has a stake in it; but the US government has the biggest stake of all.' Few at the NSC dissented. If diplomacy failed the conflict might well result in a collapse of government in London or Buenos Aires. In either case that would be a disaster for America where both Thatcher and Galtieri were seen as allies. Then there was the complex question of America's commitment to Argentina under the Rio Treaty, a mutual defence pact binding US and Latin American interests, which was seen as an essential part of the bulwark against Soviet expansion in the area. Equally there was the vital question of America's obligations to Britain under the terms of the NATO treaty: if that was ignored, then relations with Europe as a whole would be soured. The options were gone over again and again.

An early suggestion was that Vice President Bush should fly to Buenos Aires with his so-called 'crisis management team', set up after the attempted assassination of Reagan. But gradually it became clear that if anybody was going to 'raise his head above the parapet' as one NSC member put it, that would be Haig. On April 7, Haig sent William Clark a memo arguing the case for a diplomatic shuttle mission with him at the head to explore the possibilities of a settlement between Britain and Argentina. A series of telephone conversations between Clark and Haig centred round the question, 'Why you, Al?'

The answer is, of necessity, as complex as Haig's own character. In Washington it was immediately assumed that Haig was attempting to out-do his old boss Henry Kissinger, the man who virtually invented the diplomatic shuttle. Once again ambition rather than good judgment was dictating events, said the sceptics. There were others, more Machiavellian, who thought that Haig was being handed a rope to hang himself with – if the mission failed then Haig's position might be fatally undermined. But there were good reasons as well, which Haig himself argued forcibly with Clark for going ahead: he alone had the stature, clout and conviction to carry off a difficult but feasible task. With his NATO background he would have the confidence of the British, and his military experience would stand him in good stead with the Argentinians. It was the best guarantee of America's seriousness.

At a brief meeting of the NSC that evening these arguments were accepted, with only two dissenters. Reagan ended the twenty-minute meeting by sending Haig to London on the first leg of his mission, with his full backing, then left himself for a holiday in the Caribbean.

It was, perhaps, not a good omen that even before he took off for London Haig became involved in a typical piece of Washington backbiting. The first plane requisitioned by the state department for the flight was turned down on the grounds that it had inadequate communications equipment and no windows. Another one, standing by to ferry some congressmen on a trip to El Salvador, was located, and Haig rang the leader of the congressional delegation to persuade him to hand it over – which he did without complaint.

On the gossip circuit this became another example of Haig's overweening self-importance: the first plane had not been grand enough for the secretary of state. In fact the charge does not hold up. The original plane, a converted tanker, simply did not have the facilities for high-speed communication which turned out to be an essential part of the mission. But some of the mud stuck.

The Haig team consisted of a 'core' made up of the secretary of state himself; Tom Enders, assistant secretary for inter-American affairs; David Gompert, the deputy assistant secretary for European affairs; Robert Funseth, director of northern European affairs; Scott Gudgeon, assistant legal adviser, inter-American affairs; James Rentschler, a national security council staffer; and Dean Fischer, assistant secretary for public affairs. General Vernon Walters, Haig's ambassador-at-large, joined the team in Buenos Aires. On the whole the team was weighted towards European rather than Latin American interests, but there was a powerful counter-balance in Enders who was undoubtedly the intellectual figurehead of the Latin American camp.

What was striking about the accounts of the shuttle emerging from those close to the team is how little they disagreed in their assessments of both sides in the dispute. In London they felt on firm ground, dealing with a hard-line cabinet, but one which was prepared to make limited and identifiable concessions. In Buenos Aires where the line was just as hard, it was difficult to pin the junta down to any new undertakings. The question of who really spoke for the government was never fully resolved, and for nearly all the team the Buenos Aires end was a deeply frustrating experience. 'I think it finally dawned on us,' said one member of the team, 'that the junta, because of its competing interests, was unable virtually to take any decision that was different from the one it had originally taken.'

The first leg, however, was to London. On the plane Haig had his own state room in the forward section, with Enders, security guards, and communications staff also near the flight-deck; the others had writing tables distributed further down the plane. Two secretaries with electric typewriters and Xerox machines handled the mountains of paper work that accumulated. The pattern which was to emerge was for Enders, Rentschler, Gudgeon and Gompert to spend much of the flight 'hunkered down' round Haig's table, then to return to their tables to draft out position papers. Sleep was snatched in their seats.

Although there were pull-down bunks at the rear of the plane, these were all too rarely used. It was to be an exhausting schedule, but to retire to bed was not considered the 'macho' thing to do.

The team decided on that first flight that there should be three broad goals:

1. Both sides should withdraw, with the Argentinians returning their troops to the mainland, and the British fleet 'standing off' the islands.
2. Some interim authority should be set up on the islands.
3. The status of the islands should be negotiated by a certain date.

These propositions were to be put as delicately as possible to begin with, and the first trip to London was to be in the nature of a sounding-out operation rather than a bargaining session. The news that defence secretary Nott had announced a maritime blockade of the islands came as the team prepared to land, and was seen as a deliberate signal of Britain's firm attitude.

The team arrived in London on Thursday, April 8, and drove first to the foreign office, then to Downing Street. The first discussion with Mrs Thatcher was a cautious one. The prime minister had John Nott with her as well as the foreign secretary, Francis Pym, Sir Antony Acland from the foreign office, and the chief of the defence staff, Sir Terence Lewin. There were several hours of somewhat stilted talks; then everyone repaired to the study at Number Ten where Thatcher visibly relaxed. There was what one of those present described as a 'cocktail party' atmosphere, with the prime minister teasing the Americans by calling them 'you guys' and dropping heavy hints about Britain's attitude by pointing out portraits of Nelson and Wellington above the fireplace. Haig responded by telling her that President Galtieri was said to be something of a Thatcher fan. The prime minister pulled a face.

Later, over dinner, at the pudding stage – sorbet and macaroons – the conversation changed gear and Haig began to outline what the shuttle mission was attempting to do. In view of the arguments which were to arise later about American attitudes it is worth recording what he proposed:

1. That the United States agreed in principle and on principle with the British.
2. That they stood by Resolution 502 and wanted a peaceful resolution to the conflict.
3. That they saw the shuttle as a way of trying to find a 'window'.
4. That they sought a line between the important British need to stand by the principles set out by Mrs Thatcher in parliament (that is, the Falklanders' right to self-determination, the restoration of British rule on the islands, and the removal of Argentinian forces), and the minimum acceptable Argentinian position.

5. That although the Argentinians should not be seen to benefit from the use of force, they might establish some kind of residual presence on the Falklands.

It is fair to say that Thatcher's reaction was sceptical. While Pym, Nott and Acland discussed practical concessions that might be made, Thatcher continued to maintain that the important points to bear in mind were the principles she had already outlined. When Haig went on to talk of the three-stage set of ideas worked out on the plane she commented, in what was to become something of a catch-phrase for the shuttle team: 'They're just too woolly, Al.' Haig was later to use the term whenever the team came up with something he knew would be unacceptable to the British prime minister. 'It's your old friend, Woolly Al,' he would joke.

To the outside world there was little of substance emerging from the talks. In what was to become the pattern for the future, Haig appeared outside Downing Street in front of a set of microphones to announce that he was going to Buenos Aires with 'new ideas' to discuss, and then left for London's Heathrow airport.

On the first leg to Buenos Aires the team agreed that a fairly brutal set of proposals would have to be put to the Argentinians. They fell into five categories:

1. The British fleet would not turn round unless the Argentinians withdrew their troops.
2. The British were determined to use force if necessary to remove the Argentinians from the islands, and this could mean war.
3. The British had a superior military capability which meant that the Argentinians would lose in a military confrontation.
4. The United States would be unable to work with both sides in that event, and would be bound to support the British.
5. The consequences of war for Argentina would be political upheaval and economic ruin.

The atmosphere in Buenos Aires, however, was very different from the one they had just left. For a start, organisation was almost non-existent. After a preliminary session with Costa Mendez, Haig and Enders were led off to see Galtieri at the Casa Rosada while the rest of the team were left to cool their heels in a hallway, watched by ceremonial guards and deprived of coffee, telephones, and even chairs. By the time Haig returned they were in combative mood. Haig had spent most of his time trying to persuade Galtieri that the Argentinian leader had made a number of misjudgments about the British response. He said that the British were entirely serious about military action to retake the islands. Furthermore the United States would be bound to support them if it came to that. It was the first of many blunt assessments put directly to members of the junta, but Galtieri simply

132

1. SURRENDER: April 2 1982, British Royal Marines in Stanley are searched by Argentinian troops after the battle for Government House. (*Simon Winchester*)

2. THE VICTORS: Members of the elite *Buzo Tactico* who
launched a murderous attack on Moody Brook barracks; but their
plan to snatch the governor failed. (*Gente magazine*)

3. THE SPARK: An abandoned whaling station on South Georgia which Argentinian scrapmen went to salvage. They landed illegally, and set the spark that led to war. (*J. Beatty*)

4. OCCUPATION: Falkland children watch mechanised armour patrol the streets of Stanley. (*Woollmann/Gamma*)

5. REINFORCEMENT: Fresh troops arrive at Stanley. (*Perfil/Sygma*)

6. WARNING: Royal Marines training as the task force sails south (© Spooner)

JUBILATION: But in Buenos Aires they still celebrate. (© Hillelson)

9. Lord Carrington,
resigned

10. John Nott,
Defence Secretary

8. THATCHER:
Aggression must not pay.
(*Sally Soames*)

11. Francis Pym,
new Foreign Secretary

12. Sir Nicholas Henderson
Washington ambassador

13. Sir Anthony Parsons,
Britain's man at the UN

14. Rear-Admiral John Woodw
task force commander

15. Major-General Jeremy Moore,
commander land forces

16. Sir Frank Cooper,
Permanent Under Secretary
at the MoD

THE ARGENTINIANS

17. General Basilio Lami Dozo, head of the Air Force

18. Nicanor Costa Mendez, Foreign Minister

19. Admiral Jorge Isaac Anaya, head of the Navy

20. General Mario Menendez, Malvinas garrison commander

THE ARBITRATORS

21. Alexander Haig, then US Secretary of State

22. Javier Perez de Cuellar, Secretary-General of the UN

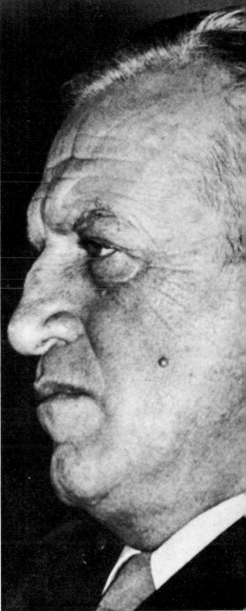

23. GALTIERI:
The Malvinas are ours.
(© Hillelson)

24. THE EMPIRE STRIKES BACK: On April 26 Captain Alfredo Astiz signs the formal surrender after British troops had recaptured South Georgia. Astiz, who is alleged to have played a demonic role in Argentina's 'dirty war' against dissidents in 1976 and 1977, insisted on adding the caveat that he had given in to 'overwhelming' force. Receiving the surrender are Captain David Pentreath (far right) of the frigate HMS Plymouth, and Captain Nicholas Barker of HMS Endurance — the Falkland's protection vessel which Britain was due to scrap. Astiz was sent back to England as a prisoner of war but was

25. Despite that setback, Argentina went on to inflict considerable damage to the task force with Exocet missiles and bombs such as these being readied for Skyhawks by mechanics at Rio Gallegos air base; the message says "Greetings to Prince Andrew", who was a helicopter pilot with HMS Invincible. But Invincible was never hit. (*Pignata/Monti/Sygma*)

SUNK: But there was an awful toll.

26. (above left) *General Belgrano.* (UP1)
27. (below). *Antelope.*
28. (below left) *Sheffield.*

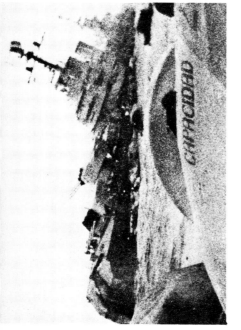

ON THE BRINK: 30. On May 12 QE2 sailed with reinforcements. (*Duncan Baxter*)
31. Argentinian troops waited for the battle. (*Sygma*)

CASUALTIES: At least
1,000 men died in the war —
of which Britain admitted
255 killed — and hundreds
injured; British surgeons
with the task force carried
out 770 operations.
32. One of the victims,
Captain David Hart-Dyke
of HMS Coventry is
re-united with his family,
his face still bearing the
scars. (*Frank Herrmann*)
33. An Argentinian casualty
waits for treatment after the
battle for Mount Longdon.
(*Tom Smith*)

PRISONERS: By the end of May it was the turn of Argentinian troops to suffer the humiliation of surrender.
34. An Argentinian soldier is led away after the battle for Goose Green in which British paratroops overcame unexpected odds.
(*Press Association*)
Eventually, 11,845 Argentians were taken prisoner on the Falklands.
35. VICTORY: Major-General Jeremy Moore celebrates the re-capture of Stanley with local children.
(*Al Campbell*)

HOME COMING: For those who survived there was the moment of joy and utter relief when they were re-united with their families.

36. A survivor from HMS Sheffield greets his wife and son. (*George Phillips*)

37. An Argentinian sailor from Narwal is hugged by his parents in Buenos Aires. (*UPI*) But will more lives yet be lost over 'those rocks' in the South Atlantic?

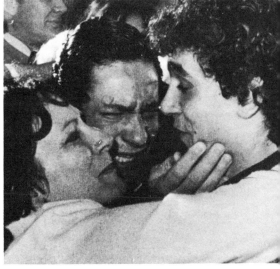

refused to believe it. He pointed out that the Argentinian claim to sovereignty over the islands was not a matter they could concede, and all his information was that the British were unlikely to retaliate. Their demands were simple: lift sanctions, stop the British fleet, and name a specific date by which negotiations must be completed. Throughout that Friday and Saturday, in the course of which there was a total of twelve hours of solid talks, the Argentinians rarely moved from that position, though they were prepared to discuss the formation of an interim administration – provided Argentinian citizens were allowed unrestricted movement on the islands and the right to buy property there.

As they talked, the Americans began to form conclusions about the four men they found themselves principally dealing with. Admiral Anaya struck them as the toughest member of the junta. He told the Americans bluntly that the British fleet was incapable of mounting a successful action 'because it will break down'. The British would rather negotiate than fight, he said, 'because all they are really interested in is oil.' The Argentinians, on the other hand, said Anaya, would fight to the death. 'My son is a helicopter pilot,' he said at one stage. 'The proudest day of my life will be when he lays down his life for the Malvinas' – to which Haig replied quietly, 'You know, when you see the body bags, it's different.'

Lami Dozo, head of the air force, was more accommodating, and seemed prepared for concessions. War, he said, might well end in stalemate. Galtieri himself seemed to swing between the two positions, alternately hard-line then prepared to concede important points. Midway through the talks he left to address a chanting crowd of 100,000 Argentinians outside the Casa Rosada, and told them: 'We are ready to punish the British if necessary.' His speech reminded everyone of the pressures he faced if things went badly. Haig was actually air-lifted off the roof of the Casa Rosada and flown over the vast cheering crowd. 'It reminded us of Teheran and the fall of the Shah,' said one aide.

As for Costa Mendez, the team took some time to make up their minds. To begin with he was helpful, even appearing as a one-man peace party. But gradually the Americans reached the conclusion that he was as hard-line a politician as Anaya, with the added problem that he was more inclined to shift positions without explanation and did not have the influence he pretended to. By the end of the weekend's talks, for example, the Americans found that he had put two entirely contradictory points: on the one hand, he said, the final terms must include a commitment to Argentinian sovereignty over the Falklands; on the other, Argentina should have the predominant role in the islands' administration.

The mood on the shuttle plane as the team flew out of Buenos Aires on Sunday, April 11, was pessimistic. Haig had spoken both to Reagan, who wondered whether the British actually needed some kind of military skirmish to save their honour, and to Clark, who suggested calling the shuttle off. But Haig was insistent that they should go for another round. On the flight to London they worked on putting the Argentinian position honestly to Mrs Thatcher without making it appear entirely unacceptable. They tackled the three problems of sovereignty, access for Argentinian citizens, and the nature of an interim administration, and tried to tailor these to the British insistence on self-determination for the islanders. They do not seem to have entirely succeeded. After a tense day round the negotiating table, in meetings directly with Thatcher, then later with her full team, both sides began to realise that the two positions as they stood were incompatible. Eventually Mrs Thatcher suggested that the British should come up with an amended text for Haig to take back to Argentina. The Americans withdrew to an office made available for them at Number Ten and waited.

When the new terms appeared, the Americans had to face the fact that little real progress had been made. The main British demands remained, with flexibility only on the date for ending negotiations and the nature of an Argentinian 'presence' on the islands. The team stayed long enough to explore just how far the British were prepared to go on each of their points of principle, then left Downing Street to talk by telephone both to Buenos Aires and to Washington.

Strangely there does not seem to have been much hostility at this stage amongst the shuttle team to what appears on the surface to have been a fairly cast-iron case of British intransigence. Thatcher's determination was actually a cause for admiration. One member of the team summed it up thus: 'I was struck by the strength of Mrs Thatcher's convictions. She felt more strongly I think than anyone in the cabinet. She was the driving force, the leading edge. She was not at all tactical. What she wanted to talk about, initially at least, were the principles involved. And in a way it was refreshing, she looked at it in historical terms, in terms of the peaceful settlement of disputes and so on. I found that quite striking, and it certainly affected the way we proceeded, because knowing the strength of her convictions, we had no doubt at all in our minds about the inevitability of the conflict and of the British success if diplomacy did not work out. It made us strive even harder to pull off a success.'

But the team were under no illusions about the toughness of the job.

'Are you more hopeful now, sir, than you were?' Haig was asked as he prepared to fly from London on Monday, April 12.

'No, not at all,' said Haig.

His despondency was not just due to British inflexibility. A telephone call from Washington had informed him that Costa Mendez was now questioning the validity of all the detailed textual negotiations in London, and despite a direct call from Haig to the Argentinian foreign minister, seeking to assure him that progress had been made, this was seen as yet another example of the junta's unreliability. The press was encouraged to believe that Costa Mendez had proposed 'some new ideas'. The truth was he had merely agreed to continue talking.

Haig decided to fly to Washington before returning to Buenos Aires, and on the way a by now thoroughly demoralised team ran over the options. This time the argument was between those, like Enders, who believed that the only approach to the Argentinians now was to try to re-establish confidence with them and help them negotiate in good faith; and those like Gompert who believed in laying down the line to them and refusing to participate in a deal which they knew would not be acceptable to the British.

The decision ended up somewhere between the two, with the emphasis on detailed discussion of the sovereignty issue, and it was here that the Americans began to sense some progress. It seemed as if the phrase 'territorial integrity' might be acceptable to substitute for the word 'sovereignty'. This had the merit of being a formula which could, just possibly, be sold to Mrs Thatcher. At the same time the talks were better organised. They revolved around a team consisting of Costa Mendez and Enrique Ros from the foreign ministry and Admiral Moya, Brigadier Miret and General Iglesias, representing the three armed forces. Only Haig saw all the members of the junta together, though Walters, who knew them well, saw them separately. Walter's *bonhomie* and endless string of reminiscences did much to keep the talks even-tempered. 'A man who combines charm with linguistic ability,' said Nicholas Henderson waspishly.

These two repeated their assurances to the junta that the British were determined to fight, and that if this happened Argentina would be defeated. Finally the message began to irritate both Galtieri and Anaya. 'It seems as if the United States has ranged itself with our opponents,' snapped Galtieri at one point. Anaya accused Haig of being little more than an agent for the British.

On the Argentinian side the Haig shuttle had begun to lose its appeal. Haig amazed them by insisting on continuing talks hour after hour, although he was patently exhausted. At least one Argentinian official thought at one point that he was in danger of having a heart attack. But Haig himself managed to arrange a much-publicised tennis game on the embassy court to demonstrate that all was well. 'What conspired against Haig was his ego,' said one senior Argentinian official. 'He never acted boorishly. He was always well-mannered and he tried to negotiate until the end. But he was not negotiating equally with the British. He went to London first then came here with a piece of paper to sign. That was not enough: outside there were signs in the Plaza de Mayo saying, "Don't sign away with ink what was bought with blood".'

Gradually any residual optimism began to seep away. The

135

Argentinians came back to insist that the word 'sovereign' should be reinserted into the text, thus destroying the delicate compromise the Americans had hoped for. A final text was drawn up but the real problem seemed now to be not so much the words on paper as the good faith of the men who had agreed to them. As they sat in their hotel discussing whether it was worth returning to London at all, a telephone call from Costa Mendez told them that Galtieri was now ready to make important concessions. He would meet them in the VIP room at the airport before they left the next day – Monday, April 19.

That morning, as the American motorcade was about to leave, there was another call from Costa Mendez. Galtieri would not, after all, be at the airport, he announced. The Argentinians would stick to their position. He apologised. 'My hands are tied,' he said. No one knew whether to believe him or not.

On the plane some modest wagers were made about where the team would be spending the next night. Enders said London. Rentschler and others said Washington. At Caracas the decision was made for them. A cable from Francis Pym in London said that, in view of what seemed to be limited progress in Buenos Aires, it was felt that the secretary of state and his aides might as well not bother to fly to London. A flight plan was filed for Washington instead. That night the bunks on the plane were used properly for the first time as the team, exhausted and despondent, took to their beds for the first decent sleep that any of them had had since the twelve-day mission began.

In view of the recriminations that later broke out over the failure of the Haig mission, it is worth pointing out that none of those who were later to attempt negotiations succeeded in getting past the major sticking points that the shuttle team had identified. Haig himself impressed the other members of his team with the calmness and patience with which he conducted himself, especially during the desperate last days in Buenos Aires, and none of those present believes he could have got further. 'For a man with a low boiling-point he was remarkably cool,' noted one of the American negotiators. 'I dare say Kissinger might have been more subtle, but I think he would only have fudged the central issues rather than resolved them.'

Nevertheless the end of the shuttle marked the beginning of a rancorous debate in Washington over what the next US move should be. Daily, in Haig's office, the case which the British had been urging since the beginning of the crisis – that America should come off the fence and side openly with Britain – was argued over. The case for staying 'publicly neutral' was put most forcibly by Jeane Kirkpatrick, and supported with varying degrees of enthusiasm by Enders and Clark. But such was the weight of public opinion building up in favour of an open commitment by America to the British side that few of those who took part believed it was a question of 'whether' the decision would be made, but only 'when', and how much aid would be given.

The tensions between Haig and Mrs Kirkpatrick, however, grew notably stronger, and details of a lively telephone call between the two found its way into the columns of *Newsweek*. According to the magazine, in the course of it Haig referred to her as 'emotionally incapable of clear thinking,' while she referred to him as a 'Brit in American clothes.'

But in this matter at least Mrs Kirkpatrick was on the losing side. On April 30 President Reagan announced that from now on America would be allying herself publicly with the United Kingdom. Military supplies would be made available and economic sanctions imposed against Argentina. 'Armed aggression of that kind must not be allowed to succeed,' said the president.

It was perhaps the last victory that Secretary of State Alexander Haig was to win inside the White House. Eight weeks later he had resigned, handing over the secretaryship to George Shultz. The collapse of the Falklands shuttle may not have been the main reason for his departure. But it helped tilt the balance of opinion against him. Washington does not take kindly to failure.

CHAPTER TWELVE

The Empire Strikes Back

'I join other right hon. and hon. members in congratulating the armed forces on the skill with which they liberated South Georgia.'
– Julian Amery MP, April 1982

'We embarked on a horrific series of events which divine providence somehow influenced.'
– diary of Major Guy Sheridan, 42 Commando, April 1982

On April 9, his third day on *Fearless*, Brigadier Julian Thompson, commander of 3 Commando Brigade, began to find his sea-legs. But conditions for him and his team of officers remained far from comfortable. Although Thompson had a cabin to himself, some of his colleagues were less fortunate. Arguably the brigade's four most vital men at this stage were those who comprised 'R' group ('R' for reconnaissance), who were to prepare the brigade's plans for the Falklands landing: Lt-Col Mike Holroyd-Smith, and Majors Rod MacDonald, David Baldwin, and John Chester. They were squeezed into one tiny cabin and Thompson added to the chaos by wandering in at frequent intervals to see how they were getting on. The man who predictably improved his accommodation was the maverick Ewen Southby-Tailyour, who ensconced himself in an officers' washroom and slept in the bath; later he moved into a cash-clerk's office, spreading his sea-charts over the cash-desk and installing a camp-bed underneath. The space crisis was eased when the group was given the *Fearless* conference room for its meetings. The historical antecedents were not auspicious: it was here that Harold Wilson met Rhodesian prime minister Ian Smith for the abortive and ultimately humiliating talks that followed Rhodesia's unilateral declaration of independence in 1965.

On April 10 'R' group received their first formal instructions from Northwood. They were brief and to the point; as summarised by one officer, they said: 'Please devise a plan to remove the Argentinians from South Georgia and the Falkland Islands.' They reflected the imperatives of the war cabinet itself: the main Falkland group was to be repossessed; the government also wanted the option of taking South

Georgia first, and not only for military reasons. The war cabinet was afraid of what a minister termed the 'Suez syndrome', whereby political opinion in Britain would become divided and the morale of the task force would fall. That minister later explained: 'We had to do something early to show we meant business, both internationally and to the British people'.

It was in this light that the 'R' group planners considered an attack on South Georgia. The more they thought about it, the more they liked it as a first objective. Once taken, South Georgia could provide a secure base beyond the range of the Argentinian air force for taking the Falkland Islands proper; and it would offer the task force a sheltered anchorage for refuelling and maintenance. It would give the politicians the quick success they evidently wanted. Consequently, and crucially, it would assuage 'R' group's principal anxieties by providing the military *more time*: time, above all, to garner intelligence and to establish air superiority. The case seemed compelling: South Georgia *should* be attacked first. 'R' group rapidly came to another conclusion: they wanted to conduct the operation themselves.

It did not take 'R' group long to demonstrate why their men were the ideal people to recapture South Georgia. From his hasty conversation with Major-General Moore before leaving Plymouth, Thompson knew that Northwood had an alternative scheme in mind, with the unlikely codename Paraquet, after the tropical bird. Major Sheridan's 'M' company, fresh from Norway, had been chosen in preference to the Borneo company as Thompson had recommended. Ironically, they now posed the main threat to Thompson's aspirations. But could Sheridan's 110 men really cope? Did anyone know how many Argentinians there were on South Georgia? There were reports of C130s flying in the area, possibly bringing reinforcements; even of a mysterious yacht, which could have inserted Argentinian special forces (in fact it was the storm-damaged yacht of Serge Briez). They were sound, if speculative, military arguments, without doubt honestly held. But they were overlaid with feelings that were common to most of 'R' group, as one member later candidly revealed. 'To put it bluntly, we wanted to have the first landing.'

Having reached that conclusion, 'R' group now embarked on a determined campaign to put it into effect. There was one immediate difficulty: the presence on *Fearless* of a group with aspirations of their own. Commodore Michael Clapp, head of the navy's amphibious warfare group, and the navy's official liaison link with 'R' group, had a team planning their own operation. Although, strictly speaking, their role was simply to position the assault ships to get the marines ashore, they too wanted a share of the action; Clapp himself had pitched in with total enthusiasm, and was even reading biographies of Ernest Shackleton. On April 11, 'R' group met Clapp's team, and smartly presented their written plans. The navy men were clearly taken by surprise. 'It was a tense meeting' one participant said later. 'Clapp's staff felt they were being railroaded – and they were.' In the end, 'R' group's John Chester sat down with the navy team and incorporated their thinking into the marines' plan – a timely diplomatic move.

That still left Northwood and whatever it was cooking up with Sheridan and 'M' company. Thompson and 'R' group now campaigned shamelessly. By telex and radio telephone, they lobbied Northwood, task-force commander Rear-Admiral Sandy Woodward on *Hermes*, and their respective unit chiefs. Their arguments reached dizzying heights: if Sheridan's group failed, it could be catastrophic for the task force; the politicians might get cold feet; the whole operation could be called off. At the same time they disparaged the Northwood scheme, referring to it not as 'Paraquet' but as the industrial poison, 'Paraquat'. One day the signal even reached Northwood: 'Kill Paraquat before it kills us'.

The issue – or so Thompson believed – was due to be resolved when the vanguard of the task force reached Ascension, where a two-part conference was scheduled for April 16 and 17. On April 15, 'R' group completed a forty-six page document, with eleven annexes, entitled 'An appreciation of the situation in the Falkland Islands'. It constituted 'R' group's presentation of their case for taking both South Georgia and the main Falklands group. But it contained a crucial tactical switch. During their campaign for the right to take South Georgia, 'R' group had begun to suspect they were losing the argument. Thompson therefore moved one step ahead and based all his arguments about the main landings on the assumption that South Georgia had already been 'secured'. It was a way of exerting pressure on the planners who would be making the final decision: ensuring that, if it was to be entrusted to Sheridan, they knew how important it was. But Thompson also hedged his bets. Even if Sheridan had first bite, Thompson wanted to come along too. He still wanted to use South Georgia as a base for the main Falklands assault: giving his men 'short, hard training periods', launching raids on the main islands, and allowing more time to gather intelligence and to take on the Argentinian air force.

The conferences where, in theory, these matters were to be decided were to be held in the *Fearless* conference room. One of the first arrivals that morning, brought in by helicopter from *Hermes*, was the fleet commander John Woodward, known universally as Sandy after his striking red hair. Aged fifty, the son of a Cornish bank manager, he sometimes gave the impression that he was surprised to find himself in his exalted position. 'I am an ordinary person who lives in suburbia,' he was to remark. 'I don't see myself as the hawkeyed, sharp-nosed hard military man, leading a battle fleet into the annals of history.' He betrayed his political inexperience when he told task force journalists that the campaign would be a 'walk-over', being compelled to 'clarify' his remarks forty-eight later. In fairness, he had been doing a desk job in Whitehall for three years when the crisis began; and to be plunged into a war must have come as something of a jolt to a man who listed his recreations as sailing dinghies, ski-ing, and collecting stamps.

Woodward's arrival was the first time 'R' group had met him in person. They did not take to him. As the conference got under way, one participant judged him: 'Very dynamic, very impatient, very keen to get on with the task in hand, but unable to relax and sit back absorbing information from all sides.' Another, even less impressed, found him 'desperately arrogant and argumentative'. A third described the atmosphere as 'frosty'.

These harsh judgments in part reflected the poor headway 'R' group made as they pressed their claims. To their fears about air-cover, Woodward replied dismissively: 'Don't bother me about air superiority.' (It was not that he discounted the air threat, more that he judged it his job to deal with it.) To the military men, he seemed obsessed by his own pet proposal to establish an airstrip at Port North on West Falkland for Phantom fighters and C130 transport planes. At the end of the first day, the best comfort that 'R' group could draw was that their own scheme had not been flatly rejected.

April 17 brought a marked improvement. This time, Thompson and his team met Sir John Fieldhouse, who had made the 4,000-mile flight from Northwood for the day: his presence thawed some of the first day's frost. In place of the unyielding Woodward, 'R' group now met someone who listened with sympathy to their hopes and fears. One participant wrote in his diary: 'My impression of Fieldhouse is first-rate. He is very relaxed but his utterly serious manner gives the briefing a sense of confidence.' He encouraged 'R' group by stressing the political need for swift action; the government needed 'a result'. Warming to his own arguments, Thompson pushed the case for South Georgia. He spoke of Gallipoli and Dieppe, and said he wanted his men to have 'a little practice' before any full-scale assault. Fieldhouse said he understood. He offered to provide another squadron of sappers, undertook to secure more helicopters from the RAF, and even hinted that another brigade could be coming out. As 'R' group later recognised, Fieldhouse had given a masterly performance that made them feel their problems were understood. It also served to obscure a crucial item of information. The decision over South Georgia had already been made, and Sheridan and his men were well under way.

Sheridan had been preparing for South Georgia from the moment that he and the 110 men of 'M' company had been detached from the main task force before its departure on Good Friday, April 9. Sheridan – as Thompson had so neatly pointed out – was an excellent choice as commanding officer. Although at forty-two he was still considered a mite impulsive, he had a formidable backlog of experience to prepare him for the unwelcoming terrain of South Georgia. An experienced Arctic explorer and mountaineer, he had led ski treks in the Himalayas and set army records for cross-country ski-ing in Norway. Major-General Moore briefed Sheridan at Hamoaze House in Plymouth on April 8, telling him that South Georgia was seen as 'a quick, easy and attractive option.' He warned that the operation might not take place at all, if there was a political end to the crisis; and all preparations were to be made in the utmost secrecy. Sheridan would have with him the 110 men of 'M' company, together with about seventy men of the SAS and its even more secretive seaborne counterpart the Special Boat Squadron, all under his overall command. Sheridan just had time to sort out his skis and arctic camouflage clothing before flying to Ascension on April 9. Two hours after it arrived, the invasion party embarked on three ships: the tanker *Tidespring* of the Royal Fleet Auxiliary, or RFA; the County Class destroyer *HMS Antrim*, and the long-suffering *Endurance*.

When, just over two weeks later, the British government announced that South Georgia had been recaptured, it implied that the operation had been a swift, surgical affair. On April 26, Mrs Thatcher spoke admiringly in the Commons of the 'professional skill' with which it had been carried out. The previous evening had seen her at her most euphoric, when she deflected reporters' questions in Downing Street with the words: 'Just rejoice at that news and congratulate our forces and the marines . . . Rejoice, rejoice.' The morning press reflected the heady air: 'Cockleshell Heroes' said *The Daily Telegraph* of the SAS and SBS, evoking a British movie about similar exploits in the Second World War. The *Daily Star* blazoned: 'Victory: Quick-Fire Marines Grab Penguin Isle.'

The rhetoric of politicians and press was at odds with reality, of course. Military operations, especially at the start of wars, are frequently beset by indecision, confusion, human error, technological failure, and the vicissitudes of fate. These are usually compensated for by human bravery and sheer bloody-mindedness. The taking of South Georgia was no exception.

On April 14, Major Sheridan advised *Antrim*'s captain Brian Young to begin detailed planning for the taking of South Georgia. The next day a Nimrod reconnaissance plane dropped written orders instructing Sheridan and Young to go ahead. The plan was for covert patrols of the SAS and SBS to go ashore from *Antrim* and *Endurance* to reconnoitre Argentinian strengths and dispositions at Grytviken and Leith. Then the main marine landing force, waiting 200 miles away on *Tidespring*, beyond the reach of Argentinian planes and submarines, would mount its attack. Things did not work out that way.

On Wednesday, April 21, the *Antrim* cautiously approached South Georgia, its glacier-encrusted mountains just visible ten miles away through flurries of snow and an angry sea: most uninviting, Sheridan

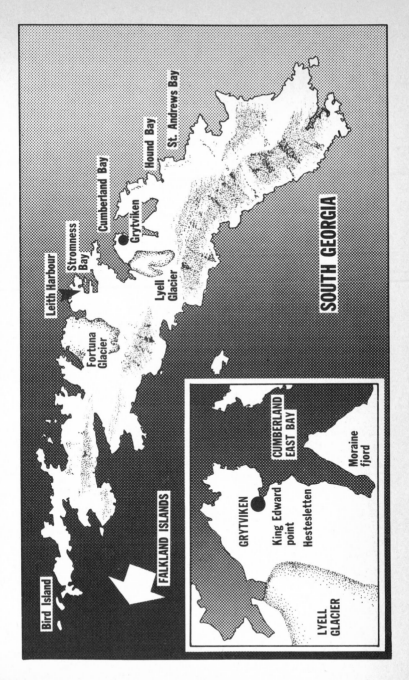

SOUTH GEORGIA

Bird Island

Leith Harbour

Stromness Bay

Fortuna Glacier

Cumberland Bay

Grytviken

Hound Bay

St. Andrews Bay

Lyell Glacier

FALKLAND ISLANDS

CUMBERLAND EAST BAY

GRYTVIKEN

King Edward point

Hestesletten

Moraine fjord

LYELL GLACIER

143

thought. At around 7.00 a.m. local time, three SAS patrols of four men each, laden with enormous rucksacks and a forbidding array of weapons, took off in two Wessex 5 helicopters from the flight deck. Their commander was a twenty-nine-year-old captain, John Hamilton. (Although this book has in general respected the request made of it not to disclose the names of individual SAS officers, the reasons for this exception will later become clear.) Hamilton's aim was to land his men on the inhospitable Fortuna Glacier twenty miles from Grytviken. In selecting that landing area, Hamilton was rejecting some experienced advice. For the three weeks of the Argentinian occupation, thirteen members of the British Antarctic Survey team had lain low on South Georgia, suffering alternately from boredom, hunger, and indecision over whether they should give themselves up. (The other members had been shipped out of Grytviken soon after the Argentinian invasion.) Hamilton collected one of the scientists by helicopter to see what information he could offer, and the scientist had strongly recommended against a landing on Fortuna Glacier. Hamilton decided to go ahead anyway. ('We're the SAS, we can walk on water,' was how one British scientist later described Hamilton's bullish attitude.)

Within forty-five minutes Hamilton and his men were back on *Antrim*. In the driving snow, which threatened to become a total white-out, the pilots had simply been unable to find the landing spots. At 10.00 a.m., the pilots tried again, and this time succeeded. The weather promptly worsened: Sheridan watched in trepidation as the barometer showed a phenomenal drop from 990 to 970 in one hour, while a seventy-five-knot wind blew up which battered the *Antrim* all night.

In the morning, what had been intended as the prelude to the recapture of South Georgia became a desperate rescue operation. At 8.00 a.m., Hamilton radioed an urgent plea for help. After a night on the glacier in winds gusting to 100 knots, he and his men were in a perilous state, with frostbite and hypothermia imminent, and needed to be extracted at once. Two Wessex 5s and a Wessex 3 took off at once but could not find Hamilton and returned to the *Antrim* to refuel. When they tried again they fared even worse. They did locate the SAS men and loaded them on board. But on take-off one Wessex 5 crashed, miraculously without casualties. Its men were redistributed between the other two helicopters; then the second Wessex 5 crashed too. The remaining Wessex reached the *Antrim* intact to report the horrifying tale. There were now seventeen men – thirteen SAS, four helicopter crewmen – marooned on the glacier who would almost certainly die if they could not be rescued by nightfall. When the Wessex 3 headed back to the glacier that afternoon, most of the helpless onlookers on *Antrim* believed, in the words of one of them, that 'there was little chance of anyone coming out alive.'

Thanks to an extraordinary piece of flying by the Wessex 3's pilot, Lt-Cdr Ian Stanley, all seventeen men survived. When Stanley landed on the glacier once more, he calculated that the appalling weather and approaching nightfall would prevent him from making another flight: this was his only chance. The capacity of a Wessex 3 is approximately five men but Stanley and his navigator Lieutenant Chris Parry squeezed all seventeen on board. They took off successfully and headed for the *Antrim*, now twisting and bucking in the roaring sea. Normally helicopters making sea landings hover neatly to one side and then slide smartly in. This was not the time or place for text-book manoeuvres. Stanley simply crashed the helicopter on to the heaving deck. But seventeen men, though shaken and very cold, were still alive, with nothing worse than cuts and bruises. Sheridan, who was keeping a diary throughout the operation, wrote that night that 'divine providence' must have intervened. He also acknowledged Lt-Cdr Stanley's part in that process: 'What a daring and good pilot Ian Stanley is.' (Although Stanley was one of three airmen later awarded the DSO for their parts in the South Georgia operation, when reports of the helicopter crashes reached the ministry of defence they produced a mood of profound pessimism, and all news of them – as we shall see – was rigorously suppressed.)

The grim fact remained that the operation was now little further forward than when it had begun. Two helicopters and a pile of equipment left on the glacier marked the extent of the SAS's intervention; and two SBS squads, deposited ashore from the *Endurance*, were faring no better. They were set down ten miles south-east of Grytviken, intending to cross the intervening Cumberland East Bay in inflatable Gemini boats. Their first attempt was thwarted by the scouring winds that had so imperilled the SAS; their second came close to disaster when ice-floes punctured their boats. They too were retrieved by helicopter, returning to the *Endurance* on April 23.

That day the SAS tried again. This time they would go ashore in Geminis, aiming for Stromness Bay, between Grytviken and Leith. Misfortune struck once more: of the five Geminis' outboard motors, only two would work. The SAS formed two convoys, one of three boats, the other of two. Halfway to shore, the lead Gemini in the two-strong convoy also broke down, causing both to spin helplessly out to sea. Although the other three boats reached the shore, the *Antrim* had yet another rescue on its hands. One of the drifting boats was found after a seven-hour search by the indefatigable Lt-Cdr Stanley, who had all but given it up for lost. The other was washed ashore on the north-east point of Stromness Bay, the last possible landfall before the vastness of the South Atlantic. Having lost virtually all their supplies and equipment, the three men aboard survived five days on the ice-cap before walking into Leith the day the Argentinians surrendered.

It should not be thought that the military and naval commanders at Northwood and on *Hermes* heard of these unfolding catastrophes with equanimity. On the contrary, Major Sheridan was called to the 'growler' – the satellite radio link, secure from Argentinian interception – with increasing frequency, to be asked what the hell was going on. Northwood and *Hermes* were also reporting anxieties of their own, which did nothing for the peace of mind of *Antrim*'s Captain Young: C130 planes were making reconnaissance flights from Argentina, and there was news of a submarine close by. At midnight Captain Young was sufficiently impressed to conclude that he should withdraw to protect the *Antrim* – and to Sheridan, the invasion of South Georgia seemed further away than ever.

Ironically, it was the reported Argentinian submarine that brought an end to Sheridan's frustrations and led to South Georgia's fall – although for a time that seemed a most unlikely outcome. On Saturday, April 24, Sheridan came under further pressure, via the growler, to 'do something'; he declined, since the SAS had still been unable to provide any intelligence about the defending Argentinian forces. The navy, meanwhile, was increasingly preoccupied with the Argentinian submarine, and early on April 25 went on the offensive. At 6.30 a.m., a Wessex 3 helicopter from the *Antrim* found the *Santa Fe*, a former US World War Two diesel submarine, travelling on the surface with apparent unconcern towards Grytviken, and dropped depth-charges which appeared to cause substantial damage. At 10.00 a.m. Lynx helicopters from the *Brilliant* and Wasps from *Endurance* renewed the attack. They fired Sea Skua missiles which apparently passed through the *Santa Fe* without exploding, although they did remove the legs of an Argentinian machine-gunner. The stricken *Santa Fe* reached King Edward harbour, close to Grytviken, where it moored with a pronounced list and oil gushing into the water.

With a feeling that events were fast slipping out of control, Sheridan decided the time had come to mount his attack. His main landing force was still 200 miles away on *Tidespring*, so he mustered all the men he could on *Antrim*: with the remaining SAS and SBS forces, and a handful of marines, he could raise seventy-five men. Since this was about half the expected opposition he knew it was a gamble, but his men, their faces blackened, ammunition bristling from their pockets, were eager for action. A frustrating three hours passed while the navy, seemingly oblivious to Sheridan's needs, remained happily pre-occupied with its victory over the *Santa Fe*. Finally, at 12.40 p.m., Sheridan's team went ashore at a grassy patch named Hestesletten and headed up the steep scree slopes of the 1,000-ft mountain dividing them from Grytviken. On the far side the *Antrim* and *Plymouth* were laying down a barrage of 4.5in shells, somewhat circumscribed by instructions from Northwood to avoid hitting the British survey buildings. At 2.00 p.m., Sheridan moved cautiously on to the ridge above Grytviken and looked down the other side. With some surprise, and a sense of anti-climax, he saw three large white flags flying prominently below. The Argentinians had already surrendered.

146

A small race now developed to see who could reach Grytviken first to accept the surrender. With the SAS forging out in front, Sheridan called up a helicopter and landed ahead. When the SAS arrived moments later, a nonplussed Argentinian officer told them: 'You have just walked through a minefield.' That evening, at the navy's request, Sheridan invited the Argentinian submarine captain and their major of marines on to *Antrim* for dinner. The navy had an ulterior motive: afraid of Argentinian frogmen or even a miniature submarine, they wanted to test the officers' reactions; when they readily accepted, the navy concluded that the waters were safe. Captain Young dressed formally in his 'number ones' and the Argentinian officers seemed grateful for the beer and wine they were given; Sheridan wondered if they might conclude that life as a PoW was preferable to a cramped and smelly submarine. He returned them to shore at 7.30 p.m., then stayed up drinking whisky until midnight. He wrote in his diary: 'A nice day.'

The next day, the gratification of victory gave way to the banalities of its aftermath. The Argentinian submariner who had lost his legs was taken on board *Antrim*. Sheridan visited a group of BAS scientists at Lyell Glacier and was clearly exasperated when they asked about damage at Grytviken. 'The politicians asked us to damage as little of the buildings as possible,' he told them, adding *sotto voce*, 'we are fighting a war, after all.' There were 137 Argentinian prisoners to be provided for, searched and documented according to the requirements of the Third Geneva Convention. Their most celebrated member was Captain Astiz, who had refused to surrender his garrison along the coast at Leith, until visited that morning by the *Antrim* and an eager detachment of the SAS. He had then insisted on inserting in the surrender document the caveat that he had given in to 'overwhelming' force. Alone of all the Argentinians taken prisoner in the war, Astiz was shipped back to Britain, where he was questioned about his notorious activities as an interrogator for the military regime. Whether this was a British propaganda ploy, or whether some deeper game was afoot, never became clear. Astiz was eventually flown back to Argentina, with a first-class air ticket, on June 10.

April 27 on South Georgia brought an unnecessary death. The navy decided to move the *Santa Fe* from King Edward Point to Grytviken jetty, with Argentinians manning the controls. In a tragic misunderstanding, a British marine shot an Argentinian sailor who, the marine mistakenly believed, had been about to scuttle the vessel. The *Santa Fe*'s captain accepted the British apologies, and the submariner was buried with full naval honours. But for Sheridan, who thought the original manoeuvre pointless, the incident soured the whole operation. The next day he left *Antrim* to join the frigate *HMS Brilliant* with the main task force off the Falklands. As he flew past South Georgia there were immaculate views up the fiords and glaciers to the mountains beyond, clear of cloud for almost the first time. That night on *Brilliant* he went to bed early, in the bunk he had been allocated in the captain's day cabin.

There is a postscript to be written, which explains why Captain Hamilton of the SAS has uniquely been named in this book. On June 10, three days before the Falklands war ended, he and a signaller were occupying an observation post overlooking Port Howard on West Falkland. But they were spotted by Argentinian troops and surrounded. Hamilton instructed the signaller to escape while he held the position. The signaller was later captured but Hamilton continued firing until he ran out of ammunition and was killed. It was the only action fought on West Falkland in the entire war; and Hamilton was recommended for a posthumous VC.

On April 22, as the desperate attempts to rescue the SAS from Fortuna Glacier were being enacted, British foreign secretary Francis Pym arrived in Washington. He had the avowed aim of discussing Haig's latest negotiating proposals, and the more covert purpose of asking the United States when it was going to come off the fence. There is no doubt that Britain was carefully coordinating its military and diplomatic activities; the action on South Georgia is the most effective confirmation of that. Pym left Washington on April 23 apparently optimistic. But by now the diplomatic game was to appear less intransigent than the enemy, who could then be blamed when negotiations irrevocably broke down.

The capture of South Georgia caught Argentina unawares. Nicanor Costa Mendez was told in mid-air that South Georgia had fallen as he flew to Washington. He was due at the state department to hear Haig's latest proposals at 4.00 p.m. on Sunday, April 25, but at 7.30 p.m. the state department announced that the meeting had been postponed at Argentina's request. Costa Mendez attacked the British action at a meeting of the organisation of American states, where a gallery of unlikely allies lined up to criticise the US. But if Argentina hoped that South Georgia would tilt the United States its way, precisely the reverse occurred.

Shortly after 11.00 a.m. on April 30 came the announcement the British had been waiting for. At the state department Haig declared that, 'In the light of Argentina's failure to accept a compromise, we must take concrete steps to underscore that the United States cannot and will not condone the use of unlawful force to resolve disputes.' The United States would immediately take economic steps against Argentina and provide Britain's forces with 'materiel [sic] support'. Although the economic moves were limited, and the military measures stopped short, 'of course, [of] direct US military involvement', they were far outweighed by the moral and diplomatic advantage Britain had gained, as the responses of the British and Argentinian governments made clear. On May 1, Pym was back in Washington to

148

meet Haig and Weinberger, jubilantly declaring afterwards: 'The last time I came to see Mr Haig in his role as a mediator. Today I have come back to consult him as an ally.'

In Argentina, the United States' declaration could have brought the conflict to an end. At 10.00 p.m. on April 29, the duty officer at the US embassy in Buenos Aires took a telephone call from a grim Thomas Enders. Argentina, Enders instructed, was to be told that the diplomatic game was over. At eleven o'clock the next morning local time the foreign ministry must be informed of the United States' sanctions, which would be announced in Washington an hour later.

US ambassador Harry Schlaudemann decided to make a last bid to avoid war. He called the US military attaché, the one man at the embassy who could be sure of reaching Galtieri. Schlaudemann told him to wear his military uniform and at midnight the two Americans met Galtieri at the Casa Rosada. As Galtieri read the list of measures to be announced the next day, the colour drained from his face. At last convinced that his friend the United States would put Britain before Argentina, he agreed to call a meeting of the junta where he would argue that Argentina should accept UN Resolution 502 and withdraw its troops.

The junta met almost at once, and argued until dawn. But Galtieri failed. He was quite unable to shift the junta's most hardline member, naval commander Admiral Anaya, who told Galtieri that they could not survive the massive protest from the Argentinian people that backing-down would cause. In the US embassy, the Americans waited all night for the telephone call telling them that war had been averted. It never came.

CHAPTER THIRTEEN

Operation Blackbuck

'The house seemed to lift off its foundations.'
– Diary of islander John Smith, May 1982

In Puerto Argentina, or Stanley as most Falklanders still insisted on calling it, resistance to the occupation was limited to small acts of defiance. For instance, at the West Stores supermarket, Ynonne Turner hid her precious stocks of sweets and chocolates from Argentinian eyes; she sold them only to locals, secretly at the back of the store.

Robert Watson, the town's dentist, was struck by the deep-seated shock that still seemed to affect most of the islanders he saw. It was greatly aggravated by the steady conversion of Stanley into a fortress. Despite Britain's proclaimed blockade, a tide of armaments and supplies arrived daily at Stanley airport, flown in by the Argentinian air force's Hercules C130s. Machine-gun nests were springing up all over town; heavier guns and anti-aircraft emplacements on the rising slopes around it.

Many people were frightened to venture out of their homes. But even indoors they were not necessarily safe. Sometimes at night the Argentinians insisted on a total blackout and the soldiers, unused to the darkness, fired at shadows. One night Stella Perry's home in John Street, which she ran as a boarding-house, was riddled by bullets. Howard Johnson, who boarded there, found all the clothes in his wardrobe perforated. Even Monsignor Spraggon's presbytery, situated just behind Saint Mary's Church, was sprayed and later the priest found a bullet lodged in the middle of a prayerbook.

In the daytime the troops often caused alarm by turning up arbitrarily on doorsteps, to search for guns and ammunition. Watson, the dentist, returned from a shopping trip with his pregnant wife, Catherine, to find soldiers had even broken into his house to search it. The young conscript posted as a guard at their front door was so troubled by the couple's return he shook visibly as they approached. The safety-catch of his automatic rifle was off, and his finger pressed dangerously on the trigger; Watson was terrified that the slightest movement would unleash a hail of bullets.

Events such as these made John Fowler, the islands' education superintendent, acutely anxious. Within a week of the invasion he had lost half-a-stone in weight. A week after that his wife gave birth to a son, and Fowler grew more and more concerned about his family's safety. An avid listener to news broadcasts from the BBC World Service, he was sure that sooner or later they would find themselves in the middle of a war. He reckoned his stone-built house in Ross Road West was solid enough but, in late April, as added protection against blast, he built a bunker in the sitting room by packing a large wooden sideboard with old clothes and surrounding that with tea chests filled with peat. Still he was uneasy, and frequently woke up in the early hours of the morning. Of course, he had no way of knowing that when he went to bed on April 30, his sleep would be spectacularly disturbed.

From the start, Air Chief Marshal Sir Michael Beetham, head of the RAF and one of the joint chiefs of staff, had been worried about the Argentinian air threat to the task force. It was a worry shared by the head of the army, General Sir Edwin Bramell – if not so much by the navy, as we shall see.

Beetham's concern leaked to the Scottish MP Tam Dalyell, who was strongly opposed to the sending of the task force and who used the information to raise questions in the Commons about the venture's chances of success. His campaign did nothing to deter the war cabinet, but it did encourage the canvassing in public of the proposition that the RAF should bomb Argentinian mainland bases.

The idea of attacking the bases closest to the Falklands, in southern Argentina, never made sense to Beetham because the logistics were too formidable. He knew it would take seventeen in-flight refuelling tankers to get just *one* bomber from Ascension to southern Argentina and back. That many were necessary because the tankers themselves would require refuelling as they circled the South Atlantic waiting for their rendezvous; and, to give some margin for emergencies and error, two extra tankers would also have to be put up for each bomber, as standbys.

And it was no good sending one bomber. It is incredibly difficult to hit something as narrow as a runway, especially from two miles or more above the ground, out of range of ground defences. Without laser guidance – which requires 'smart' bombs and someone on the ground to guide them in – the best chance lies in dropping the bomb load across the runway at an angle of about thirty degrees; the calculation is that by this method there is a 50-50 chance of getting one bomb in a load of twenty-one on the target.

But one bomb might not be enough to knock out a runway. In the end the RAF decided it would have to send at least four bombers to hit one base. That meant putting up seventy-six refuelling tankers. Even supposing there were enough planes available – and sufficient crews to fly them – Wideawake air base on Ascension islands simply did not have the parking space.

Beetham advised the war cabinet that it was logistically feasible to bomb the bases in northern Argentina, which would have little effect on the enemy's operations but which might provide a salutary shock. But despite all the public talk, that was always regarded as politically and diplomatically impossible: a prospect before which all the ministers quailed.

However, there were no such inhibitions about bombing the runway at Stanley airport. The logistical problems were the same as bombing southern Argentina but in this scenario one plane and one bomb on target might be enough: it would deny the runway to Argentina's fighters and bombers, though not necessarily to the Hercules and Pucara, a light but lethal plane which the Argentinians had been importing onto the islands; it would, perhaps most significant of all, also give the Argentinian garrison something to think about. Beetham stressed that it meant mounting the biggest RAF operation since the bombing of Germany, and that the chances of putting the runway totally out of action were 'slim'. Nevertheless, he was told to get on with it.

On April 13, the day after the Easter holiday – and, incidentally, the day John and Veronica Fowler's son was born in Stanley – four Vulcan bombers and five flight crews were detached from their regular duties with Strike Command. The Vulcans, once the vanguard of Britain's nuclear deterrent, had been made obsolete by Polaris and were due to be scrapped once the Tornado multi-role combat plane came into service; but they were all the RAF had that could possibly fly the longest bombing raid in history.

The operation was given the codename 'Blackbuck', and for sixteen to eighteen hours a day the crews practised dropping dummy 1,000 pound bombs on RAF ranges on the Isle of Man, Cape Wrath and into the sea off the Yorkshire coast. They concentrated on the techniques of low-level flying and, more important, air-to-air refuelling. During their brief respites, ground technicians worked to modify the planes, fixing new refuelling probes and conventional bomb racks.

By April 28 they were ready and the Vulcans were flown to Ascension island. Two days later, Northwood pressed the button for Operation Blackbuck to proceed.

Given the sheer scale of the enterprise, it is not surprising that something went wrong. But few people would have predicted that all the hours of preparation and final checking would be for nought – because of something as prosaic as a faulty window. Squadron Leader John Reeves of 50 Squadron, the man chosen to deliver Britain's first major blow against the Falklands' garrison, had been in the air for just three minutes when he broke radio silence to report that he could not pressurise the plane because a cockpit window refused to close; he had to turn back. The news thoroughly amazed the crew of Vulcan number XM 607 from 101 Squadron who had followed Reeves into the air, but only as back-up, in case of just such an emergency. They had fully expected to be called back to Ascension. Now – on a diet of beef, ham and cheese sandwiches and flasks of hot coffee – they faced fifteen hours of continuous flying, seventeen refuelling operations, and who knew what at 10,000 feet over Stanley. In the somewhat cramped quarters behind and below the flight deck, and separated from it by a short step ladder and a curtain, the bomb aimer, Flight Lieutenant Bob Wright, settled down to pass some of the time with a paperback novel. Its title, he swears: *Birds of Prey*.

Because refuelling was so crucial to the mission, the Vulcan carried, in addition to its five-man crew, Flight Lieutenant Dick Russell, who was seconded from the RAF wing which operates Britain's twenty-three Victor K.2 tankers. His job was to oversee the Vulcan's aerial matings when, at 300 m.p.h., the pilot, Flight Lieutenant Martin Withers, had to guide the bomber's probe into a basket, looking like a giant shuttlecock, trailing sixty feet behind each tanker, to make a male-female connection. The two planes had then to fly in perfect symmetry until the fuel had been transferred.

It is as difficult as it sounds, especially at night, but everything went smoothly until the rendezvous with the fourth tanker, when Withers was told over the radio by the Victor pilot that the instrument panel was showing the basket had a fault. He flew alongside and Russell shone a torch through the darkness to try and make out what was wrong. All seemed in order so Withers decided to 'simply stick it in and see.' It worked.

And just before 4 a.m. on May 1, 150 miles from Stanley, the Vulcan began its descent to 300 feet to escape radar detection until the last possible moment – forty miles out – when it would have to regain height to at least 10,000 feet to avoid being shot down. Bob Wright put down his paperback, and checked his instruments once more. During the flight he had repeatedly gone over the routine he would have to perform – calculating the approach to the target and feeding the information into a computer which in turn would issue simple flying instructions to the pilot. All Withers had to do then was to keep the wings level; the computer would release the bombs. A specially installed Carousel Inertial navigation system (bought off the shelf from British Airways) showed that after their marathon journey they were only two miles off course.

As they began climbing, the Vulcan's early warning system loudly announced they had been picked up on radar. It was another minute before they would reach their supposed safety 'floor' – out of range of the Tigercat missiles, sold to Argentina by Britain. Withers turned off the wailing alarm and switched on the ECM (electronic counter measures) to jam the tracking radar. They were now twenty-five miles from the target.

The co-pilot, Flight Lieutenant Peter Taylor, spotted the lights of

Stanley below through a break in the heavy cloud. To Withers, it all seemed so peaceful and quiet he found it 'eerie'. Wright made his final checks: bombdoors open; wings straight; target pinpointed. 'It was all going smoothly, like training.' At 4.23 a.m., twenty-one 1,000-pound bombs cased in iron – nearly ten tons of high explosives – began falling at intervals of a quarter of a second.

The Vulcan was still three miles from the airport, out over the sea; the momentum would take the bombs the rest of the way. Withers veered sharply starboard in a routine evasive manoeuvre. He later reflected, 'How sad it was. It took just eighteen seconds for the bombs to hit the ground. It seemed so cold-blooded because they were not hitting back. There was no flak.' A single codeword was flashed to Ascension and thence to Northwood to report mission complete: 'Superfuse'. All they had to do now was get home.

John Fowler had just been roused by the sound of one of his children crying. He settled the child down and went to make himself a cup of tea. In the sitting room he noticed the fire in the grate was barely alight so he bent over to liven it up with a poker. As he gave the peat a jab there was a shattering, trembling bang. Breathless from the shock, he gradually realised that the explosion had taken place far away and in the direction of the airport.

Watson, the dentist, almost fell out of bed when he heard the explosions and felt 'the earth shuddering'. He knew instinctively that the British were hitting back. For the first time in a month he felt elation.

It was a very different feeling to what the crew of the Vulcan were experiencing. Their first rendezvous on their home run was not until they were some 400 miles south of Rio de Janeiro. As they turned for home they saw their fuel consumption had been much greater than predicted; they had barely enough left to make it. And if, for any reason, the tanker was not there when they arrived, they faced calamity. They would have to ditch in the South Atlantic; doing so near enough to a ship able to pick up their distress calls would be miraculous.

There was, as it turned out, no need to worry on that score because the tanker was there. But then came a heart-stopping shock. The two planes apparently mated correctly, but instead of flowing into the Vulcan's tanks, the fuel gushed over the windscreen totally obliterating the pilot's vision; Withers could see neither the tanker nor the probe. It was as if the bomber had been engulfed in a car-wash. Frantically he operated his windscreen wipers but they had no effect.

Bob Wright, alerted by some energetic swearing, ran up the steps to the cockpit, brushed aside the curtain, and craning forward found a small spot at the bottom of the windscreen through which he could just see the probe and the basket, imperfectly connected. He started shouting directions to Withers: 'Up. Down. Left a bit . . .' He expected to be told to shut up, but Withers followed his crude directions and they worked: 22,000 pounds of fuel began to flood into the bomber's dangerously empty tanks. The crisis over, the crew relaxed and tuned their high frequency radio to the BBC World Service in time to hear the news of the raid. It seemed uncanny. 'They were talking about us and we weren't even home,' said Wright. 'We had to pinch ourselves.'

It turned out that, within the limited parameters forecast by the RAF, Operation Blackbuck had been a total success. Reconnaissance pictures taken soon after, by Harriers from the task-force, showed one sizeable crater in the centre of the runway; the other twenty bombs had, as expected, landed either side of the tarmac where the only real damage would have been to Argentinian morale. However, the runway was still available to the Hercules and the Pucaras, though this fact was ignored in official British announcements.

It was to remedy this loophole, and to attack the airstrip at Goose Green, that later that morning every Sea Harrier in the task force – twelve from *Invincible* and eight from *Hermes* – began a series of raids. But this time the Argentinians were on the look-out and the Harriers met a dense barrage of anti-aircraft fire and missiles.

In Stanley, John Fowler heard the crump of ack-ack fire, then the whine of a jet. Going overhead 'a bit slow', and crossing from west to east, he saw a fighter suddenly engulfed by black puffs of smoke. Fowler willed the pilot on, and was puzzled why he did not turn on his after-burners and escape. Then he saw a brilliant white flash explode against the sky, and the plane fell. The pilot apparently made no attempt to eject. Argentinian troops on the slopes shouted with jubilation, and jumped up and down. Fowler felt quite sick. It was not until later, when something prompted him to get out his eldest son's aircraft recognition book, that he realised the Argentinians had shot down one of their own Mirages. 'I laughed my head off,' he said.

Indeed all the Sea Harriers had returned safely, though one of them had taken a shell through its tail. And later that day, they shot down two more Mirages and a Canberra B2 bomber which came out from the mainland seeking revenge.

That same day, May 1, the first SAS and SBS units were put ashore on East and West Falkland by helicopter. The war had started in earnest. Almost immediately, it was to get out of hand.

CHAPTER FOURTEEN

Death of the Big Ships

'The whole principle of naval fighting
is to be free to go anywhere
with every damned thing the navy
possesses.'
– Sir John Fisher, First Sea Lord, 1914

The duties of Petty Officer William 'Billy' Guinea, of the nuclear-powered submarine *HMS Conqueror*, included, among many other things, 'ships identification'. In practice that had always meant being able to identify one Russian ship from another because they were the only ones *Conqueror* stalked – until April, 1982. Once invasion became inevitable, Guinea was ordered to bone up on the Argentinian navy 'which, frankly, was not something we had bothered about too much.' He raced around *Conqueror*'s base, at Faslane in Scotland, looking for reference material, but there was none. The best he could do was persuade the base photographer to copy the pictures in *Jane's Fighting Ships* and enlarge them.

Thus equipped, *Conqueror* sailed for the South Atlantic on April 4. She had a new captain, Commander Chris Wredford-Brown, who seemed to the crew 'a bit reserved'; but this was his first command. Also on board for the first time was Surgeon Lieutenant Commander Chris 'Mac' MacDonald; the need for a surgeon was something the crew found puzzling, and slightly disturbing.

On the two-week journey down to the Total Exclusion Zone which *Conqueror* was to enforce, the Attack Team and the Fire Control Team practised constantly because they believed in the dictum that a submariner's first mistake is likely to be his last. Once there, and on patrol, the overwhelming impression is one of stunning boredom. The crew took six-hour watches. Off duty, they slept or watched war movies or amused themselves betting for preposterous stakes: Billy Guinea bet his fellow petty officer Billie Budding a cup of tea for every Englishman on board – against a cup for every Scot – that Scotland would beat England at soccer; they and he lost and Guinea had to brew 105 cups, there being only three Scots in the company. For 'the more overweight of us' the surgeon organised a sponsored 'slim' to raise cash for a spastics home in Helensburgh; between them, the crew lost £300-

worth of fat. Their only knowledge of the outside world came courtesy of Northwood: a daily summary of what was in *The Times*, plus 'rubbish from Westminster'.

The routine abruptly changed 'at least twenty-four hours' before 4 p.m. on May 2 – the crew refuses to be more precise – when *Conqueror* detected three large ships. *Jane's* is an excellent reference work and Billy Guinea had no difficulty in identifying them: two Argentinian destroyers, *Piedra Buena* and *Hipolito Bouchard*, and the venerable 10,650-ton cruiser, *General Belgrano*.

The order from London to sink the *Belgrano* was undoubtedly the most controversial decision of the war. In the House of Commons, John Nott found no difficulty in justifying it:

'This heavily armed surface attack group was close to the total exclusion zone and was closing on elements of our task force, which was only hours away. We knew that the cruiser itself has [sic] substantial fire power, provided by 15.6 inch guns, with a range of thirteen miles, and Seacat anti-aircraft missiles. Together with its escorting destroyers, which we believe were equipped with Exocet anti-ship missiles with a range of more than twenty miles, the threat to the task force was such that the task force commander could ignore it only at his peril.'

To which the officers of the *Belgrano* say: not true. They were, they claim, on patrol, forty to fifty miles south-west of the exclusion zone, on a bearing of 270 degrees, sailing west *towards* the Argentinian mainland; they had specific orders *not* to enter the zone.

In the circumstances, of course, Argentina would claim that the *Belgrano* was an innocent victim of unprovoked aggression, but it must be said that some British MPs also found Nott's account unconvincing: What did 'hours away' mean? inquired the shadow foreign secretary Denis Healey; fifty miles? a hundred miles? three hundred miles?

Nott dodged the question, as well he might – not because of some perfidy on his part, but because the extent of the exclusion zone had never been properly defined, at least to the crew of *Conqueror*. The British had declared it as 200 miles around the Falkland Islands, but where was the centre point from which they should calculate the radius? Petty Officer Guinea, whose duties included navigation, had no specific orders to answer that question so, in consultation with Commander Wredford-Brown, he selected a point in Falkland Sound – which divides East and West Falkland – and simply drew a circle. There was, of course, no way of communicating that arbitrary decision to the Argentinians. And anyway, no matter where the line fell, the truth is that any Argentinian warship venturing more than a very few miles from shore, was regarded by the task force as dangerous.

The *General Belgrano* had sailed from Argentina's southernmost port of Ushuaia on Monday, April 26. There were just over 1,000 men on board, 300 of them raw recruits with an average age of eighteen. Whatever she was doing when *Conqueror* first found her it was clearly of no immediate threat to the submarine, or the rest of the task force, since the decision as to what action to take was referred to Northwood and, in turn, to Mrs Thatcher's war cabinet. It was the war cabinet that gave the order for her to be attacked.

Conqueror might have simply crippled her. She was armed with Mark 24 Tigerfish torpedoes which can be set to explode in the proximity of the target, rather than on impact, thus reducing the damage. But Tigerfish is extremely expensive; some estimates say £500,000 a time. It is also, in the opinion of some submariners, unreliable; the fact that during the trials – off Malta in 1967 – a test Tigerfish independently changed course by 180 degrees, and very nearly sank its launch submarine, is well known in the navy.

In any event, Commander Wredford-Brown ordered his torpedo officer, Billie Budding, to load the tubes not with Tigerfish but with vintage Mark 8 torpedoes, *circa* the Second World War.

At 4 p.m. on May 2, the first torpedo, fired without warning or challenge from less than three miles, hit the *Belgrano* on the port bow, killing the eight or ten men who were there. The second hit her stern, killing or trapping at least 250 men; most of those victims were in the ship's canteen or in their sleeping quarters. She began taking on so much water that within ten minutes she was listing about fifteen degrees to port; ten more minutes and the list was twenty-one degrees.

Comandante Hector Bonzo, her skipper, decided he had no choice but to abandon ship. The problem was how to give the order, since all of the communications equipment, external and internal, had been destroyed in the explosions. In the end the order was passed from man to man by word of mouth.

Seventy self-inflating rafts, each with room for twenty men, were put over the side, mostly to port where, because of the ever-increasing list, the crew could walk down the side.

It turned out that some of the rafts had been punctured by flying metal so there was overcrowding with up to thirty men to a raft. Some of the men had been badly burned by the blasts – none of them were equipped with anti-flash masks or gloves. It was noticeable that the burns victims were 'perfectly passive, no screams, no panic'; they were easy to handle because they were in deep shock. (Our description comes from one of the *Belgrano*'s senior officers who agreed to give a lengthy interview to our colleague Isabel Hilton, on condition he was not named.)

There were anxious moments when the floundering *Belgrano* threatened to roll on top of the rafts which could not get clear because most of the men were covered in oil, and their hands slipped on the wooden oars; there was nothing for it but to paddle with their hands.

The rafts were about 100 yards from the ship when it began to go down, stern first. Those who had the strength sang the national anthem.

As dusk came, about 6.30 p.m., a north-westerly wind began to rise and the waves grew, overturning one raft from which all the occupants disappeared. The remaining survivors tied the rafts together, in two groups, with rope. They closed the flaps on the canopies to keep out the water, and prepared to spend a stormy night.

The officer Hilton interviewed described what happened on his raft: 'To be honest, I hadn't really expected the men to behave so well. There were two other officers with me, and we began to tell little tales about each of our provinces, about where we lived. We made each person sing a song. We told stories. And what was more important, we prayed. That reinforced one's faith, especially during the moments when we were tossed about as though we were on a trampoline. We never knew when we might be thrown out of the raft, so we were sitting in our lifejackets waiting to cut through the canopy if it started to sink. We prayed continuously in the hope that while we did it would not happen.'

There was one severely burned man on that raft who could only avoid aggravating his agonising injuries by crouching on his knees. For thirty hours – which is how long it took before help arrived – he did not utter a word. He was the first man taken on board an Argentinian rescue ship; half an hour later he died. In all, 368 of the crew of the *Belgrano* perished.

In the aftermath, some of the blame for the high toll was placed on the two escorting destroyers. Since they were not attacked, Nott told the Commons, they should have been able to go to the assistance of the damaged cruiser. 'Fewer might have died,' wrote the *Daily Mail* taking up his theme, 'if the two destroyers ... had not fled as soon as the torpedoes struck, leaving the crew of the *Belgrano* behind.'

That was nonsense. It was *Conqueror* that fled, pursued by both destroyers which, for two terrifying hours, hunted her with sonar and Hedgehog depth charges. Some of the submarine's crew found the experience worse than anything they had imagined: 'I thought I'd been scared before,' said Guinea, 'but I'd never been *that* scared.' Any doubts the crew had about their new and reserved captain evaporated. Under fire he was 'very cool' – and *Conqueror* escaped unscathed.

After the war, when she returned home to Faslane, Commander Wredford-Brown said he thought that in the long run the sinking of the *Belgrano* had saved lives. That is probably true in the sense that, thereafter, Argentina's warships did not venture out to sea again – thus fulfilling a prediction widely offered at the time in Britain and the United States that hers was a one-shot navy; 'Sink one and you've sunk the lot,' as one notable American defence expert put it.

Nowadays, however, navies do not fight only with ships. And when, two days later, Admiral Anaya took his revenge, it came from a most unexpected quarter.

The man primarily responsible for Exocet, the missile which was to become a household name in Britain and Argentina – and the instrument of greatest alarm to the task force – was a French engineer named Émile Stauff. The father of six children, a podgy man with a Gallic moustache and an extremely deep voice, he does not come across as someone who likes the idea of people being killed by his inventions. Nevertheless, since 1946, his 'engineer's curiosity' has led him to develop for the French a whole range of lethal weapon systems – Milan, Hot Rod and Roland among them – which have been sold around the world with huge success.

Stauff conceived the notion of a 'cheap', easy-to-use anti-ship missile, capable of destroying a large modern warship, some twenty years ago. But his research work, conducted in the barrack-like offices of Aerospatiale just outside Paris, progressed slowly, largely because the French defence ministry was unenthusiastic about the idea, and kept the project chronically short of funds.

All that changed in June 1967 when, in the course of the Six Day Middle East war, an Israeli destroyer was sunk by a single missile fired by a small Egyptian patrol boat. As a consequence, defence ministries everywhere began to re-think the future of naval warfare. And in France, Stauff suddenly had all the development money he could use.

He spent much of it on designing some complex electronics, a lightweight battery and, most important, a supremely sensitive radio altimeter that would give his missile its particular deadliness. Exocet is the French name for a species of flying fish and Stauff's ambition was for his 'fish' to fly a similar trajectory, skimming the waves – thus making it difficult to detect and almost impossible to stop. He succeeded. A British junior minister was among the foreign dignitaries who attended the trials in 1967, and so impressive were they that Britain was among the twenty-six countries which subsequently ordered for their navies 1,800 Exocets, at around £300,000 a time.

So, too, was Argentina. However, her navy went further than most customers by ordering not merely the original surface-to-surface version, which can be fired from ship or shore, but also a later breed of Exocet, designated by Aerospatiale as AM 39, and designed to be fired from aircraft. To carry them the navy also ordered, at a cost of $160 million, fourteen Super Etendard fighters made by the French company, Dassault. It was a potent package, and in 1981, the *Comando de Aviacion Naval Argentina* began selecting its most experienced naval pilots to form the Second Attack Squadron.

The pilots were sent to Toulon, in south-west France, then to Landivisian in Brittany, for familiarisation training with the

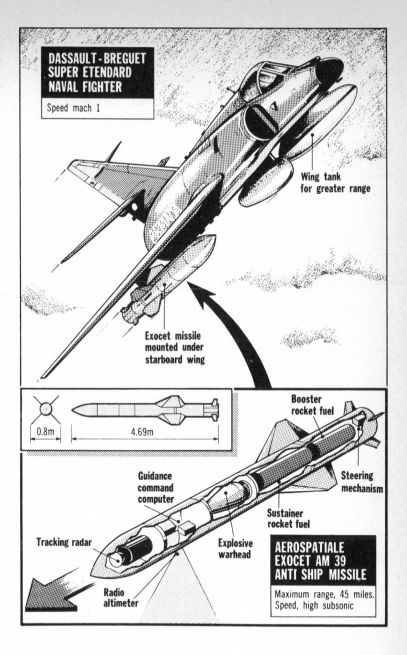

DASSAULT-BREGUET SUPER ETENDARD NAVAL FIGHTER

Speed mach 1

Wing tank for greater range

Exocet missile mounted under starboard wing

0.8m

4.69m

Booster rocket fuel

Guidance command computer

Steering mechanism

Sustainer rocket fuel

Tracking radar

Explosive warhead

AEROSPATIALE EXOCET AM 39 ANTI SHIP MISSILE

Maximum range, 45 miles. Speed, high subsonic

Radio altimeter

161

Etendard. In late 1981, deliveries of the hardware began: the first five Etendards and the first five Exocet AM 39s. From then on, Argentina had the capability, in theory at least, to deliver a catastrophic blow against any ship, however large. An AM 39 is a 'fire and forget' missile, with its own guidance system to take it to a target up to thirty miles away, travelling ten feet above the waves at 680 mph, or close to the speed of sound, to deliver 363 pounds of high explosive with enormous kinetic energy.

All of which might have given the captains of the task force ships considerable pause for thought as they came within range of the Etendards. For with the possible exception of the two frigates *Broadsword* and *Brilliant* – which were the only ships armed with short-range Sea Wolf missiles – none of them had any weapon that might shoot down an Exocet. It did not cause alarm because Britain believed it was highly improbable that Argentina could launch an *aerial* Exocet attack.

The reason for that awful miscalculation was partly an accident of time, partly the duplicity of what one observer later described as 'the limbs of the French empire'.

As we have already said, the French government proved to be Britain's most resolute ally in this crisis. It not only backed sanctions against Argentina to the hilt; it also provided Britain with tactical help by sending Mirage fighters – similar to those supplied to Argentina – so that British Harrier pilots might better rehearse shooting them down. To Argentina's fury, the French government also provided intimate details about the *Aviacion Naval*, its Etendards and Exocets.

The French revealed that the moment Argentina chose to invade the Falklands had coincided with the planned departure of a team of Aerospatiale technicians to Buenos Aires, to assist in the 'matching' of the missiles to the planes; a complicated business which involved making sure that the missile launcher, attached to the wing, would accurately interpret the pilot's wishes as to the precise target before he 'fired and forgot'. As part of its sanctions, the French government ordered Aerospatiale to cancel the mission, and the technicians did not go to Argentina; the British were so informed.

As a result, the ships of the task force sailed south with the belief that the enemy could not launch an aerial Exocet attack. For instance, during the long voyage, Captain Jeremy Black of *Invincible* – the deputy task force commander – briefed the crew at some length on the dangers of particular weapons including surface-to-surface Exocets. But the AM 39 did not appear on his agenda.

It might have been a very different story if the British had known one crucial fact: when the Falklands crisis began, a French technical team was already in Argentina, had been there since November 1981, was not recalled – and, from April 2 onwards, gave enthusiastic help to get the Etendards and the Exocet-launchers ready for war.

The leader of the nine-man team, Hervé Colin of Dassault, told us they remained in Argentina because they were never ordered to pull out, even though he was in contact with his company throughout the war: 'I wouldn't say that we were forgotten, but let's say that here we were, and nobody asked us to go home.'

So, throughout the early days of the crisis, and *after* sanctions were imposed, the team worked at the Base Espora headquarters of Second Attack Squadron, helping the Argentinians with the key task of fitting and testing the missile launchers and the control systems.

Colin explained what happened: 'Essentially the aircraft has a box inside which gives the missile instructions and a missile launcher which goes under the wing. Once you have fitted those and tested them to ensure that they are working, it is relatively simple to mount the missile.'

Testing the system is 'a little delicate'. Fortunately for Argentina, Aerospatiale had supplied the necessary kit which allowed the French technicians to discover that three of the missile launchers had developed faults. 'We corrected those, completed the tests, and we were then over ninety per cent sure that it would work,' said Colin. When, on April 19 and April 20, the Etendards flew south to their war base which we believe was at Rio Gallegos – where the Exocets themselves were fitted – the technicians volunteered to accompany the squadron. It was deemed unnecessary; Argentina now had her killer punch.

The crew of *HMS Sheffield* thought they would not have to go to war. When the crisis erupted on April 2, they were not far from Gibraltar, on their way home after four-and-a-half months at sea – a long time for a destroyer – and Captain Sam Salt went on the tannoy to say: 'Don't worry, chaps, we have our orders to go home arriving on April 6, as planned.' Six hours later he was obliged to announce: 'Forget what I said; we are steaming south.' The men took it remarkably well, partly because they thought they would never get further than Ascension.

In fact, *Sheffield* was one of the first surface ships to reach the Total Exclusion Zone – sent ahead to establish a British *status quo* as far south as possible, in case some diplomatic solution was imposed. And once there, the crew knew that if there was trouble, they would always be in the front line because *Sheffield*'s job was to act as the forward air defence picket, nearer Argentina than the main body of the fleet, to give warning of an attack. She was, frankly, expendable.

In addition, she was very ill-equipped against any form of low-level attack. Her main weapon was the Sea Dart missile which has a range of forty miles and a reputation for accuracy against high-flying targets. It also has some debilitating drawbacks. Unlike Sea Wolf, it relies on other radar to detect the target and on human beings to decide if it is hostile. Unlike Sea Wolf, it can only take on one target at a time. And unlike Sea Wolf it cannot hit anything flying at under 2,000 feet. Since

Argentina's navy was equipped with Sea Dart, it knew all about these limitations; indeed, in late April, the Etendards practised dummy attacks against her own destroyers.

On Tuesday May 4 – two days after the death of the *Belgrano* – *Sheffield* was once more on picket duty, south east of the Falklands, some twenty miles in front of the rest of the fleet. She was at 'Defence Stations', the second highest state of readiness, with half the 270 crew on watch, half resting. It had been a quiet day. The crew's main concern was that the Argentinians might take their revenge for the *Belgrano* by attacking the task force with submarines.

Just after lunch, Lieutenant Commander Nick Batho, the operations officer, picked up the briefest of radar contacts with an aircraft approaching from the west. He had no possible way of knowing that one of a pair of Super Etendards had just emerged from radar deadground, where they could not be seen, in order to take a bearing on *Sheffield*; having done so, the plane dropped down below the radar horizon once more.

Batho informed the officer of the watch, Lieutenant Peter Walpole, of a 'possible contact' and then got on with the job of trying to analyse what it was. It could have been an enemy aircraft. It could equally have been a Harrier – which in terms of radar picture and electronic signal emission is very similar to an Etendard – or a helicopter. Or nothing at all.

Up on the bridge Walpole did not call 'Action Stations' – and thus probably saved many lives because if he had done so the ship's corridors would have been full of running men when the Exocet hit. As it happened he and Lieutenant Brian Layshon, the pilot of *Sheffield*'s helicopter, were the best aircraft recognition men on board and they both studied the horizon waiting for a bomber, if that is what it was, to appear. Walpole was looking across the starboard bow. Suddenly in the far distance he saw a puff of smoke. He failed to recognise what it was, but then neither he nor anybody else had ever seen an Exocet approaching head on at near supersonic speed.

When it was about a mile away Walpole and Layshon said, almost simultaneously, 'My God, it's a missile.' Four seconds later it hit the starboard side amidships, a few feet above the water line. It penetrated at an oblique angle as far as the main engine compartment, where it exploded with devasting force. (Claims published in Britain and America that the Exocet failed to detonate, and that all the damage was done by kinetic energy and the propellant fuel, are discounted by *Sheffield*'s officers. Captain Salt told us: 'I was there, and there is no doubt that the warhead exploded.')

The blast went upwards and outwards, wrecking the galley, spreading as far forward as the Operations Room and as far aft as the Damage Control HQ and the Machinery Control Room. It instantly robbed the ship of most of its electrical power, the communications

HMS SHEFFIELD: The killer blow

How attacking jets fly under ships radar

Spotter Etendard | Attacking Etendard

HMS SHEFFIELD

RADAR DEADGROUND

HMS SHEFFIELD

No 2 Deck

DAMAGE CONTROL HQ   Air Intakes

MECHANICAL CONTROL ROOM

GALLEY

Communications Centre

Operations Room

CABLE DUCTS

Corridor

MAIN ENGINES

MISSILE STRIKES SHIP AT AN ANGLE

165

equipment and all pressure in the fire hoses. Fires started over a wide area, fed by some highly combustible materials such as the PVC covering four miles of electrical wiring, and within twenty seconds *Sheffield* was filled with black, pungent, suffocating fumes.

The bridge was evacuated and those crew who had been below decks – those that had survived – began scrambling through the hatches. Captain Salt, who was on his way to the bridge from his cabin when the .Exocet hit, donned a gas mask and attempted to survey the damage. The starboard gangway was impassable but he could see that huge metal doors were distorted, metal ladders had been ripped from their mountings, and below him on the starboard side, the jagged metal surrounding the gaping hole was already glowing red hot. While Lieutenant Layshon took off in the ship's helicopter to fetch help, the crew attempted to fight the fires – with buckets of sea water.

Twenty miles away on *Invincible* they could already see the plumes of smoke rising on the horizon. Two frigates, *Arrow* and *Yarmouth*, were despatched to her aid, and for four-and-a-half hours there was a desperate fight to save the ship. But it was always hopeless. And with paint on the superstructure beginning to blister, the decks too hot to stand on, and the missile and ammunition magazines in danger of exploding, Salt had no choice but to give the order, 'abandon ship'.

The Etendard pilots had no idea of what damage they had done, or even if they had hit anything at all.

All that they could say was that they had followed their mission briefing, and it had seemed to go like clockwork. En route from Rio Gallegos they had refuelled in mid-air from Hercules C130s and then relied on the Etendard's sophisticated inertial navigation system to take them to the area where they knew – from aerial reconnaissance – the task force was patrolling. On their final approach they had hidden in radar deadground until the last moment when they had momentarily climbed to find their targets. On the radar screens they had seen the blip of a medium sized ship and, beyond it, a much larger one which they assumed and hoped was *Hermes*. They each took a target, fed into their computers the respective bearings, instructed their Exocets how low to fly (there are three levels to choose from), turned on the cameras that would record each launch for later analysis, and fired. Even as the missiles dropped towards the sea, the planes had turned for home.

Back at base, all they could do was wait for news – from the BBC World Service.

Later, when the war was over, Isabel Hilton became the first journalist of any nationality to visit the Etendard squadron and she found its leader, Captain Jorge Colombo, still puzzled as to how *Hermes* had escaped. 'When the English communicated that we had hit *Sheffield* we thought, "Wait! What happened to the other missile?"

We remained almost certain that it went towards *Hermes* – or at least an aircraft carrier.'

The best guess is that it was fired from too great a range, ran out of propellant and simply fell into the sea. But the Second Attack Squadron still had three Exocets left. The pilots analysed the film of their first attempt to sink *Hermes* or *Invincible* – and bided their time.

As for the French, their weapons industry was well pleased with its products. In a full page advertisement published in the French armaments magazine *Heracles*, the copy writer enthused: 'The first engagements in the Falklands conflict have spotlighted three French weapons systems among those equipping Argentine Armed Forces. The destroyer *HMS Sheffield* was put out of action and the aircraft carrier *Hermes* was injured by two air-to-surface Exocet AM39 missiles fired from a Super Etendard ... Besides the personal drama involved in these engagements, how can one not be struck by such a small number of Argentine arms being successful, facing the important offensive and defensive means of about two thirds of the powerful Royal Navy?'

CHAPTER FIFTEEN

The Last Chance for Peace

'The question at the moment is: Have both
sides seen enough blood drawn to make
them have second thoughts?'
– UN official, May 1982

'I don't mind about you, but I'm going
down there to win the war.'
– Rear Admiral Woodward, April 1982

BRITISH WARSHIP SUNK BY ARGIES cried the *Sun* newspaper's massive headline next day. HMS SHEFFIELD HIT AND
SUNK: SEA HARRIER SHOT DOWN said *The Daily Telegraph*,
while the *Daily Star* put it more concisely: SUNK! In fact the *Sheffield*
had not yet gone down. The hulk was to float for another six days until
it was dispatched to the bottom by plastic explosive.

But there was no denying the almost palpable shock which ran
through the nation that morning. 'The worry I live with hourly,' Mrs
Thatcher had said only the day before, 'is that the Argentine forces
might attack by sea and get through to our forces and sink some of our
ships.' Now it had happened, and the reactions of ordinary men and
women reflected the way in which, overnight, the war had become
real, sobering, unpredictable. 'Somehow I never thought they could
get at us like that,' said a Sheffield steel-worker. 'A few casualties, yes.
But one of our ships – that's war, isn't it?' 'We've got to hit back,' said a
London railway porter. 'Bomb the mainland I say. If you don't punish
a bloke who picks your pocket he'll steal your wallet next.' There was
little sign of weakening in the national resolve. 'We've got to stick with
it now' was just one of the sentiments expressed by a group of morning
shoppers in Birmingham.

The mood in the war cabinet that day reflected all those feelings,
with John Nott perhaps most shaken of all Thatcher's ministers. 'It
has been a dreadful event,' he confessed to the House of Commons.
But the first effect of the sinking was to infuse Britain's diplomatic
efforts with new energy and put the foreign secretary Francis Pym
firmly on the offensive again. Whereas only that weekend he had been
at best condescending, at worst airily dismissive of the various peace
initiatives, now he was to give them renewed and serious attention.

And for the time being he had the full backing of his prime minister to press for a solution.

The divisions within Mrs Thatcher's cabinet between the so-called 'war group' and the 'peace group' were real ones, but they were not as predictable nor as fixed as they were portrayed in the press at the time. In the first phase of the conflict, before the war proper began, the ministers who belonged to the inner cabinet had indeed divided into two definable groups. In the first were Thatcher, Nott, and Cecil Parkinson, the Tory party chairman. They had a clearer, less anxious view of the military option than did the foreign secretary Francis Pym and the home secretary William Whitelaw. The latter two not only had a temperamental preference for compromise they had also, unlike the others, both served in World War Two. They knew what war was like, and they had a much stronger view of what seemed to them the absurdity of this particular war as it loomed closer than the others did. It would be too simple to say that they were against the war while the Thatcher group was for it. What would be nearer the mark would be to say that they had a bias against going to war, while the Thatcherites had a bias in favour of retrieving the national honour.

As time went on, the dividing lines grew blurred. Each, according to one source close to the war cabinet, deviated from their 'norm' from time to time. The most regular doubters were Nott and Whitelaw. Nott – febrile, nervy, subject to rapid changes of mood – alarmed the cabinet more than once with his ability to press some military point, then pull up to say: 'My God, I hope we're right.' Equally Whitelaw would unexpectedly veer from dove to hawk at certain moments.

But there was one division that remained consistent, and this was between Mrs Thatcher and her new foreign secretary, Francis Pym. In a perfect world the prime minister would not have given Pym the job in the first place. They had never really got on. While preserving the niceties of behaviour they were in reality less like colleagues than rivals, circling watchfully around each other in a state of constant mistrust. In the sudden vacuum created by Carrington's departure, Pym, strong within the party and the House, was in the end the obvious candidate. But he was far from ideal in Thatcher's eyes. He lacked her single minded will. He actually wanted the peace missions to succeed even when she felt that they were becoming a farce, and he was the last of the war cabinet to concede that war was inevitable.

It is against this political background that the last real chance of achieving a peaceful settlement of the Falklands conflict must be judged. While there is good evidence for believing that after the Haig shuttle had failed, the more hawkish members of the war cabinet viewed the peace moves as little better than a charade, and even found the possibility of their success a positive embarrassment, Pym took them entirely seriously, and bent all his energies towards a solution. The failures of the next few weeks were to depress him deeply.

There is still a mystery about the first of those peace initiatives: the intervention of President Fernando Belaunde Terry of Peru. On the surface it seemed to have all the ingredients of possible success – yet it met with indifference or hostility at various stages from both sides in the conflict. Even in retrospect, some of that mystery still lingers.

Dr Belaunde, the first democratically elected leader of Peru after twelve years of military dictatorship, had first intervened mid-way through the Haig shuttle when he urged a seventy-two-hour truce which was accepted by Argentina, who admitted it was greatly to her advantage, and ignored by Britain. But it was not until after Haig's mission had failed, that the Peruvian proposal took the shape of a draft treaty.

It was drawn up in consultation with Haig – and therein, perhaps, lay its disadvantage, since it was inevitably tarred with the American brush. It was based on a ceasefire, a mutual withdrawal of forces, temporary administration of the islands by a third party, and a fixed time for settlement. Haig, all too familiar with the sticking points, suggested three additional clauses: a guarantee to respect the 'interests' of the inhabitants, the establishment of a group of mutually acceptable countries to see that the plan was carried out, and the deliberate omission of any discussion of sovereignty.

Aware of the disadvantages of the American association, Belaunde moved cautiously – so much so that in the early stages some of the main actors in the drama were unaware of what he was proposing. Francis Pym, who arrived in Washington on the weekend of May 1, appeared vague when questioned about the contents of the 'Peruvian proposals'. And when, on Sunday May 2, Senor Javier Perez de Cuellar, secretary general of the United Nations, and a fellow Peruvian, went to dinner at the New York residence of Britain's UN representative, Anthony Parsons, where the third guest was Pym, reporters sensed something akin to bafflement in Perez de Cuellar's face when they questioned him at the door about the Peruvian initiative. Once inside he had to catch up with events.

At the foreign ministry in Buenos Aires, the proposal was taken much more seriously. 'The most tragic thing in this whole business was what happened to the Belaunde proposal,' a senior official told us. 'I was in the room when Costa Mendez came in and said: "*We have an agreement. We can accept this.*" Everybody was very excited. Two hours later, we got the cable telling us you had sunk the *Belgrano*.' The proposal was dead. On May 7, the Peruvian government announced that it had decided not to proceed further at this stage, for fear of prejudicing its relations with the junta.

The withdrawal of the Peruvian peace plan allowed Pym to blame the Argentinians for its failure. There could, he said, have been a ceasefire within twelve hours if it had not been for their 'intransigence'. But Pym knew perfectly well that neither side had ever given the Peruvian ideas a proper chance. What had appeared, on the surface, to be the most promising initiative of them all, was consigned to the shelf before it had even been taken out of its wrapper.

Meanwhile events had moved to the United Nations, where Britain's diplomatic efforts had been bent, with great singlemindedness, towards one simple aim: keeping the Falklands issue out of the Security Council. Having won Resolution 502, the British knew that if they ever went back to the Security Council they would almost certainly be presented with something far less effective. 'There was nothing more we could get from the Council,' said one British official. 'Our job was to keep them at bay. There were a few alarums and excursions and there were quite a lot of people who had to be spoken to quite firmly from time to time. But by and large we succeeded beyond all expectations. If anyone had said at the beginning we could keep it out for so long I wouldn't have believed them.'

Before that, however, the secretary general himself had begun to make his first delicate moves to resolve the Falklands matter.

It was the *The Times*'s United Nations correspondent who noted, with fascination, the way in which Javier Perez de Cuellar prepares his dry martinis. First he places precisely two drops of vermouth into a frosty ice-cold glass, then puts the glass into the freezing compartment of the refrigerator to chill further, next to a bottle of dry gin. No olive is added, no lemon peel, no ice to dilute the potency of the mixture.

The method is meticulous, the attention to detail unerring. To draw an analogy between Perez de Cuellar's dry martinis and his diplomacy would not be entirely misleading.

Perez de Cuellar's succession at the United Nations had been greeted with relief by most member-states who had grown tired of the high-handed approach of his predecessor, Dr Kurt Waldheim. Waldheim had believed in 'high-profile' diplomacy. Perez de Cuellar, poet, music-lover, bibliophile and intellectual, believed in precisely the opposite. It was typical of him that when he was being canvassed as the new secretary general, he was relaxing in his beach house in Peru without a telephone while the other candidates were scouting for votes in the corridors of the UN. When he was elected he was able to point out quietly that since he had not asked for the job, he consequently had no debts to pay. He did however bring six years of experience as a senior UN hand: he served as under secretary general to Waldheim, and he worked as a special representative in Cyprus and Afghanistan. He had also acted as an observer during the elections in Rhodesia. Knowing that he would be regarded from the outset as a 'third world' secretary general, he took care to choose his staff from a broad geographical spectrum. When the Falklands crisis broke he distanced himself from both camps.

His preparations for intervening in the affair were characteristically modest. As the Haig shuttle got under way, he remained on the sidelines, but began putting together a diplomatic task force of senior officials to study the options. Then on Sunday May 2, he put his first proposals, separately, to both sides, and discussed them in detail at dinner that night with Pym and Parsons.

It has to be said that the British never appeared anything except suspicious of the UN negotiations. But Parsons had great respect for Perez de Cuellar, and over the following weeks was to attend some thirty meetings with him in the secretary general's wood-panelled conference room on the 38th floor. The Argentinians, now represented by Enrique Ros, attended a similar number. The two sides in the dispute never met together. Neither knew directly what the other was proposing. Perez de Cuellar was the conduit. He was, however, according to one of the negotiators, 'much more than a post office. He would warn us where there was no chance of our position being accepted, and suggest possible ways round the problem. The talks were between three professionals who knew each other. They were conducted in a very orderly, straightforward way.'

For the first week there was little real movement as both sides decided how to play things. Then, following the sinking of the *Sheffield* and the war cabinet's decision to step up diplomacy, the mood changed. Pym deliberately softened the British position – to the fury of Tory back-benchers – by dropping the key phrase Mrs Thatcher was so fond of: that the islanders' views were 'paramount'. 'I am not worried about how the vacuum is filled,' said Pym. 'No door is closed.' On May 6 Parsons went to see Perez de Cuellar with a very clear British demand. The Argentinians, he said, must drop their claim that recognition of their sovereignty was a precondition of talks. If they did not the talks would cease. But if they did, then real progress might be made.

For four days Ros said nothing in public. Then, on May 11, he gave reporters one enigmatic sentence. 'I am bringing back some very interesting answers,' he announced. In fact the Argentinians had made the single most significant move in the whole sweep of the Falklands negotiations: they had indeed dropped their demand for sovereignty.

It is still a matter for dispute as to whether the bets were hedged and whether it was therefore a genuine move forward. It was to be obscured by contradictory statements from Buenos Aires – not least by Costa Mendez – and by public scepticism from the British who said they were unable to believe in the Argentinians' good faith. But in retrospect the British team concede that, at the time, it was indeed a breakthrough.

Perez de Cuellar certainly thought so. He urged the British to concede something in return, and what he got was the acceptance of a UN administrator as a substitute for a British governor. By May 14, therefore, he was cautiously optimistic. He thought that he had got agreement on these issues:

1. Negotiations to be conducted in good faith, with a December 1982 target date.
2. A ceasefire and withdrawal under UN auspices.
3. An interim UN administration with Argentinian and UK representatives.

Points undecided included certain parts of the interim administration, particularly the exact role of the islands' council, details of the withdrawal, and the argument over whether the agreement would cover the Falklands alone or also South Georgia and the Sandwich Islands.

It was at this point that Parsons decided to take stock, to commit what he believed had been achieved to paper, and to fly back to London for an on-the-spot appraisal by the boss – Mrs Thatcher.

There are those at the UN who still maintain that this move effectively scuppered the chances for peace. 'When I see people putting their views down on paper,' said one UN man, 'I see people preparing their excuses to break off negotiations.' The same UN source felt nothing but foreboding at the idea of Thatcher putting the delicately phrased agreement to the test.

This is not entirely fair. The British team considered that the negotiations had reached a crucial point and that they had to take stock. They had been in constant touch with the foreign office by cable, but the next stage, they knew, would mark the point of no return, and they needed to be sure there were no misunderstandings. Parsons himself suggested the trip, and the idea was accepted. Not everyone at the UN viewed his departure with concern. Indeed the Argentinians themselves considered it an extremely hopeful sign.

Parsons and the Washington ambassador Nicholas Henderson flew back on May 15 to be greeted at London airport by a barrage of questions which both carefully deflected. That Sunday they drove to Chequers, the prime minister's country residence, where the inner cabinet was assembled. What took place during the seven hours of talks that followed was pivotal in determining the future course of events. 'We all realised that it was a last chance,' said one of those involved. 'We knew that if we failed to get a deal a lot of people were going to die.'

The main theme in the course of the discussion, much of which was directly between Parsons and Thatcher, concerned clarity. Parsons knew that certain points in the document contained potential traps and he was determined that everyone on the British side should be aware of them. His view was that while it was up to the prime minister and the cabinet to decide how far Britain was prepared to go, it was his responsibility to tell them where the 'bottom line' of the agreement in front of them really lay. It had always been his view that the UN favoured vagueness in drawing up agreements in order to win maximum support, and that this often led directly to misunderstandings which might otherwise have been avoided. His instinct therefore, throughout the talks with Thatcher, was to spell out particular passages, rather than to leave them obscure. Quite often, surprisingly, it was he rather than the prime minister who leant in the direction of toughness and clarity rather than delicacy and ambiguity. One example was the section dealing with how withdrawal of troops should be dealt with. The draft left it deliberately vague. Parsons insisted that since withdrawal was going to happen the terms should be spelt out precisely. On the other hand, when Thatcher tried to insist that self-determination for the islanders should be written into the agreement, Parsons pointed out that this would never be accepted by the Argentinians and it would be better simply to refer to article 73 of the UN charter which covers the interests of the inhabitants of non self-governing territories.

The British claim that they did not change their position significantly during the Chequers talks. There were alterations to the draft, they admit, but not major ones, and all these did was to underline facts which some UN officials would have preferred to leave vague. To that extent only did it harden the British position. But, even so, that meant the martini which Senor Perez de Cuellar preferred to stir gently, had been shaken instead.

On the other hand, by the standards of Britain's past positions, it was a radical document. Gone was the British governor. In his place was a UN administrator. Gone was the insistence on self-determination. In essence the Argentinians might, by accepting the agreement as it stood, have achieved the end of British rule in the Falklands, if not precisely the beginning of Argentinian rule. 'My God, if the British had gone a quarter this way in April we'd have had ourselves a deal,' said a member of the Haig shuttle team later.

Everyone thought the Argentinians should accept it. Jeane Kirkpatrick was convinced it was a good deal and she talked with Enrique Ros throughout the whole of one evening and until 2 a.m. the next morning, in an attempt to persuade him. 'It was simply self-defeating madness for Argentina to reject it,' she recalled. 'I pointed out that if they wanted a negotiated settlement of the Falklands dispute they could have it. It did in fact represent a great deal of flexibility on the part of the British government, but it was couched in language so that nobody saw it – and least of all the Argentine government. I was trying to point out to them that it really constituted the achievement of Argentina's aims and that if they accepted it and got out, they had won, as it were. I also tried to tell them that if they did not accept it this was the end of the negotiating track, and there would be war.'

In retrospect many of the Argentinians who were at the UN agree. 'Surely this was the time for us to assess our position,' said one. 'If we were going to win the war, then of course we could forget the British proposals. But if we were in trouble then obviously now was the time to accept the proposal, or something like it.'

Which was exactly what the British thought they would do. 'We thought they would accept ninety per cent of our proposal and give us a difficult ten per cent to decide on.'

But they did not. At 11.15 on the night of May 18, Perez de Cuellar called Parsons and told him that he had the Argentinian response. Perhaps, he suggested diffidently, Parsons would prefer to wait until the following morning before discussing it? No, said Parsons, he thought he might come round and collect it right away. One glance told him the worst – the Argentinians had retreated from their earlier undertakings. Even sovereignty was back on the bargaining table. The game had been played and lost.

On the very day that the United Nations talks broke down in New York, *HMS Fearless* sailed into the waters of the Total Exclusion Zone off the Falklands. The symmetry of these two events is almost *too* striking: it suggests a ruthless mastermind, dictating the twin destinies of war and diplomacy with an eye to the ultimate coincidence of both.

But there was nothing predictable about either of them. The defence planning that led finally to the British invasion was just as agonised and almost as tortuous as the negotiations for peace had been. And although, in the detailed account that follows, the parallels between the two are at times almost irresistible, it is actually the remoteness of one from the other that is ultimately striking.

On April 19, the day when the Haig shuttle, crestfallen, flew out of Buenos Aires for Washington, the military planners on *Fearless* received a jocular, if heavy-handed, message from Rear Admiral Woodward. It ticked them off for failing to get on with the job in hand. Woodward's staff, it said, had worked out that the Falklands consisted of 4,700 square miles of territory with 10,000 Argentinians on them. This meant that there were only .47 Argentinians to every square mile. Why can't we just go down there and round them up? chided the task force commander. The joke had a serious edge to it: Woodward was getting impatient. The previous day he had given the order for the main task force to sail south from Ascension, leaving the planners on *Fearless* and the commandos on *Canberra* to sort out their problems. 'I don't mind about you,' he had told one of them, 'but I'm going down there to win the war.' Brigadier Thompson was sufficiently moved by the seriousness of the situation to give up drinking for the duration of the campaign.

The dispute between the land force commanders and Woodward had been a dominant feature of the intensive planning discussions on *Fearless* which had occupied the past two weeks, and Woodward's departure infuriated some of the planners who were left behind. 'He was fanatically keen to get to the islands,' said one, 'but he did not seem to understand how ill-equipped we were. We had a British Rail task force, not the *Nimitz*.' The SAS were even more angry. Most of their men and materials were on two of the ships that had sailed south on Woodward's order, but some of their equipment was still ashore on Ascension, while the SAS commanders were on *Fearless* which stayed behind. So now one of the smallest unit of the whole campaign was spread across the South Atlantic in three ships and on two bases.

The crucial decisions preceding an invasion had yet to be made. Only three days earlier, at the first Ascension conference, the planners had still been considering four possible options for 'Operation Corporate' as the retaking of the islands had been codenamed. They lost the argument to launch their assault from South Georgia. Now they fell back on three remaining choices. These were:

1. To establish a base at Ascension Island, mount a series of selective raids on the Falklands, then, when reinforcements were ready, launch a major operation to establish a bridgehead. The principal advantage of this was that it gave the landing forces time – for intelligence-gathering, training, and establishing naval and air superiority around the islands. It would not guarantee quick results.

2. To sail south to the Exclusion Zone, remain at sea, mount selective raids, then establish a bridgehead. Again this offered time, and had the advantage of maintaining limited security for the naval force against air attack while still offering some overt military action. But it meant the main land force having to spend more time at sea in bad weather where the risks from enemy air attack were still considerable.

3. To establish a bridgehead on the islands as soon as the ships arrived from Ascension. It would be politically attractive because it was fast and it would maintain momentum. But it allowed only minimum time for intelligence-gathering and for special forces' operations on the islands, and no time at all to establish naval and air superiority. It also placed the land forces ashore at great risk. It had always been the least-favoured alternative of them all.

But now, faced with the political imperative of getting on with the job at speed, the planners were forced to apply themselves to Option Three – the one they had already virtually written off in the Ascension document.

The question of a direct assault on the islands had been debated hotly ever since the 'R' Group had boarded *Fearless* and recovered from their bout of sea-sickness. Now it received their total attention. They held no set meetings, nor did they have anywhere specific to work. Life was 'a constant discussion group' according to one of them.

The unofficial 'chairman' of the group was Major John Chester, thirty-eight, tall and chubby-featured, with a calm reassuring manner. As brigade major, Chester acted both as administrator and liaison officer for the planners.

Lieutenant Colonel Mike Holyroyd-Smith, forty-two, leader

of 29 Commando Regiment, Royal Artillery, was the 'father figure' of the group. A big, bluff, hearty man who smoked his pipe incessantly, he had more men under his command than any of the other planners, and his vast military experience demanded his colleague's respect.

He was convinced that the key to a successful landing was to find a location where artillery could be brought easily ashore and protected. Well versed in missile warfare, he argued that the navy would not have the capacity to neutralise the Argentinian air force.

Major Rod Macdonald, thirty-four, the commando sapper chief, was the youngest of the group. A tall, loose-limbed, intense man, he threw out ideas with an enthusiasm and excitement that was compelling. Occasionally impulsive, he was to admit later that some of his early ideas erred on the rash side.

Major David Baldwin, thirty-seven, was the unofficial group 'secretary'. A small, rather shy, retiring officer, he kept meticulous notes of the discussions and collated the ideas that emerged.

There were two other officers, not part of the group, who nevertheless played important parts in the planning stage. One was Michael Clapp, fifty, who was responsible for *how* the landing would be carried out, rather than where and when. He liaised with Chester. Tall, elegant, and unfailingly courteous, Clapp had been in the navy since the age of seventeen and had seen battle service in Singapore and the Far East. He had commanded a Buccaneer air squadron and, as captain of a minesweeper, had helped round up gun-runners off the Borneo coast. He was less of an 'ideas' man than an organiser.

Finally, there was the irrepressible Ewen Southby-Tailyour, whose encyclopaedic knowledge of the Falklands coastline was to be so crucial. The fact that Southby-Tailyour was referred to fondly as an 'overgrown schoolboy' by one member of the group should be taken as a reference to his infectious enthusiasm rather than to any lack of military experience on his part. In fact Southby-Tailyour had seen service with the marines in Aden and the Yemen, and had then commanded some forces supplied by the British government to the Sultan of Muscat and Oman; he had become the first marine to win the Sultan's bravery medal in action against guerrillas. But he was undoubtedly an eccentric. A small, solidly built figure with white wavy hair, he was full of charm and outlandish ideas. His final report from Greenwich naval college (written by Vice Admiral Halifax who was now closely involved with the Falklands planning team at Northwood) had said: 'This officer prefers fighting to writing and is not recommended for further staff training at this establishment.' Southby-Tailyour probably regarded that as a compliment. His great passion is sailing. He calculates that he has sailed a total of 120,000 miles, of which 10,000 have been on his own. Undoubtedly the most useful of these voyages were those around the Falklands in 1978, when he sailed in and out of the many bays and inlets, busily sketching the coastline. The governor of the day complained about the amount of time he spent in his boat rather than commanding Naval Party 8901, which is what he was supposed to be doing. But then the governor can hardly have known how valuable the exercise was to be.

Southby-Tailyour's military connections were as impressive as his local knowledge of the Falklands. His father had been commandant-general of the marines. He had gone to the same prep school as Sandy Woodward (though, of course, much later) and had attended it with Peter Cameron, who commanded the 3 Brigade air squadron on the Falklands. He had trained in the marines with Guy Sheridan, and been in the same class at Warminster infantry school as Colonel 'H' Jones, commanding officer of 2 Para. Finally, as a young subaltern in 4/5 Commandos, he had served with the man who now commanded him, Brigadier Thompson. (The two were close friends – Thompson was the only man Southby-Tailyour would entrust with his beloved sailing-boat.) Southby-Tailyour thus had an intimate knowledge of many of the officers who would be taking part in Operation Corporate, as well as the terrain where it would be put to the test.

The problem which dominated the thoughts of all these men as they wrestled with the landing plans was the threat posed to the task force by the Argentinian air force. 'From Day One we were concerned about the air threat,' wrote one of them. 'I think we became obsessed by it, and rightly so.' It was this which led to their main dispute with the task force commander, Rear Admiral Woodward.

It had been a key assumption in the first Ascension document that amphibious operations onto the islands would only be carried out under cover of total air superiority. Woodward had argued that this was the navy's responsibility, not the land force commanders', and they felt he had somewhat brusquely dismissed their fear that it could not be achieved. His proposal was for a landing at Port North on West Falkland some 115 miles west of Stanley. (It was there that he wanted an airstrip built from which Phantoms and C130s could be flown and British air superiority established.)

Macdonald had been asked to prepare an airstrip plan for Port North just two days before the first Ascension conference. He had responded by saying it was impossible: without seeing the ground or knowing of what it consisted, all he could provide would be a limited strip for Harriers.

So tense became the argument with Woodward over the question of how or whether the air threat could be countered that some 'R' group officers actually sent cables back to London pleading for their own superiors to fly out to Ascension to argue their case. A number of them did so to attend the second day's conference, and finally Woodward on *Fearless* agreed that the North Bay landing idea would have to be dropped.

But the air threat continued to worry them. 'This invasion is only possible if we bomb the mainland and/or take out their navy,' wrote one of the planners. 'But both would cause political problems.' And later: 'It is now clear that we have no air superiority. We are being told that Harriers may be based between the islands and the mainland. J. T. [Thompson] is very worried about *Canberra* ... he [Woodward] still believes it can be done by the Navy and is raising the level of expectations at home by his messages.'

Thompson tried to calm his colleagues' fears by arguing Woodward's case for him. He pointed out that the navy was being forced to play a new game of warfare. No one had fought a missile war before and Woodward was rightly concerned about protecting his flagship, the *Hermes*. Against that, pointed out Thompson, the land force commanders were doing the same thing they had been doing for 2,000 years. 'The only difference between Hannibal and us,' he said one night, 'is that he went by elephant, and we are going to walk.'

But still the 'R' group were concerned. They worried about the presence of civilians on the Falklands, and about the number of casualties London would tolerate. A study prepared in Whitehall told them that ten per cent of casualties would be acceptable, but twenty per cent would not. In the end the overwhelming constraint was shortage of men. Classical amphibious landing theory dictates a three to one troop advantage. But the task force had little more than 3,000 commandos and paratroopers against what was assumed to be some 9,000 Argentinians. Instead of three to one in their favour, it was three to one against.

It was with this in mind that the planners had to run through the various possibilities. These had included, initially, a direct landing at Stanley itself. The SAS commanders had argued for an Entebbe-style raid, landing at Stanley airport, driving into town, and gunning down the Argentinian high command. Back in Britain, several test-runs had even been carried out at a remote Scottish airfield until information about the strength of Argentinian defences on the road to Stanley had begun to emerge.

Various seaborne landings at Stanley had also been canvassed. The captain of *Fearless*, Jeremy Larken, had suggested backing his ship into Stanley harbour and letting men pour out from its dock in landing craft. Other naval officers proposed sending in the five supply ships and doing the same thing. At one point the question of whether it was possible to get a large number of men onto the islands by helicopter was examined. Airborne landings from Sea Kings had never been tried before, so a new system, with the helicopter hovering thirty feet above the sea was tried out, using thirteen senior officers and a private from 3 Para whose birthday it was. 'It was the most high-powered stick that ever jumped into the sea,' said one of the participants afterwards.

None of these plans, however, came to anything. All assessments showed that there simply were not enough men to take Stanley frontally. Besides, no one knew whether the harbour was mined or not.

In the end, the 'R' group accepted that the landing would have to be elsewhere, and the paper they offered at the first Ascension conference concluded: 'given the imbalance of force ratios . . . and our very limited assault capability . . . a front assault on Port Stanley would have little chance of success.' Two separate appreciations, one carried out by Jeremy Moore's staff, which had moved from Plymouth to Northwood, and one prepared for the cabinet, had quite independently reached the same conclusion.

Macdonald, who had originally argued for the direct assault, but who later conceded that it was 'a rather cavalier idea, based perhaps on my own lack of experience', now proposed the nearest thing: landing at a nearby bay and moving swiftly into Stanley. His plan was to seize a piece of land with a helicopter assault, bring in the supply ships to build up a beach-head and break out for the capital within twenty four hours. 'He wanted to land next to the town and just go Whap!' said a colleague. The most promising places for such a landing were Uranie Bay on the south side of Berkeley Sound, or Cow Bay on the Atlantic coast to the north.

Holroyd-Smith, the gunner, opposed the 'Whap!' idea. He argued that it would be difficult to guarantee getting all his gun batteries ashore in such a short space of time and that a force, once landed, would be highly vulnerable to air attack. He favoured landing some distance from Stanley. Thompson at first was undecided, and for a long time leant towards Macdonald's view. He liked the idea of Uranie Bay which would, he felt, allow the commandos to get quickly up Mount Estancia onto the high ground that dominated Stanley to the north. On the other hand, he was haunted by the possibility of an immediate Argentinian counter-attack. In the end he vetoed the Macdonald plan; his thinking was reflected in the Ascension document: 'The imbalance of forces, lack of initial assault capability and subsequent inability to maintain a rapid rate of advance across country with appropriate fire support for a practical period, precludes an attack against Port Stanley by 3 Commando Brigade (without reinforcement) in any time frame. The landing force as currently constituted cannot retake Port Stanley.'

The debate had at least cleared the air. Now Thompson and his staff could concentrate on the task of finding a landing site where they could consolidate and from which they could advance on Stanley, just as Holroyd-Smith had argued from the beginning. On the evening of April 17, Thompson and Southby-Tailyour laid out the maps on the floor of Thompson's cabin, and 'brainstormed' a place called San Carlos bay.

There was nothing new about San Carlos as an idea. Indeed Southby-Tailyour had ringed it on his map back in Plymouth on the weekend of the Argentinian invasion, and had scribbled next to it, 'sheltered, dominated, good ops [observation positions]. 65 miles to Stanley; 92 miles by sea.' On the journey to Ascension he had returned to it with interest as he went through the twenty-one bays on East Falkland which he had detailed; the twenty-one West Falkland options; the site at Low Bay in the south favoured by Woodward and Port North which was the Rear Admiral's beloved airstrip choice.

Now Southby-Tailyour noticed that the others kept returning to San Carlos too. It was far enough from Stanley to minimise the risk of counter-attack, and provided the Falkland Sound was navigable and not blocked by mines, it afforded a deep enough anchorage to get a large flotilla of warships close enough to shore to protect the troops from air attack. The navy was keen on it because it would ensure they got a slice of the action, and Thompson liked the idea of reaching agreement with the navy on *something*. In addition, there were close surrounding hills where Rapier batteries could be installed. It was also politically attractive – the British could get onto the islands with maximum impact and minimum risk. As Thompson later told reporters, Mrs Thatcher 'could turn round to Galtieri and say, "You are at Port Stanley, but I am somewhere else. Ya Boo!"'

The planners' principal worry, apart from the air threat, was the lack of information about the enemy at San Carlos. Indeed lack of intelligence about Argentinian dispositions had plagued the 'R' group's deliberations all along. 'The real problem with sorting out where to land on the islands,' noted one of the planners, 'was that we didn't know anything about the place.' Although Southby-Tailyour could describe every bay and harbour on the Falklands, he knew nothing about Argentinian dispositions. And to begin with, neither did anyone else. There were no US satellites passing over the islands, and no high-level 'spy' planes available. There was no background information from embassy sources – 'virtually nothing ever came through,' said one of Thompson's aides.

Finally, after SAS patrols and the SBS had landed secretly on May 1, some material began to trickle in, supplemented by intercepts of radio traffic between Stanley and Buenos Aires. 'But for a long time,' said one of the planners, 'we relied on the BBC and press cuttings for all our information on Argentinian strengths and intentions.'

On April 29, the day the Americans decided that they would finally get off the fence and come out openly on the side of the British, Major General Jeremy Moore flew to Ascension Island to confer with his commanders. By this time San Carlos was third on the list of possible landing sites (Cow Bay held first place, followed by Uranie Bay). The 'R' group argued strongly against Woodward's option of Low Bay on the Lafonia plain because of the lack of protection, but in summing up to Moore they urged that 'the name of the game was "stay flexible"'.

Then, on May 5, the mood changed. On *Canberra* the news about the sinking of the *Sheffield* heightened the tension; suddenly everyone felt acutely vulnerable. With agonising coincidence, the ship's company was told that the medics would be collecting 1,000 pints of blood; a signal had gone back to London ordering 300 pairs of crutches; someone heard that there were 2,000 body-bags on board.

On the same day a signal arrived from *Hermes* in the Exclusion Zone that the task force would only be kept operational for another month. Something had to be done quickly. Then, a week later, a task force frigate successfully navigated the Falkland Sound and reported several important findings: there were no Argentinian troops to be seen; no mines; and ample room for *Canberra* and the warships to get in. The SAS confirmed the absence of enemy troops around San Carlos, to Thompson's amazement.

The decisive vote for San Carlos can be pinned to a meeting held on May 10 in the conference room on *Fearless*. Present were the unit commanders called across from *Canberra*. The majority backed the San Carlos option though they were worried about the complexity of the landing plan. Thompson ordered no one to mention the name outside the room. Although there was to be some further wavering, the die was cast. Two days later at a meeting on *Canberra* Thompson produced a set of hand-written draft orders for the landing at San Carlos and laid them on the coffee-table. There was a silence of some seconds as everyone absorbed the realisation that this was finally it.

At nine minutes past one on the next afternoon – May 13, the day the British in New York were drafting the document on which the UN peace talks were finally to founder – a Sea King helicopter lifted off from the mid-ships flight-deck on *Canberra*. It was carrying the unit COs from the commandos and paras across to *Fearless* for a final conference with Thompson; where they were given their final instructions. The meeting lasted two and a half hours. The room was crowded: Clapp, Larken, Thompson, Macdonald, Holroyd-Smith, Chester and Baldwin were all there; everyone, in fact, who had, over the past agonising weeks, been bound up so intimately in refining the most crucial strategic decision of them all.

Everyone, that is, except one: Ewen Southby-Tailyour did not attend. He spent the afternoon in the wardroom trying to come to terms with the enormity of the decision in which he had played so major a part. That night he wrote in his diary: 'I am beginning to have a period of self-doubt. The responsibility is beginning to bear down on me. I am worried about mines in the Falkland Sound, and I am worried about the accuracy of everything I have told them.'

But it was too late for that.

CHAPTER SIXTEEN

D-day

'It was an exploit which captured the imagination of our people.'
– Defence Secretary John Nott, May 1982

'We knew someone would turn up sooner or later.'
– Falkland Islander, May 1982

The Special Boat Squadron is one of the more retiring units of the British armed forces. Unlike its army counterpart, the Special Air Service, it has never performed in anger on the British mainland as the SAS did when it stormed the London Iranian Embassy in 1980; and the SBS has never received the publicity bestowed on the SAS – protesting its modesty, yet secretly gratified – since that event. Whereas many people in Britain know that the SAS is based in the market town of Hereford, few have been aware that the headquarters of the SBS are an unprepossessing set of barracks and boathouses, discreetly labelled 'Amphibious Warfare Training Centre', in the Dorset coastal resort of Poole. Some members of the SAS have an unmistakable air of brashness about them; the men of the SBS seem somehow more quiet and modest. This impression partly results from a deliberate decision by the SBS to avoid elitism, for no one may serve in the unit for more than three years. It also reflects the homely attitudes revealed by a recent conversation with its commanding officer, whose name we have agreed not to divulge.

Reporter: 'What special equipment did you take to the Falklands?'
Officer: 'Marks & Spencer polo-neck sweaters.'

It was therefore altogether appropriate, while 'R' group went through its final agonies over where to land and rumours of an imminent invasion swirled in Britain, that men of the SBS should have been ashore in the San Carlos region since May 1. They were part of a wave of around a dozen four-man SBS squads dropped on the Falklands by helicopter to reconnoitre possible landing sites, while SAS teams also conducted reconnaissances and searched for targets for diversionary raids on the day of the landing itself. One of those SBS squads, with a clear view down to the settlement of Port San Carlos, was led by a thirty-six-year-old sergeant from Taunton in Somerset, a man of slight though muscular build, shy and somewhat introverted, whom we shall call Johnstone. With him were a corporal and two marines whose designations were Swimmer Canoeists 1, 2 and 3. They wore civilian clothing, bought mostly off-the-shelf in sports shops, such as anoraks and long-johns; but including at least one Marks & Spencer pullover.

Johnstone's team had been landed among the Inner Verde Mountains some ten miles from their designated observation point. They spent their first two days hiding in 'scrapes': eighteen-inch cavities they excavated in the peat, covered with chicken wire and hessian netting, and then meticulously replanted with grass. They carried rifles, grenade-launchers, anti-tank rockets, grenades, pistols and knives. But these were to be used only in self-defence, for their principal tools were binoculars, night sights, and a 60x telescope. On their third night ashore they set up their post in a natural cave they had thankfully found among tumbled rocks on Camerons Ridge, less than a mile across Port San Carlos Water from the settlement itself. From there, they began their task of observing the Argentinians they expected to see, in at least company strength, below. They were flabbergasted: there weren't any.

By night, Johnstone reconnoitred the shore, searching for beaches with steep shelves where landing craft could come close, and access to the hinterland. He also looked for sheltered anchorages, free from kelp. By day he and his squad kept up their watch. The only Argentinians they saw arrived by helicopter, briefly checked the settlement, and then departed. Other squads in positions around the San Carlos basin came to the same conclusions. When the SBS teams were withdrawn on May 16, they reported that there were good beaches, safe anchorages, and – above all – no Argentinians.

To Thompson, of course, it all seemed too good to be true – and he was right. There *were* Argentinians at hand on the day of the landing, who had arrived after the SBS parties withdrew and inflicted casualties just when it seemed that the British would emerge miraculously unscathed. But until then the main obstacles the landing force encountered were not Argentinian, but largely – though not entirely – of their own making.

In the week that followed the final conference on *Fearless* on May 13, tension mounted by tangible degrees. On May 15, all civilians on board *Canberra*, including journalists, were told they were now under military discipline; *Canberra* tested its machine-guns that afternoon, loosing them off at the height of a force 8 gale. The next day, a Sunday, an air raid red alert interrupted the church service held in the cinema, and in his weekly message over the ship's tannoy, *Canberra*'s captain, Dennis Scott-Masson, predicted 'an interesting and intriguing week'. On Monday, brigade press officer Captain David Nichols arrived from *Fearless* to brief journalists on the landings, revealing that Rear Admiral Woodward had admitted he had 'insufficient capability to provide twenty-four-hour air superiority', but promised to 'do his best'. The journalists were forbidden any further contact with their offices.

On Tuesday, May 18, the military units were given their landing plans. The commander of 42 Commando's 'K' company, Captain Peter Babbington, told his men to go in hard and kill the officers. Major Mike Norman, the man who had commanded the Stanley garrison when Argentina invaded, said much the same. Having joined *Canberra* at Ascension – and briefly taken amiable charge of the resident press corps – he now briefed 'J' company of 42 Commando, who included some original members of naval party 8901, how to select their targets. 'When you're shooting people,' he told them, 'pick the man who is waving his arms about.'

This curious instruction was a disguised tribute to an SAS party which had raided Pebble Island on West Falkland on May 15. The SAS had spent forty-five minutes sabotaging aircraft before a group of Argentinians arrived, including a man waving his arms and shouting orders. The SAS promptly shot him and the others ran away – a lesson that Norman now pointed up. Tragically, eighteen of the successful SAS squad had drowned when the helicopter transferring them to *Hermes* crashed into the sea, almost certainly because an albatross flew into its engine. This news – though not the probable cause – was broken to the journalists on *Canberra* on May 19.

On Thursday, May 20, like a condemned man's breakfast, the food on *Canberra* improved dramatically, when the P & O chefs offered steak for breakfast, lunch, and tea. That evening, Lieutenant Colonel Vaux addressed 42 Commando. He warned that the landing would be unlike any previous fighting they had known, particularly in Northern Ireland, where casualties took precedence; here they would not. 'If we stop to pick them up we could slow the advance and incur more – they will have to wait.' But the Argentinians could be beaten by 'shock action', and Vaux pleaded: 'let the buggers surrender'. He ended by wishing his men 'a very short and very decisive holiday – good luck to you'. Across on *Fearless*, Lieutenant Colonel Malcolm Hunt said much the same: 'May your god go with you. Good luck.'

A parallel gathering was held by a small number of senior officers on *Fearless* earlier in the day. They included several members of 'R' group who happened to be present when Julian Thompson walked in holding a piece of paper. It bore the single code-word PALPAS – final confirmation from Northwood that the landings should go ahead. Thompson said: 'Gentlemen, we go.' The officers then toasted the Falklands flag, which Ewen Southby-Tailyour had produced.

The flag bore an incongruous hole – the result of one of Southby-Tailyour's more adolescent escapades. Before leaving the Falklands in 1979, he had stolen the flag from the governor's flagpole, storing it in his house on Dartmoor. An appreciative mouse had found it there and munched its way neatly through one corner. Increasingly consumed with guilt, Southby-Tailyour had offered the flag to Hunt when they met at Brize Norton some six weeks before. Hunt promptly told Southby-Tailyour to put the flag back – which is precisely what he intended to do.

The British plan for D-Day was simple – if any plan that entails silently landing 3,000 heavily-laden men and thousands of tons of equipment by night from a fleet of eleven ships can be called simple. 40 Commando and 2 Para would go ashore first, landing on 'Blue Beach One' and 'Blue Beach Two', either side of San Carlos settlement. Then 45 Commando would go into 'Red Beach One' at Ajax Bay, with 3 Para landing last at 'Green Beach One', east of Port San Carlos. The landings would start at 1.30 am local time, and all the units should have secured their land objectives by first light six hours later. With the inevitable threat from the Argentinian air force, speed was of the essence.

The first thing that went wrong was the weather. In an attempt to delude the Argentinians over the landing site, the fleet had first steamed boldly south-west towards Stanley. The ploy required clear skies so that the fleet could be seen: instead there were clouds, wind and rain. By the time the fleet had turned into Falkland Sound, towards its true objective of the San Carlos basin – when every commander in the force was fervently hoping for cloud cover – the weather had cleared. At 12.30 a.m. on D-Day, May 21, there was a brilliant night sky with a myriad stars above and the outline of the shore plainly visible ahead. Despite the danger it portended, it was a moving sight.

The second thing that went wrong was an attempt by the SBS to make a silent capture of a group of Argentinians who had been discovered on the headland dominating the north entrance to San Carlos Water, known as Fanning Head. The Argentinians, of course, should not have been there in the first place. The SBS had reported that the area was not defended, but on the eve of the landings their commander had sent a four-man patrol from the frigate *Brilliant* to make a final check. As they paddled towards Fanning Head they saw lights and then heard men talking in Spanish. They turned round and paddled furiously back.

The SBS was given the task of eliminating the Argentinians before the main landings, if possible by persuading them to surrender. Two dozen men were landed on the shore, together with marine Captain Roderick Bell, who could speak fluent Spanish. They moved up, then Bell called to the Argentinians through a loud-speaker to give in. Some came forward and others seemed willing to do so. But a few remained out of earshot on the far side of the hill. They opened fire and bullets

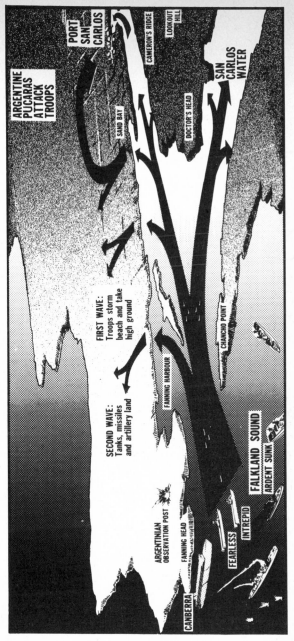

British landings at San Carlos, May 21 1982

ripped into a sergeant's rucksack. The SBS responded instantly and after a brief gunfight some Argentinians lay dead while others were captured, or appeared to have fled into the night.

It was thus to the alarming sound of gunfire that the main landing force prepared to embark – and a chapter of accidents now unfolded. First, 40 Commando were unable to leave *Fearless* in their landing craft because the pump filling the embarkation dock broke down. The *Fearless* captain, Jeremy Larken, took a considerable risk in opening the dock gate to allow the sea to flood in, which could have swamped the landing craft, but they survived. Then the men of 2 Para had immense trouble clambering off the *Norland* – which had no dock at all – into their landing craft. They had missed most of the practice at Ascension; anyhow, it was hardly the paratroopers' customary method of going into action. One man fell and broke his pelvis, and when 2 Para did get away they set off in the wrong direction until fetched back by Southby-Tailyour, whose task that morning was to guide each landing craft in to its beach.

40 Commando and 2 Para were supposed to link up to cross the 'line of departure' – the naval equivalent of the army's 'start-line' where the assault is deemed to have begun – and to land together either side of San Carlos settlement. They were already an hour late at the line of departure and 40 Commando – by prior agreement – forged ahead, to avoid the risk of the two battalions firing at each other if San Carlos proved to be defended. In the event, it was not; but 40 Commando had other problems, when it found that its designated landing site was obstructed by overhanging rocks. The drivers of the light tanks at the front of the landing craft were unable to disembark, compelling the troops behind to squeeze past them in the dark and then wade through alarmingly deep water. Eventually the light tanks found somewhere else to go ashore.

And so 40 Commando liberated San Carlos settlement. Its commander, Lieutenant Colonel Malcolm Hunt, found thirty-one islanders there, most of whom had fled from Stanley. 'C' company commander Captain Andy Pillar raised the Union flag, a ceremony dutifully repeated for press cameras at first light. The islanders seemed strangely unimpressed; Hunt thought the settlement manager 'not cool, exactly, but muted'.

Meanwhile, the remainder of the landing force was making its inelegant way ashore. 2 Para finally reached Blue Beach Two. Both 45 Commando and 3 Para encountered difficulties similar to 2 Para's in climbing into their landing craft. 45 Commando went ashore next, followed last of all by 3 Para, who had cruised along their beach in search of a suitable landing site, with a man in front probing for hidden rocks with a pole. It was broad daylight by the time all were safely ashore. Just twenty-seven minutes later, *Canberra* received its first air-raid red alert of the morning. Not for the first or last time in the Falklands war, it was a close-run thing.

With greater ease than they had effected their landings, each battalion now secured its first objectives. 40 Commando stayed in San Carlos; 2 Para headed up Sussex Mountains to protect the beach-head from attack from the south. 45 Commando secured the disused refrigeration plant at Ajax Bay, while 3 Para moved into Port San Carlos. There they made the first tangible contact with the enemy, apart from the incident on Fanning Head. Somewhat disturbingly, for the intelligence had predicted quite the opposite, they found that some forty Argentinian soldiers had been at Port San Carlos the previous night. They had departed in some haste, leaving behind half-eaten meals, several regimental swords, and some medals confiscated from Mike Norman's men in Stanley three months earlier. 3 Para were keen to go in pursuit but were instructed to help secure the beach-head.

The fleeing Argentinians, it later turned out, were led by a young infantry officer, Lieutenant Roberto Oscar Reyes, who had distinguished himself two weeks earlier by hitting the manager of the San Carlos settlement in the face with the butt of his pistol. On his retreat to Port Stanley, Reyes left a trail of destruction worthy of a Wild West outlaw, holding up islanders at gunpoint, stealing clothes and food, and shooting livestock. But he had already exacted a greater toll from the British, for he caused the only deaths they suffered that day.

For long after the Falklands were recaptured, the commanding officer of the SBS was to blame himself for what happened. He had of course erroneously reported that the landing zones were undefended – the result of withdrawing his patrols five days before D-Day. He was also aggrieved that the four-man SBS squad who discovered Argentinian troops on Fanning Head had promptly retreated, instead of pressing on to see what else they might find. These omissions need not have mattered if the news of 3 Para's discoveries had reached the helicopter pilots with the task force; tragically, they did not. In the firm belief that the land was clear, a Sea King lifting Rapier missiles took off for Port San Carlos. It was accompanied by a light Gazelle armed with rockets and a machine-gun. As the two helicopters rounded Camerons Point, Reyes' men fired on them from below. The Sea King escaped but the Gazelle was hit. The Royal Marine pilot, Sergeant Andy Evans, though fatally wounded managed to ditch into the sea. For fifteen minutes Reyes' men machine-gunned Evans and his crewman, Sergeant Ed Candlish, in the water, but missed. Finally, Candlish managed to drag Evans ashore; he died in his arms.

A few minutes later, the tragedy was re-enacted. Candlish watched in impotent horror as another Gazelle headed in the same direction. It too was brought down, crashing and bursting into flames. Both its pilot and crewman were killed. Among the men who rushed to the wreckage to pull the victims out was the anguished SBS commander who had reported the area clear.

Another powerless spectator was surgeon commander Rick Jolly. He took off from *Canberra* in a Wessex helicopter when the first Gazelle was shot down and arrived just after the second crashed. 'I ran up,' Jolly said later, 'and there were the two aircrew, both dead, their chests soaked in blood and it was obvious they had been hit in the air by machine-gun fire.'

The medical officers had been forbidden to take bodies back to the task force but Jolly ignored his instructions and loaded them into the Wessex. In part he did so out of respect for the dead men: 'I was not going to leave them out on the hillside.' He also wanted to deliver a warning.

'*Canberra* had been attacked all day but I think that some of those on board felt a bit distant. "We're not going to be hit", well that's what some people were saying, and then those dead guys came in. It was at that point that my colleagues realised we were in a shooting war.'

That evening, aboard the landing ship, *Sir Galahad*, the Brigade Air Squadron held a memorial service for the three dead men – the first of many similar services to come. Afterwards, Peter Cameron, the squadron's commander, and his men got royally drunk. But well before dawn, they were back in their helicopters ready to face whatever response to the invasion Argentina might provide.

PART 3

CHAPTER SEVENTEEN

The Blackbird and the Falcon

'Well, I think that some of the experts rather
exaggerate the value, the strength of the
Argentinian air force. ... Their Mirage aircraft
really are a decade behind the Harrier, and
beyond that their other aircraft are not particularly
modern, some of them are very old,
and the Harrier is a very effective aircraft. ...
So I think we must not exaggerate their air
situation. It is certainly significant and
we must watch it, but we must not exaggerate it.'
– Defence Secretary John Nott, May 9, 1982

The task force lexicon included three primary nicknames for the Argentinians: 'Argies', of course; 'bean-eaters', because of the supposed national appetite for *habicheula*; and, most frequently heard, 'spics'. It was natural enough that men on their way to fight should demean the enemy. The danger lay in underestimating him. And though much of the Argentinian army, and most of its navy, did prove to be as irresolute as many people had predicted, any contempt for the 'bean-eaters' of the *Fuerza Aerea Argentina*, the air force, was fatally misplaced.

But it was only too easy to miscalculate the threat. On paper the Argentinians had two advantages – a vast superiority in numbers and land bases. However those were almost totally countered by the fact that the nearest base, Rio Gallegos, was almost 400 miles away from the mid point of the islands, Falkland Sound. That meant that the Argentinian pilots were always flying close to the limits of their range and thus had precious little 'loiter time'; time to find a target or engage in a dog fight.

And in every other respect, the odds were heavily stacked against the *Fuerza Aerea*. Their training was good – some of it done with France, some with Israel – but it had been carried out almost exclusively over land and, as the pilots were quickly to discover, over sea they were much more vulnerable to radar detection. Not one of their commanders, let alone their pilots, could boast real combat experience. They were up against a vast array of missiles and guns from ships and, after San Carlos, from land. And in the air, as John Nott said, their aircraft were deeply inferior. They had blackbirds; the British had falcons.

That analogy comes from Colonel James MacManaway, a veteran pilot with the United States marine corps, whom we asked – before the fighting started – to assess the likely outcome of an air war. The main threat to the task force, in terms of numbers, lay with the three Argentinian squadrons (I *Escuadron* of the Fourth Brigade, and IV and V *Escuadrons* of the Fifth Brigade) that were equipped with sixty-eight American-built A4P Skyhawk fighter-bombers. Their opponents in the air would be Royal Navy Sea Harriers, and the RAF version, the GR3. As it happened, both the Skyhawk and the Harrier were conceived to meet the need for attack planes that would not require long fixed runways to operate from, and they are approximately the same weight and size. The similarities end there.

'The Harrier will not only outfly and outgun the Skyhawks,' said MacManaway, 'it will happily do so on a two to one basis. Even then the Harrier will seem like a falcon, swift and lethal, and the Skyhawks like blackbirds, big and clumsy,' he said.

His view was a partisan one in that the US marines have long been among the staunchest champions of the vertical-take-off Harrier and, after the RAF, the largest operators. They were equipped with 110 British Harriers in the mid-1970s and they hoped that a good performance by the plane in the Falklands war might help to overcome the navy's opposition to their plan to buy 340 of an advanced version, developed and built by McDonnell Douglas. Still, the technical evidence for MacManaway's assessment was overwhelming.

Argentina's Skyhawks were well over twenty years old, refurbished models of one of the earliest versions of the plane; formidable in their day but now obsolete. (They were sold to Argentina by the US Navy in 1966.) They had since been fitted with a more modern weapons-aiming sight, but even that was distinctly inferior to the Head Up Display that the Harrier pilots had to aid them in a dog fight. And, in low level flight, the Skyhawks were 100 mph slower.

When it came to weapons things were supposedly more even. In theory, the Skyhawk and the Harrier both carried the same 'primitive' version of the Sidewinder air-to-air missile which, because it seeks the heat from the jet exhaust of the target, needs to be fired from *behind*. But, in great secrecy, the British had dipped into their NATO war stocks to hurriedly equip the Harriers with the latest generation Sidewinder, the American-made AIM9L, which has a guidance system sensitive enough to be fired from any aspect. (NATO war stocks are supposed to be untouchable, except for a crisis in Europe; Britain was able to raid the shelves because the Americans agreed to supply 100 replacement Sidewinders immediately.)

To cap it all, the Harriers had the ability to jump, not merely off the

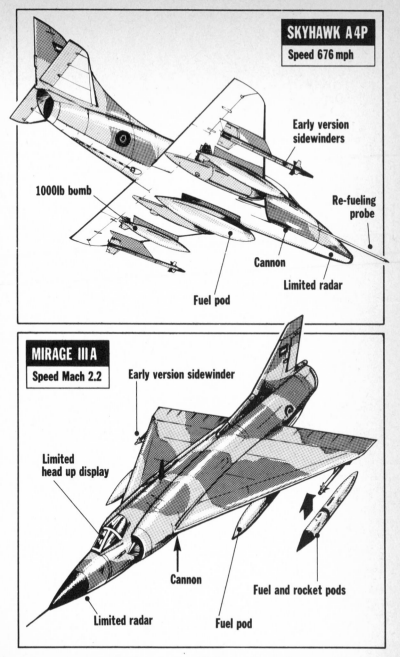

SKYHAWK A 4P
Speed 676 mph

Early version
sidewinders

1000lb bomb

Re-fueling
probe

Cannon

Limited radar

Fuel pod

MIRAGE III A
Speed Mach 2.2

Early version sidewinder

Limited
head up display

Cannon

Fuel and rocket pods

Limited radar

Fuel pod

ground but also in mid-air. The technique known as 'viffing' (vectoring in forward flight) is possible because the Harrier's jet nozzles rotate downwards to give vertical thrust for take-off. Early on in the plane's career pilots discovered that rotating the nozzles downwards in flight caused rapid deceleration but also a *gain* in altitude. The advantage this gives in a dog fight is not hard to imagine: a Harrier pilot who finds the enemy on his tail, simply viffs, is very rapidly overtaken – and the hunter becomes the hunted.

In addition to Skyhawks the Argentinian air force did have 44 supersonic fighters, for convenience described as the French Mirage III, though in fact more than half of them were the Israeli version of that plane, the Dagger. They could fly at Mach 2.2 (more than twice the speed of sound) but only at high altitude. In low level flight they were not much faster than the Harriers, and no better armed than the Skyhawks.

All in all then, the air war promised to be no contest. MacManaway reckoned that Argentina's only hope of inflicting real damage on the task force was to stage mass attacks. If they were to put up, say, twenty aircraft in waves, some would get past the Harriers, and a few would get past the British fleet's missiles, and reach at least those ships on the periphery. From his experience of staging mock attacks, MacManaway believed it would take fifty or more planes to get through to the carriers, *Invincible* and *Hermes*. Either way, the Argentinian losses would be horrendous.

The question was, did the bean-eaters have the stomach for it?

Basilio Lami Dozo and the Argentinian air force grew up together. The *Fuerza Aerea* was established as a separate branch of the armed services in 1946. Lami Dozo joined it immediately as a seventeen-year-old cadet at the *Escuela de Aviacion Militar* in Cordoba, Argentina's second city. There he came under the considerable influence of the men who shaped this new officer class with a high level of technical ability – and stern, right-wing ideology.

On the flying side, and on the techniques of aerial warfare, the tutors were mainly emigrés from the German Luftwaffe; most notably, Hans-Ulrich Rudel. Although only thirty years old, Rudel was already a legend. In the course of the Second World War he had flown, according to German records, 2,530 missions in Stuka dive bombers. In the process he had helped to destroy Warsaw, and he had accounted for 519 tanks, one battleship, one cruiser, one destroyer and seventy landing craft. He was shot down thirty times and eventually lost a leg; he simply re-learned to fly with one foot for the rudder pedals, and became the most-decorated German officer of the war. In 1945 he was arrested by the Americans but was soon released because of his injuries, and went to Argentina. In the next few years he passed on his skills to the likes of the young Lami Dozo, and preached

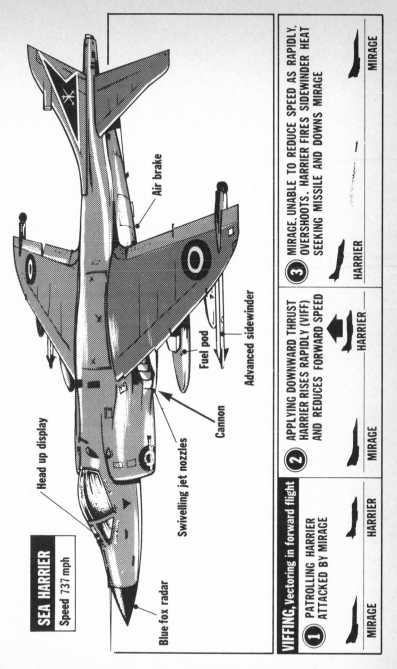

SEA HARRIER
Speed 737 mph

Head up display

Blue fox radar

Swivelling jet nozzles

Cannon

Fuel pod

Advanced sidewinder

Air brake

VIFFING, Vectoring in forward flight

① PATROLLING HARRIER ATTACKED BY MIRAGE

MIRAGE   HARRIER

② APPLYING DOWNWARD THRUST HARRIER RISES RAPIDLY (VIFF) AND REDUCES FORWARD SPEED

MIRAGE   HARRIER

③ MIRAGE, UNABLE TO REDUCE SPEED AS RAPIDLY, OVERSHOOTS. HARRIER FIRES SIDEWINDER HEAT SEEKING MISSILE AND DOWNS MIRAGE

HARRIER

MIRAGE

ultraconservatism. He also wrote a book, *In Spite of Everything*, which supported most of what the Nazis had done.

Right-wing nationalism, this time with a catholic tinge, was also the creed of another of Lami Dozo's tutors, Jordan Bruno Genta, who perhaps provided the strongest influence on air force thinking. Genta, a prolific author, spouted all the standard obscenities against freemasons and Jews; more important, he composed a doctrine for the air force which justified military intervention in politics and argued for devotion, not to the constitution or the law, but to 'God and the motherland'. Any action the military might have to take in defence of the motherland was excused by 'God's will'. (This kind of thinking, best summarised in his book *Guerra Contrarrevolucionaria*, led to Genta's death. He was murdered in 1974 by Montonero guerrillas who believed he had inspired the 'Triple A' death squads.)

All of which might help to explain one of the great paradoxes of the Falklands war. On the one hand, Brigadier General Lami Dozo – who became head of the air force in 1981 – emerged as the most prudent member of the ruling junta, and supposedly the least enthusiastic exponent of the invasion. On the other hand, once the deed was done, 'only God' could judge their actions, he said; and once war became inevitable, none fought harder and longer than Lami Dozo's pilots in defence of the motherland. 'We will die before we are dishonoured,' he said while visiting one of his bases, at Comodoro Rivadavia, in late April. Many of his army and navy colleagues said much the same; Lami Dozo meant it.

In their first sorties, flown while the task force was in open sea, the air force had no success, and lost three Skyhawks and two Mirages. But the British landings at San Carlos subtly altered the odds. Now that at least some of the warships sat in Falkland Sound, there was no need to waste precious 'loiter time' looking for a target. And now the pilots could make their final approach over land – West Falkland – as they had been trained, where the hills would hide them from radar detection until the very last moment.

At about 10 a.m. on May 21, the first Skyhawks and Mirages lifted off from their mainland bases and headed due east. In the next hours and days Britain was to learn that, given almost fanatical courage, even blackbirds can be lethal.

CHAPTER EIGHTEEN

Bomb Alley, Death Valley

'Do [the government] intend, in pursuing an
ultimate military victory, that the awful
tragedy that is unfolding should be
continued to its bitter end?'
– Tony Benn MP, May 1982

Friday morning, May 21, was clear and soft with a pale blue sky, the sun just showing through some light cloud on the horizon. The atmosphere on board *Canberra* was astonishingly calm. P & O officers, in their blue and white uniforms, wandered around the promenade deck, taking the air after breakfast, and getting their first real look at the Falklands. The big white ship was so close to the shore they could see the waves breaking on the rocks. There was no noise at all; it was as though, by some mistake, they had anchored in a little bay off the west coast of Scotland.

The illusion was shattered at 8.03 a.m. Christopher Burne, the senior naval officer on board, was in a toilet when the warning came over the tannoy: 'Air raid warning red'. He ran up to the bridge where marines in camouflage gear – with little pieces of torn cloth woven into their helmets – raced to man the machine-guns. It was a false alarm. There was another one thirty-five minutes later. At 8.43 a.m., yet another, but it turned out to be a British helicopter and everybody on *Canberra* laughed. Five minutes later they came.

On shore, where the paratroopers were still digging themselves in, platoon commanders blew their whistles and yelled, 'Down ... get down ...' There was, in the main, no cover at all and men just hugged the ground.

The raiders were not yet the Skyhawks and Mirages from the mainland but Pucaras, which arrived from the direction of Stanley to the south-east, flying so low they were almost grass-hopping. As they attacked both the men ashore and the ships, two were shot down almost immediately, but they kept coming. Our colleague, John Shirley, watching from *Canberra*'s bridge, thought how tiny they looked, like model aircraft. Then one of them turned and headed for the ship, and Burne shouted 'engage, engage' to the machine-gunners, and red tracers began to streak into the air. Through the lens of his camera Shirley could see little pimples of white appearing on the edges of the wings as the Pucara fired back – at *him*, or so it seemed. He dropped the camera and thought, 'What in God's name am I doing here?' Then the plane was gone, chased in vain by a Blowpipe missile. Burne said: 'I think we can expect more attacks like that for the rest of the day.'

That was a prelude that left one frigate, *Argonaut*, damaged. Twenty-one minutes later, the first Skyhawks and Mirages arrived to begin an extraordinary day-long mass assault by seventy-two aircraft that would leave the fleet reeling.

Perhaps one of the best witnesses to what happened during those awful hours was Rick Jolly, the surgeon commander, if only because he had a bird's-eye view. When the main attacks began he was in a Wessex helicopter that had gone to *Argonaut* to pick up a casualty of the Pucaras. As they were hovering, the ship's deck officer began furiously waving his arms; the pilot of the Wessex, Mike Crabtree, put the machine in a steep dive and said on the intercom: 'Air raid red. Skyhawks coming in.' Seconds later two flew over the top of them.

On the tactical radio net to which all the ships and helicopters were tuned, *Argonaut* reported the attack: 'Two bombs on the flight deck. Magazines in danger. Another strike coming in.' Aboard *Fearless*, the command ship which was at the entrance to San Carlos Water, Commodore Michael Clapp grabbed the microphone: 'Keep firing. Keep firing. Over.' *Argonaut*: 'Roger. Out.' The helicopter bolted across the sea to Fanning Head where Crabtree hoped they would be safe, and from where they had a grandstand view of what was to follow.

To their left, in San Carlos Water just south of Fanning Island, sat *Canberra*, a huge white whale of a target in the now brilliant sun. Near her was *Fearless*. In front of them, in the neck of water leading to Falkland Sound, were the frigates *Yarmouth* and *Plymouth*, with the cruiser *Antrim* steaming figures of eight, 'like a mother tiger guarding her cubs'. To their right, out in the sound, forming the first line of defence – the 'gun line' – were five frigates, *Ardent*, *Broadsword*, *Brilliant*, *Argonaut* and, furthest out, *Alacrity*.

On the radio net, came the next warning: 'Hostiles. 170 (degrees), five miles and closing.' Almost as soon as it was said, four Mirages appeared in the sky, diving on *Antrim*, their cannon shells splashing in the water, making a trail which ended inexorably against the ship's side. She was firing back with everything she had, and the pilot of the fourth Mirage thought better of it, and banked away from the exploding traces until he was going straight for Fanning Head – and the helicopter. A gunner named Gleason cocked the machine-gun. Jolly unplugged his headset and ran for his life, throwing himself into a nearby ditch. When the Mirage had passed harmlessly overhead – despite Gleason's efforts to bring it down – Jolly went back to the Wessex and plugged in again, and Crabtree said, ruefully: 'Oh, you back with us Doc?' The surgeon felt thoroughly ashamed.

Out over the Sound, a thin white line rose up into the sky towards a speck on the horizon. There was a puff of dirty white smoke, with a fireball in the centre of it, and debris began trickling down towards the sea. *Brilliant* came on the radio net and said: 'Splash. One Skyhawk.' A little white later, in roughly the same vicinity, Jolly saw some white splashes followed by a bigger yellow one and he thought, 'Great, another splash.' Then a pall of black smoke began to build and over the net someone said, 'What the hell is that.' They quickly worked it out: 'Jesus, it's *Ardent*.'

HMS Ardent, one of the Royal Navy's latest Amazon class frigates, had been opened up like a tin can by two 1,000 pound bombs that landed on her aft deck. Her major systems were severed and she went out of control at eighteen knots. She was thus defenceless when two more planes attacked in a pair, and dropped ten more bombs into her gaping wound.

Crabtree decided to leave Fanning Head to offer *Ardent* what help they could. He flew the Wessex first to *Fearless* to refuel and collect stretchers, and then on to the tower of smoke that now enveloped the stricken ship. As they passed over her, Jolly, who was sitting in the helicopter's doorway, could see 'the fires of hell' burning inside her: fierce orange flames that made her entire stern look like the insides of a furnace. Most of her 230 crew were at the bow, dressed in their 'once only' survival suits. They were waving at the helicopter and pointing off the port quarter.

About seventy-five yards from the ship there were two men in the water, bobbing up and down in the six-foot swell. 'Got them,' said Crabtree, and he put the Wessex in a steady hover while a crewman lowered the strop. But neither man could help himself, and one of them, his life jacket deflated, was clearly drowning.

There was no alternative but for Jolly to go down and get him. They put the surgeon in a harness and lowered him down on the winch, and at the last moment he realised he had forgotten to earth himself, to get rid of the build up of static electricity that is a consequence of riding in helicopters; he hit the water and felt the 'bang' and wondered how navy divers – who jump from helicopters to perform their rescues – ever got used to it.

Oblivious to the very real possibility that *Ardent*'s magazines might explode at any moment – and exhibiting the kind of blind flying skills that time and again were to earn helicopter pilots extraordinary reputations in this war – Crabtree manoeuvred the Wessex until Jolly could grab the drowning man and lift him, with some struggle, to safety. Then he had to go down and do it all again.

The second man lay in the water with a deep gash across his forehead, blood trailing away in the water downwind, staring at the suspended Jolly as though he were the angel of death. He was too big a man for the surgeon to lift. So Jolly removed the hook from his harness, attached it instead to the man's life jacket, wrapped his arms around him, signalled 'winch us up' – and hoped for dear life that the jacket could take the strain. It did and Crabtree said: 'Well done, Doc. Bloody marvellous. Well done.' Having disgraced himself at Fanning Head, at least in his own eyes, Jolly felt very pleased with his redemption.

Meanwhile, *Ardent* was going through her death throes. Her stern had been consumed by the fire and it was only a question of time before she blew up or sank. Her captain, Alan West, made 'probably the hardest decision of my life' and gave the order to abandon ship. Some of the men cried; so, too, did West. It was later established that twenty-four of her crew had been killed, and thirty injured.

And still the attacks continued. *Canberra* seemed to be the main target, though there is a question mark over that: given the persistence and the success of the Argentinian pilots that day, it is curious that they never managed to hit such a large and defenceless target; perhaps, as they claim, they did not try.

But it did not seem that way to those on board. As the ship shuddered from the shock of bombs exploding in the water around her, John Shirley lay under a table in the Meridian Room with Lieutenant Colonel Nick Vaux of the marines, discussing whether the experience was more or less unpleasant than being fired at by the Provisional IRA from the Divis Flats in Belfast. Vaux said that on balance he preferred the Divis Flats.

Early the next morning, on orders from London and under the cover of darkness, *Canberra* removed herself from the firing line and sailed to the eastern perimeter of the Total Exclusion Zone, well out of range of Argentina's planes.

The warships, of course, could not retreat. The damage inflicted on them in that first day was unbelievable: *Ardent* sunk; *Argonaut* badly damaged; *Antrim*, *Brilliant* and *Broadsword* all hit by bombs which failed to explode.

They failed to explode for two main reasons. Some of the bombs, supplied by the United States, were up to thirteen years old and their wiring had deteriorated. Others were released from such a low height that arming mechanisms did not have sufficient time to drive the detonator against the charge before the bombs hit – an error in flying technique which the Argentinian pilots eventually learned to correct.

But for that grace, Britain might have lost a quarter of the task force's fighting ships. There was worse to come.

The view from the Argentinian cockpit was no less terrifying. To escape radar detection, the Skyhawk and Mirage pilots had decided they must fly the last 150 miles to the attack zone at no more than *ten feet* above the waves. Thus the sea spray was often over their wings, and for those who returned to base the first priority was to have the planes rigorously hosed down to get rid of the encrusted salt.

At such low altitudes their altimeters simply did not work so they flew by the seat of their pants, hoping to spot any exceptional wave before they collided with it. Once, and if, they reached a British ship they then employed their most hair-raising technique, described by one Skyhawk pilot as follows: 'The missiles don't lock on to you until they have been travelling for about 200 metres, so you have that amount of time to home in on your target. You then veer from side to side as hard as possible until you're within launching range. You dive straight towards the ship, release the bomb at 150 metres, then keep travelling straight, as low as possible – preferably clipping the mast where the missiles can't get you. As soon as you're past it, you bank as steeply as you know how. The bomb has a delayed action so it doesn't blow you up as well as the ship – you hope.'

As they screamed away they had one chance to look back and see what damage they had caused. One pilot described the extraordinary sight of aluminium plates from his victim 'flying into the air like confetti'.

That left the problem of dodging the Harriers on the way home. The Argentinian pilots had great confidence in their own skills. In particular, the Mirage pilots reckoned that when it came to combat flying they were as good as the Israelis – and they reckoned that they were the best in the world. Still, they had great respect for the Harrier pilots and with no spare fuel to 'loiter' they believed their best chance was to return the way they had come – as fast and as low as they dared. Some of them did not make it and were forced to eject. The inadequacies of their ejection equipment made them extremely angry; some of the pilots who were rescued and got back to Argentina had grotesquely distended mouths and eyes bulging abnormally from the sockets, as a result of the extreme G-forces.

(Advice on the problematic Skyhawk ejector seats came from an unlikely quarter; an American air force major who, at the outbreak of hostilities, was attached to the Argentine air force under a military aid scheme. Unlike his counterpart in the navy, the major was not asked to leave by his hosts. His US superiors ordered him to stop flying after April 30, but he continued to go to his Buenos Aires office in the air force building, Edificio Condor, every day. 'They had a few problems keeping the planes flying and sorting out the ejector seats that I was able to help them with,' he said.)

The information on Argentina's pilots comes from a respected Argentinian journalist named Luis Garasino who, in late May, was allowed to spend three days visiting air bases in the south.

The pilots admitted to him that they had suffered considerable losses – as many as fifteen planes in one day. But overall, they said, the casualties had been less than half of what they had been warned to expect, which was seventy-five per cent of all their pilots. (Whether *all* of the Argentinian pilots were so warned is a moot question. Lieutenant Ricardo Lucero, twenty-nine, who ejected over San Carlos on May 25 and was rescued by *Fearless*, said he had been 'immensely surprised' by the level of anti-aircraft fire because he had been told it would be minimal. Lucero also said that, in a six day period, more than half his squadron had failed to return; his superiors said the missing aircraft had been 'redeployed' to other bases but, suspecting the truth, the pilots now called Falkland Sound 'death valley'.)

According to Garasino, morale in the *Fuerza Aerea* was unmistakably high: the atmosphere at bases like Rio Gallegos was not unlike Biggin Hill at the height of the Battle of Britain; and Argentina's 'young finest' were equally careless with their lives.

There was, undoubtedly, an element of propaganda in all this for on Saturday, May 22, when they might have pushed home their advantage, most of the Argentinian pilots stayed at base; only two marauding Skyhawks came in low over West Falkland and when Harriers raced to intercept them, they turned tail.

The British took advantage of the lull to supply the bridgehead with all the equipment and vital supplies it needed and to establish batteries of Rapier anti-aircraft missiles.

The lull, however, was merely that. At precisely 2 p.m. on Sunday the warships in the 'gun line' – or 'bomb alley' as it was now inevitably called – saw the first two Skyhawks appear out of the hills of West Falkland. They flew over the Sound north of the ships, then turned hard right to fly down the waterway as low as their pilots dared.

A Rapier missile fired from the shore claimed the first plane, and the second dropped its bombs short. But then came the main attack, wave after wave of Skyhawks and Mirages, determined to swamp the defences.

HMS Antelope, a sister-ship of *Ardent*, claimed two 'splashes', and a share of a third, then she herself was hit; two 500 pound bombs crashed through her decks, killing a young steward on the way, and buried themselves in her engine room. They did not explode but *Antelope* was in no condition to go on fighting, so her skipper, Captain Nicholas Tobin, sailed her into San Carlos Water for repairs, and to have the bombs defused. Staff Sergeant Jim Prescott of the Royal Engineers was attempting to do that when one of them exploded and killed him instantly.

The explosion tore a hole in her starboard side, from the waterline to the funnel; all Captain Tobin could see was pipes and smoke and flames pouring out. The fire was unstoppable and she had to be abandoned. For hours photographer Martin Cleaver watched her burn from the deck of another ship, waiting for the flames to reach the missile magazine. By the time they did – providing the most spectacular photograph of the war – Cleaver's fingers were so cold he could barely release the shutter. The next afternoon, her back broken, *Antelope* sank.

On Monday they came back again. For a change, the Mirages led the Skyhawks, twenty-four of them in all. Harriers from *Hermes* and *Invincible* – both of which throughout this period stayed well out to sea, out of range – raced in to intercept and, over Pebble Island, a British pilot claimed the first 'double kill' of the war: two Mirages which he said he shot down with two Sidewinder missiles. But it was not totally one-sided. One of the giant landing ships, *Sir Galahad*, took an unexploded bomb through her side and had to be evacuated. One of her sister ships, *Sir Lancelot*, was also hit.

By the end of the day, the claimed tally of Argentinian aircraft shot down since the landings stood at twenty-six. The tally of British ships sunk or hit by bombs which had failed to explode was ten.

If it is possible to measure these things, then perhaps the score was about even, but there is no doubt that the British commanders were becoming increasingly alarmed. They awaited Tuesday, May 25 – Argentina's national day and a day when something spectacular was bound to happen – with trepidation.

Captain Jorge Colombo and his Super Etendard squadron had been waiting their moment for three weeks, since the sinking of *Sheffield*. On national day they learned from what Colombo describes as 'all the reconnaissance, particularly aerial reconnaissance', that a very large ship was heading west towards Falkland Sound where she would be well within their range. They could hardly believe their luck; two more of the precious Exocets were carefully prepared.

But before the navy pilots could attack there was a problem to be resolved. Between the Etendards and their target, ten miles north of Pebble Island, the task force had posted pickets, guarding the entrance to Falkland Sound. One of them was *Coventry*, a sister ship to *Sheffield*. Unlike *Sheffield*, however – and learning from that lesson – she was accompanied by the frigate *Broadsword*, armed with the short-range Sea Wolf missiles. The air force was given the job of neutralising them.

The first two attempts, in the morning, failed because the Skyhawks were detected by *Coventry*'s radar – and as many as five were shot down. But at 3.30 p.m. came another larger wave of Skyhawks, escorted by Mirages. This time the planes took the route over West Falkland where they could hide among the radar clutter caused by the hills. While three of the Skyhawks turned south to make the run down 'bomb alley', at least six more turned north and headed for *Coventry* and *Broadsword*.

Coventry could not possibly cope alone and, as it turned out, *Broadsword* could be of very little assistance. Sea Wolf is undoubtedly a formidable deterrent to low flying aircraft – in the words of British

Aerospace, the manufacturer, 'she will hit three out of four planes and the other one, you hope, will be frightened away'. But it has a serious weakness: it is a 'point' defence system, meaning it is only concerned with *self*-defence. (Its guidance computer detects, identifies and fires the missiles at hostile targets automatically.) Thus, *Broadsword* could only defend *Coventry* by getting between her and the Skyhawks, to make herself the target. There was no time. *Coventry* was hit by three bombs which *did* explode; she took a heavy list to port within five minutes and capsized within twenty. Her commanding officer, Captain David Hart-Dyke, literally walked down her side to the water; his life raft was punctured by the superstructure as she rolled over.

Nineteen men died. But for sheer heroism on the part of a lot of people, it would have been a great deal worse. For example, Chief Aircrewman Alf Tupper, the winch man on a helicopter summoned from *Fearless*, volunteered to be lowered into the sea and then unhooked his lifeline in order to guide rescuers to wounded seamen from *Coventry*; according to his commanding officer, Tupper was directly responsible for saving forty or fifty lives.

The air force's job done, two Super Etendards took off, probably from Rio Gallegos. They hid below British radar until from somewhere between fifteen and thirty kilometres away – Colombo would not say: 'it's a commercial secret' – they each fired one Exocet. Then they flew home to wait for the BBC to tell them what they had hit.

It turned out to be neither of the aircraft carriers but something almost as big, the requisitioned cargo ship, *Atlantic Conveyor*. Air force pilots thought it was a 'waste' of two Exocets. Colombo was more philosophical: 'We had our priorities, it's true. But instead of hitting a number one target, we sank some other ship, well and good. All welcome. Why not?'

Why not indeed. The destruction of the *Atlantic Conveyor* – which cost the lives of twelve men – was the most serious single logistical blow the British ever suffered.

First of all, having transported the RAF's reinforcement Harriers from Britain on her long flat decks, *Atlantic Conveyor* acted as a seaborne parking lot for any planes not on patrol or on standby; there was simply not enough room to accommodate all the Harriers on *Invincible* and *Hermes* comfortably, so *Atlantic Conveyor* was used as an occasional third aircraft carrier to ease the crush.

More important, when she was hit the ship was on her way to San Carlos with vital supplies. They included four giant Chinook helicopters, each capable of carrying up to eighty troops at a time which were to have played a crucial role in the advance on Stanley. Three were lost; a fourth survived only because it happened to be flying at the time. Also lost were at least six Wessex helicopters, sufficient tents to accommodate 4,000 men, mobile landing strips for the Harriers that would have allowed them to operate from shore, and a vital water desalination plant.

The consequences were abrupt and disastrous. They led eventually to a tragedy near a place called Bluff Cove. More immediately, Brigadier Julian Thompspon was obliged rapidly to re-design his plan for the advance on Stanley.

That day, by coincidence, Thompson had been called from his headquarters at San Carlos to the command ship *Fearless* to talk to Major General Richard Trant from Northwood. Thompson had wanted to await the arrival of reinforcements before advancing from San Carlos. But Trant *ordered* him to press ahead without further delay. The brigadier was literally drawing up plans to employ the helicopters from *Atlantic Conveyor*, when he learned they no longer existed. He tore up the paper and began again.

The order to advance was confirmed in a signal the next morning. Thompson called a meeting of his unit commanders, some of whom despaired at the news. Major Gerry Wells-Cole, the deputy assistant quarter master was 'at his wits end' because he simply did not know how an advance could proceed without the supplies and equipment lost with the ship.

Thompson was 'testy'; he ignored everyone's objections and kept repeating that the units *had* to move; they would walk to Stanley, if necessary. (He was later to say that the army boot or, as he called it, the LPC – 'leather personnel carrier' – was the most important piece of equipment they had.)

In his unit's official war diary, Lieutenant Colonel Malcolm Hunt of 40 Commando described May 25 as 'the lowest day of the campaign'. He added: 'The mood in San Carlos is sombre.'

There is a startling postscript to this episode. In London the ministry of defence deliberately announced that the *Atlantic Conveyor* was still afloat, and much of her valuable cargo might yet be saved.

Whether it was that temptation that lured the Super Etendards out once more, or whether it was simply their determination to sink an aircraft carrier, we may never know. Either way, on Sunday May 29, Argentina launched her first navy/air force combined attack – and her last remaining air-launched Exocet.

Captain Colombo says his squadron was already planning its final assault, when: 'The higher-ups asked if we had any problem if they added four aircraft from the air force, four A4s [Skyhawks] to attack the *Invincible*. They said, 'You attack with Exocets and they will follow in and attack with bombs.'' ... We said, no problem.'

The idea was that two Etendards, with their inertial navigation systems, would lead the Skyhawks to the target area, find the *Invincible*, and fire the last remaining Exocet. The Skyhawks would then follow the smoke trail of the missile and deliver the *coup de grâce* with their bombs. And that is what happened – or almost.

The Etendards found a large blip on their radars, which they took to be *Invincible*, and one of them fired the last Exocet.

The Skyhawks followed it in. The missile got there first bcause it was faster. On the radio, the leader of the formation, Lieutenant Jose Daniel Vasquez said as follows: 'I am seeing it. It is an aircraft carrier. There are flames and a lot of smoke. The missile hit it squarely. Now I am going towards it in the trail left by the rocket. Now . . . bombs away . . . Attention, number two. Confirm the damage. I am turning away to the right.' Before he could say any more, Vasquez was shot down and so was the second Skyhawk; the other two fled.

That evening in Buenos Aires confident rumour – as opposed to wild press speculation – had it that *Invincible* really had been put out of action.

The rumour, and Colombo, were wrong. Argentina had just wasted her last Exocet on the hulk of *Atlantic Conveyor*, the ship she had already killed. That evening, London time, the MoD quietly announced that the huge lady had 'sunk'.

CHAPTER NINETEEN

The Other Casualty

'The essence of successful warfare is secrecy.
The essence of successful journalism is publicity.'
– British regulations
for war correspondents,
first issued, 1958

'My noble friends and I neither expect nor
wish that, on this kind of subject at this
kind of time, government statements should
be in the least bit informative ...'
– Lord Mayhew, House
of Lords, May 1982

It was as sombre a morning as Britain had known since that terrible day when the *Sheffield* went down. The headlines spoke of another British warship 'crippled', 'damaged' or 'badly hit'. There was no further information available, but since even Ian McDonald, the ministry of defence's impassive spokesman, had described it as 'bad news', everyone expected the worst.

'Is it the *Canberra*?' a nervous reporter had asked at the previous evening's defence briefing. There was no direct reply to the question, and in the silence that followed rumours had begun to circulate: there had been a fearful disaster; at least 300 men had died; the task force was pulling back in disorder. Even the ministry was left in ignorance of the true facts. They had been told that the ship involved had capsized quickly – and that probably meant no survivors.

When, therefore, John Nott rose to his feet in the House of Commons at 3.32 that afternoon, it was with something close to relief that MPs heard him announce the name of the ship, the *Coventry*, and the scale of the losses: twenty dead and a further twenty injured. He revealed at the same time the loss of the *Atlantic Conveyor*, and said that four of her crew members had died (though in fact the final death toll was twelve, including her master, Captain Ian North). The news was indeed 'bad', but it was nothing like as bad as had been feared.

But the way in which the information was handled provoked an attack on the ministry's system of news management. For more than twelve hours, anxious relatives of men serving in the task force had been left in suspense, not knowing which ship had been hit, or how many lives had been lost. Nott later conceded that the name of *Coventry* should have been released earlier: 'In retrospect it may have been the wrong judgment,' he told the House.

The battle lines between the ministry and the media, however, had been drawn virtually from the start of the conflict. As in all wars the interests of the two were entirely divergent: one wanted the suppression of facts, the other wanted their widest dissemination. The main distinction between the Falklands war and most other modern conflicts was its remoteness: at 8,000 miles distance suppression was relatively simple to achieve, since communications were entirely in the hands of the ministry of defence.

The man with the major responsibility for how the world should hear about the war, and how much it should be told, was Sir Frank Cooper, permanent under secretary at the ministry of defence. A powerfully-built former RAF pilot, whose long career in the civil service had included the rigours of the Northern Ireland office where control of information is a daily matter of life and death, Cooper was in no doubt where his first responsibility lay. 'Obviously the public has got a right to know,' he was to say later. 'But I do not think it has got an unlimited right to know. You have got to give a very high priority to the security of our forces and the success of our operations.'

To ensure this happened, Cooper decided early on to take the job of press relations in London out of the hands of the MoD's regular PR department, and give it to his own civil servants to handle. Thus the men who were on familiar terms with reporters and were used to pressmen's demands, were denied their normal role and deprived of access to real information. Instead, a series of briefings by civil servants was instituted. These ranged from what became known as 'the concourse', the daily press conference chaired by the MoD's official spokesman, Ian McDonald, to private briefings for defence correspondents, and even more private ones for national editors.

It was McDonald who became the most public expression of Cooper's policy. Known unkindly as the 'speak-your-weight machine' his slow, deliberate and immaculately modulated voice was as familiar on radio and television as the weatherman's. Since he was on the TV news virtually every night, he rapidly became a national figure, his faintly detectable Scottish burr and his severe bespectacled features immediately associated with important announcements of victories – or defeats.

McDonald had early on set himself two apparently irreconcilable ground rules: never knowingly to lie, and never knowingly to endanger the safety of the task force. He is confident that throughout the crisis he never broke either rule. But there were some close calls.

Since he sat in on all the meetings of the chiefs of staff there was no doubting the fact that he knew a lot, and defence correspondents devised all sorts of ways of trying to prise it from him. On one occasion, a decision had been taken not to release the news that two helicopters carrying SAS troops had crashed on South Georgia while the island was still in enemy hands. But most people were aware that a landing was imminent and McDonald was pressed to say whether the task force had landed or not. He paused momentarily, then said, no, they had not. Strictly speaking, he would argue later, this was the truth. The SAS, being special troops, were not part of the main task force, only attached to it. Anyway, they had crashed, not landed.

On another occasion he was asked about insistent rumours that *HMS Hermes*, the fleet's flagship, had broken down. The question was asked in various forms but he was always able to give a consistent denial. Luckily, he was never simply asked whether one of the aircraft carriers was in trouble. This he would have found more difficult to deny since the other carrier, *Invincible*, *had* developed engine faults on the way down to the South Atlantic, and had been delayed for twelve hours as a result.

But McDonald's most formidable weapon was silence. Whatever the rumours emerging from Buenos Aires – where claims of British casualties were consistently exaggerated, often to great propaganda effect – he would refuse to confirm or deny anything until he was completely certain of it. At one point this led to an extraordinary state of affairs where Argentina was admitting to the loss of two of her Skyhawks, while McDonald in London would only confirm that *one* had been shot down.

There were, however, occasions when the MoD, while not lying directly, certainly misled journalists with the calculated intention of deceiving the enemy. The false impression that the submarine *Superb* was on patrol in the South Atlantic, when in fact she was limping back to Britain, was never denied; and prior to the landings at San Carlos, everyone was actively encouraged to believe that there would be no such operation – only a series of hit and run raids.

Cooper later argued that this was entirely justified in the circumstances of war, but it also undermined his authority and influence with journalists thereafter. 'I don't know if it confused the enemy,' said one defence correspondent, 'but it sure as hell confused the rest of us.'

This sense of frustration would frequently boil over at some of the MoD briefings – particularly at those chaired by Cooper for the national editors. Although the purpose of these meetings was to establish a relationship of trust and confidence between the MoD and the editors, who were supposed to be responsible figures, they rapidl developed into slanging matches. Most editors believed the MoD being deliberately obstructive. Television networks complaine no live pictures were being got back, although in their op technology was available. Newspaper editors complained that copy was being delayed by anything up to thirty-six hours.

To both these charges the response was simply that 'operational' communications came first. Anything that might interrupt vital messages had to be delayed or abandoned. Thus live TV transmission was deemed impossible. There would be 'voice overs' but no pictures, and TV reporters had to learn to be radio men instead. The only way of getting television and even still pictures back was by ship. 'Our photo-transmission speed is currently twenty knots,' said Cooper at one point.

Then there was censorship, carried out at both ends of the conflict. The twenty-eight journalists who sailed with the task force were accompanied by seven censors or 'minders' from the MoD, as well as by military press officers attached to each unit. Their job was to ensure that no potentially damaging information was transmitted to London, and since this frequently led to suppressing or excising the names of serving men or the revealing detail of military action, they were deeply unpopular with the journalists to whom such material was their life blood.

At the ministry in London there was another layer of supervision, to make sure that reports did not give aid and comfort to the enemy, or threaten the security of operations. Frequently the two sets of censors were at odds.

Thus some correspondents with the task force were told in no uncertain manner that there should be no reference to the raids on Stanley by Vulcan bombers: 'You won't even be able to tell your wives or your children about the Vulcans when you get back,' warned a press officer. That evening the BBC reported the MoD's announcement of the Vulcan attack, and the unhappy 'minder' found himself confronted by a group of very irate reporters.

Kim Sabido, a radio reporter with IRN, wanted to give a moving account of the bomb disposal expert who had died while trying to defuse the bomb which destroyed *Antelope*. The story was killed on the grounds that it would reveal to the Argentinians that their bomb fuses were incorrectly set. That evening, Sabido listened in suppressed fury as the cause of the explosion on *Antelope* was put out over the BBC's World Service.

Sometimes the anger was even more justified. John Shirley of *The Sunday Times* filed a story which included the sentence, 'Only the weather holds us back from Stanley.' This was changed without his knowledge to, 'Only the *politicians* hold us back...' John Witherow of *The Times* wrote of the 'failure' of the Vulcan raids, and found this had unaccountably been transmitted as the 'success' of the raids. A report of a disastrous night encounter between two British units who had opened fire at each other by mistake, became a victorious fire-fight with the enemy.

But these were isolated incidents. Following the landing at San Carlos, what most reporters found more frustrating were the sheer logistics of getting and transmitting information. In the tense hours before San Carlos the needs of journalists came bottom of everyone's list of priorities. Some found themselves on ships heading away from the action rather than towards it. Others were on the scene but miles from the nearest communications point. Still more wrote stories, gave them to press officers for transmission, then discovered – sometimes days later – that their precious story was jammed into someone's pocket, quite forgotten. A helicopter delivery system set up to carry reporters' copy in brown envelopes marked Press broke down because the pilots, flying fifteen hours operational duties a day, did not have time to worry about such minor concerns as deadlines. And, since all reports from the Falklands were 'pooled', individual credit for a well-written story sometimes went to the wrong reporter.

To journalists who were frequently subjected to the same misery and danger as the soldiers they were accompanying, the frustrations were almost intolerable, and the bitterness they felt towards the 'minders' grew to the point where the two groups refused even to have a drink together when they finally reached Stanley. Frequently the system broke down altogether. At one stage, the 'SatCom' (satellite communications) centre at Ajax Bay, from which all stories were filed, was simply blown away. The one Chinook helicopter that had survived from *Atlantic Conveyor* landed too near and the draught lifted the SatCom tent bodily into the air, overturning the vital transmission dish. For several hours there was no communication at all between the Falklands and London.

On the whole though, the television and radio reporters – Michael Nicholson of ITN, Brian Hanrahan of BBC television, Kim Sabido of IRN and Robert Fox of BBC radio – were able to send back regular and often graphic voice reports. The print journalists felt the frustrations much more, with one exception.

Max Hastings, writing for the *Daily Express* and the London *Standard*, and filing a weekly column for the *Spectator* magazine, managed to send back eloquent and remarkably detailed stories. Somehow, wherever he was, he appeared to have access to communications in a way that others did not. Hastings' secret was partly to have established good relations early on with those officers he judged would be best placed to help ensure his stories got to the right place, and partly to file copy that was congenial to the army.

'Most of us decided before landing that our role was simply to report as sympathetically as possible what the British forces are doing here today,' he wrote in one story under a heading 'None of Us Can be Neutral in This War'. In justification he quoted his father, a noted war correspondent in the Second World War: 'When one's nation is at war, reporting becomes an extension of the war effort.'

It should be added that Hastings' material, though sometimes biased, was always well-written and gave an excellent impression of what conditions on the Falklands were like. But the facilities he was afforded to ensure that it got back to London frequently infuriated his colleagues. At one point three reporters at San Carlos, who had agreed to surrender their places on a helicopter for much-needed reinforcements, watched in amazement as Hastings was bundled onto the same helicopter by an SAS unit. Even the commando officers were taken aback: 'I gather Lord Hastings is here,' said one, coldly. Interviews with senior officers, denied to others, were laid on for Hastings. And on one notable occasion the SAS allowed him to file his material – a flattering account of their exploits – on their own network from the heights of Mount Kent back to SAS headquarters in Hereford, in the West of England, from where it was telephoned to the MoD in London. The ministry held on to it for a week.

The argument over patriotism and objective reporting spread to Downing Street as well where Mrs Thatcher, not surprisingly, held strong views. She was particularly incensed by the BBC which seemed to her on occasion to be positively subversive in its coverage of the war. 'There are times when we and the Argentines are almost treated as equals,' she complained. One BBC programme, *Panorama*, which canvassed dissident opinion within the Tory party, roused her to a full-blooded attack on the BBC in the House of Commons.

One person surprised by her vehemence was former US secretary of state Henry Kissinger. He was struck far more by the backing which the government was mostly receiving from the media. 'If we could have got the support for our Vietnam policy that the prime minister has for her Falklands policy, I would have been the happiest man in the world,' he said.

Some of that support verged on the embarrassing. The tabloid *Sun* which had, throughout the conflict, labelled itself as 'The Paper that Backs our Boys', ran a series of strident headlines such as 'Stick it up Your Junta!', and, perhaps most jarringly, on the sinking of the *Belgrano*, 'Gotcha!' A *Sun* reporter with the task force, scrawled 'Up yours Galtieri!' on the side of a British missile, and wrote next day that it had been sent on behalf of the *Sun*'s readers; and when Mrs Thatcher attacked the BBC, the *Sun* leapt into the fray with a leader announcing: 'There are traitors in our midst'. It was promptly labelled 'the Harlot of Fleet Street' by its rival tabloid, the *Daily Mirror*.

The people of Britain seemed largely unmoved by such hysteria. A poll taken after the BBC row showed that eighty-one per cent of the population believed that the BBC had behaved in a responsible manner throughout the Falklands crisis. Unlike the fevered atmosphere which had prevailed during the Suez crisis twenty-five years earlier – when newspapers that questioned Britain's aggressive role lost readers hand over fist – no great discrimination could be detected amongst newspaper readers in 1982. Most papers put on circulation, and the increase was spread evenly amongst the patriotic and the sceptical.

In the aftermath of the war, as a House of Commons committee examined all the charges and counter-charges of censorship and irresponsibility, jingoism and patriotism, bias and objectivity, it was hard to avoid the conclusion that the Falklands war had merely reinforced the prejudices of both sides. The press collectively felt that the ministry of defence had had a terrible war: 'I have to tell you, Sir Frank,' thundered one editor during Cooper's final briefing, 'that this will go down in history as a monumental cock-up.'

The ministry of defence, on the other hand, believed they had got it about right. Pressed to say what lessons they had learnt from their handling of the news, an official thought hard, then said: 'Next time, we'll cut down on the number of journalists.'

In Buenos Aires the same problem was tackled rather differently. A vast mass of uncheckable information, much of it inaccurate, leaked out from the armed forces. But as far as the official spokesmen were concerned, hard facts were as scarce as they were at the ministry of defence in London.

The Argentinian equivalent of Ian McDonald was a sonorous disembodied voice which delivered official, numbered communiqués. The voice never became as familiar as McDonald's, but there were certain parallels of style and the pace was almost identical.

The communiqués assured the people that the news issued by the junta would be 'evaluated in volume as well as content to avoid inaccuracies and the creation of false expectations'. Where no news was made public, it added, people should be confident there was no important news to announce.

Government directives to editors and news agencies instructed them to practise self-censorship 'so that press censorship and other restrictions would not be necessary'. Editors were told that the publication of news which 'could damage the morale of the nation should be avoided'.

Editors were not told how the strictures were to be enforced, except to be assured that they themselves were responsible. Any medium violating the decree would be closed down and the editor arrested. In fact, the measures were rarely invoked: the only closure came late in May, when the agency *Noticias Argentinas* published a story alleging that supplies to the troops on the islands were less than adequate. The closure was temporary and occasioned a considerable outcry.

There were greater risks for those few foreign correspondents who ventured outside Buenos Aires. The worst sufferers, three British journalists, were arrested in Rio Grande on April 13. Simon Winchester of *The Sunday Times* and Ian Mather and Tony Prime of *The Observer* were to spend the war in the world's most southerly jail, in Ushuaia, facing charges of espionage. At the time of writing, although they are released on bail, those charges still stand.

Just as in Britain, journalists complained about the parsimonious supply of official news. Instead, a heady mixture of rumour and disinformation was indiscriminately published. The *Invincible* and the *Hermes* were both sunk several times by the press which also regularly printed stories of British atrocities: perhaps the most persistent was that the British machine-gunned in the water the survivors of ships they had sunk.

The Argentinian television commentator, Jose Gomez Fuentes, asked after the surrender about his role as a journalist, said: 'If there is a war in my country, I will give information which unites the country and I will omit everything which does not. Now this is called disinformation. What's that? I don't understand it.'

CHAPTER TWENTY

The Battle for Goose Green

'In the darkness you cannot use bayonets, it is also much harder to
aim your weapons. The only way you can kill people in that
situation is to get right against the trench and throw a couple of
grenades and then machine-gun it, and then get on.'
– Major Chris Keeble,
second in command 2 Para,
August 1982

'Our training is very realistic but of course when it's for real you
are seeing your own comrades die.'
– Sergeant Ian Aird,
5 Platoon, 'B' Company, 2 Para,
August 1982

Major Chris Keeble, second in command of 2 Parachute Battalion, is a
tall, wiry man, with silver-grey hair, boyish good looks, and a
disconcerting resemblance to that model Englishman Mike Brearley,
recent captain of the England cricket team. His home is a converted
vicarage in a village a tidy distance from 2 Para's headquarters at
Aldershot. The lawn is neat, the flowerbeds tidy – Keeble tends them
himself – and the interior of the house, with its stripped pine furniture,
is fashionable, though not ostentatiously so. There are ample signs of
Keeble's young family: four children – Benedict, 9, Justin, 7, Anna
Louise, 4, and Emily, 1 – all cared for, with evident devotion, by
Keeble's wife Jenny.

It is August, 1982: just over two months have passed since Goose
Green, the first major land battle of the Falklands war, that also proved
to be its bloodiest. 2 Para, who fought the battle, lost eighteen men; the
Argentinians who opposed them lost 250. For Keeble, at the age of
forty, it brought perhaps the most serious test a senior officer can
expect to face. Halfway through the battle 2 Para's commanding
officer, Lieutenant Colonel Herbert Jones – known universally as 'H' –
was killed. With 2 Para dangerously bogged down, Keeble moved into
the front line to take command. He led 2 Para to victory twenty-two
hours later.

Keeble has decided, not without reservations, to describe 2 Para's battle. Baring its soul to the public is not in the nature of the military establishment; nor, probably, is it in Keeble's own character. But Keeble has concluded that he should do so, for three principal reasons. He is, quite simply, proud of his men's achievement, and wants it told. He wants to pay tribute to Colonel H. Above all, he wants the truth about Goose Green to be known. Within days, even hours, of the battle, disturbing rumours were circulating: 'H' died through foolish recklessness; the paras killed more Argentinians than they needed to; after a British officer was shot accepting a white flag, the paras went on a murderous orgy of revenge. Each of these rumours contains an element of truth. Keeble hopes that he can show them in a new light.

Keeble speaks in the familiar polished tones that Sandhurst imparts to its alumni as recognisably as any charm school. Through his account, a picture emerges of a professional soldier unswervingly dedicated to his craft: and not any professional soldier, but a member of the Parachute Regiment, with its own traditions and attitudes, and a distinctive fighting style. 'Read Arnhem,' says Keeble simply. 2 Para was formed in 1941, after Churchill had directed that Britain should raise parachute units to match the Germans'. In August 1944, 2 Para's Colonel John Frost and his men held the north end of Arnhem bridge on the Rhine for three days, in the face of almost continuous German attacks. 'That was his mission and that was what he did. It is an unwritten philosophy that doesn't put a limit. Anything is possible.'

By the same philosophy, paratroopers on the offensive do not stop until they have won their objective. 'Casualties are a secondary facet. Because people are dying around and beside you, you cannot let yourself say, "I can't hack this because people are dying". You have *got* to keep going. You must achieve your mission, that is more important than anything else.' A handful of casualties early on can spare hundreds later: 'If you go hard and fast, you invariably save casualties. Maintain the momentum, and what you can do with ten blokes now may take you 100 blokes two hours later.'

There is an obvious corollary. As Keeble explains without embarrassment, if you are prepared to take casualties, you are prepared to inflict them too. 'Our people *are* extremely aggressive. They *are* trained to fight, not piss about. You can't mince it. You have got to kill the enemy, you have got to destroy that machine-gun, before he destroys you. When you fire anti-tank rockets into a trench a lot of people die. If you have four people in a trench and a grenade comes in four people die. Every trench you attack you *destroy* it. You jump in the trench and rake it with fire and if you see an Argie it's either him or you. There is no time to take people out and say, "stand over there and be a good prisoner of war". You deal with the trench, and then you head on.'

Keeble calls this 'gutter fighting'; and however ruthless it seems, it contains an inherent logic. War may indeed be hell, he implies; but if so, hellish methods must be used. It presents him with no great moral dilemmas. He is a devout and practising catholic, who attended the catholic boarding school of Douai in Berkshire before proceeding to Sandhurst at the age of 20, in 1961. He arrived in the Falklands with a simple guiding precept. 'As far as I was concerned, here was a guy who was occupying a piece of terrain which we wanted back. We were going to get it back, there was no *question* of us losing, there was no question of them winning. It never entered anybody's mind whether they were good or bad.' Near the end of the battle, when Keeble was negotiating a surrender, he met an Argentinian officer and pointed out that they were both catholics. He added: 'I don't want to kill you but if I have to I will.'

Keeble's religion also assisted him in reaching certain conclusions about his own fate. 'Death does not worry me in the slightest, I have no fear of dying at all.' And in the battalion as a whole, says Keeble, 'There is quite a lot of importance attached to religion ... I think that has a part to play in the success of the unit.' He believes it contributes above all to its fellow-feeling, to that intangible yet vital military quality termed morale. 'That was really what drove 2 Para. It's two-thirds morale and one-third combat power. You have a team of friends who will actually die for each other, and certainly after Goose Green they had been welded by fire, literally.' When they reached Stanley at the end of the campaign, 2 Para was the first unit to enter its red-stone cathedral: 'to pray for our dead and for our success'.

The account of the battle for Goose Green that follows is based to a large extent on Keeble's own description, though not entirely. Other sources helped inform the planning stage; a 2 Para sergeant described scenes on the battlefield Keeble could not have seen; the BBC's reporter Robert Fox, who accompanied 2 Para throughout, assisted with important details, although he was not a party to our conclusions; and John Shirley of *The Sunday Times* helped with background information.

In strict military terms, Goose Green was an unnecessary target. 'Let's be objective,' says Keeble. 'To succeed in the Falklands there was little point in attacking Goose Green because the centre, the capital, is Stanley, and if you want to capture the country you capture its capital, if you want to defeat the enemy you must capture its army. Both were in Stanley, so why go for Goose Green? That's a question which needs answering.'

Keeble's doubts were shared by many of the officers who attended a fraught planning meeting at San Carlos on May 26, after Major-General Trant had given Thompson his abrupt instruction to move out of the bridgehead. Goose Green is a settlement, in normal times the home of some eighty islanders, astride the narrow isthmus that connects the two halves of the main East Falkland island. As the military planners' maps showed, the Argentinian forces occupying Goose Green were scarcely blocking the main path from San Carlos to Stanley, for they could quite simply be bypassed. Originally, Goose Green was merely to have been raided in a bid to destroy its airstrip, from which Argentinian Pucaras were operating. Under the pressure from Northwood, Goose Green became a prime target because – to put it crudely – no one could think what else to do. As usual when a decision is imposed through force of circumstance, substantial arguments in its favour came welling up, and the attack assumed a new rationale. It would be a clash of arms that would demonstrate the land forces' resolve to the Argentinians, to the British people, even to themselves. As Keeble put it: 'It would be a thermometer – you could test the water. I think that is probably why we went.'

And so, in 2 Para's improvised headquarters in a shepherd's refuge named Camilla Creek House, H and his company commanders planned their battle. It presented them with a new kind of warfare, as Keeble explains: 'Generally speaking, the British army is constructed to defend, to go to NATO and dig themselves in and stop the Russian hordes.' This time, 2 Para would be taking the offensive. But H in particular relished the moment. Since leaving Eton to go to Sandhurst, he had been a soldier dedicated to the point of obsession, and even spent his spare time playing war-games; the attack would be the apotheosis of his career.

2 Para's advance would start at the sea inlet of Camilla Creek at the northern end of the isthmus, three miles from the goal of Goose Green. Approximately halfway, two features blocked their way. On the west shore, by the ruined building of Boca House, was Boca Hill; parallel to the east was Darwin Hill, with Darwin settlement nestling between it and the shore. Both hills were ominously well-defended with enemy machine-gun emplacements and a complex system of interlocking trenches; in its depressing lack of cover, the terrain reminded Keeble of Salisbury Plain: 'no vegetation at all, completely bare-arsed'. H allocated one company of 110 men to each obstacle: 'B' company would take the west flank, to Boca House; 'A' company would aim for Darwin Hill. A third company, 'D', would move between them, following the gentle ridge that formed the backbone of the isthmus. H would command the operation from the front line, taking with him the dozen or so men who formed the battalion's tactical headquarters, TAC HQ, and following a track down the middle of the battle-ground. Keeble says: 'It was to be a very tightly controlled operation with H up front to see exactly what was happening.' If it seems surprising that the battalion commander should expose himself to the risks of the front line, that also stems from the traditions of Arnhem, where the paras' General Roy Urquhart led a dash through German positions in an

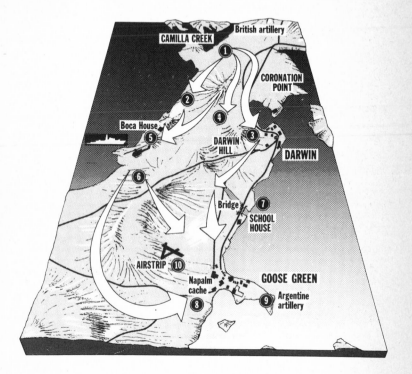

The Battle for Goose Green: [1] Companies from 2 Para began their advance from a sea inlet at Camilla Creek. [2] 'B' Company of 110 men took the west flank, heading for Boca House, but soon ran into stiff resistance from Argentinian troops. [3] Meanwhile 'A' Company headed for Darwin Hill and also became bogged down. By dawn, they were well short of their objective. [4] 'D' Company TAC HQ advanced on the central front and attempted to support the attack on Darwin Hill but, in the process, Lieutenant-Colonel 'H' Jones was killed. Major Chris Keeble took command and, [5] sent 'D' Company to attack Boca House which was also bombarded by a ship offshore. The fight was all over within minutes and, [6] the Paras began a two-pronged advance on the airstrip and the settlements at Goose Green. [7] 'C' Company which had been held in reserve, then took the toughest objective School House. Not one of the defending troops survived. [8] The Argentinians had large stocks of napalm but little of it was used and, [9] the big radar-guided guns were silenced by Harriers. [10] The airstrip fell without a fight; and 1,600 Argentinians had been defeated by 450 paras.

attempt to reach his divisional headquarters. Keeble adds firmly: 'The only way to lead is to lead. From the front.'

For weaponry, 2 Para had fifty-six machine-guns, double the number they would normally reckon to carry. It was in part to compensate for other failings. The advance troops were to be supported by 105 mm artillery, Milan wire-guided missiles, and a section of snipers, all firing from the far side of Camilla Creek. But 2 Para had also tried to enlist armoured support from the light tanks of the Blues and Royals, part of the Household Cavalry, only to be told that they were required for 'other priorities'. They also hoped for air support, but fog and low cloud were to rule this out for most of the day.

As for manpower, the intelligence from SAS reconnaissance patrols predicted that the two sides would be equally matched. 'We reckoned they were about a battalion, so it would be one for one,' says Keeble. The intelligence was wrong: the Argentinians had a superiority over 2 Para of almost four to one. If the true odds had been known the attack might never have taken place; on this occasion, ignorance was bliss.

If that disadvantage proved a blessing in disguise, another incident almost certainly did not. On May 26, two days before the attack, 2 Para believed it had been dealt a mortal blow by its own side. That morning the 2 Para officers were buzzing with the news that the BBC World Service had broadcast that the attack on Goose Green was about to begin. The brigade information sheet called the broadcast 'a serious security leak', and for several days the reporters on the Falklands found themselves cold-shouldered even though they were quite blameless. The damage, in fact, began with a World Service press review quoting somewhat premature British newspaper reports that Goose Green had already fallen; and it was compounded by official reports throughout the day that the British had begun to move from San Carlos, and that 2 Para themselves had been in action five miles north-east of Darwin – a reference to an abortive reconnaissance patrol 2 Para had dispatched. In the Falklands these niceties were scarcely appreciated, and H was beside himself with anger, threatening to sue both the BBC and the ministry of defence for 'manslaughter'. 2 Para's gloom was added to when two prisoners, captured and questioned on the afternoon of April 27, left their interrogating officer in no doubt that the Argentinians at Goose Green were expecting an attack.

But to compensate, the more phlegmatic Keeble believed, 2 Para had its renowned morale – and the tedious spell 2 Para had spent dug in on Sussex Mountains after the San Carlos landing had left them itching for action. 'The question, when we were sitting there, was not whether we were going to get killed from the air, but when are we going to get off this mountain and go banjo the enemy?' His bullishness was reflected by H when he spoke to his fellow officers on the eve of the attack. He conceded that the battle plan seemed disjointed: 'We are taking small bites at the cherry all the time, and we are going to bite our way through.' But he added – referring to the earlier plans for Goose Green – 'This is not a raid anymore. It is a full battalion attack by day and night. We've really got to hit them hard.' Yet even H, apparently, was not free from all doubt. BBC reporter Robert Fox met him in Camilla Creek House on the night of May 27. 'I've never been involved in anything like this before,' Fox confided.

'Neither have I,' H replied.

At 2.30 a.m. local time on Friday, May 28, the three forward companies of 2 Para crossed their 'start line', near a bottle-neck entrance to the isthmus only 400 yards wide. It was still dark, and pouring with rain. The bottle-neck was an obvious place for mines but to their surprise and relief, 2 Para found it clear. From Brenton Loch to the west, *HMS Antrim* was firing a 4.5 inch gun in support, but as they crossed the start-line it fell silent: it had jammed. The Argentinian artillery started up as soon as they reached the isthmus, shells crashing down haphazardly around them, together with some wild machine-gun fire. They aimed to make as much progress as possible before first light around 6 a.m., to compensate for the lack of cover. Both 'A' company in the east and 'B' in the west moved forward steadily towards the first Argentinian positions, which they attacked with machine-guns, grenades, and 'throwaway' 66 mm anti-tank rockets. They were soon taking casualties of their own, although no one yet knew how many. Later, when day came, they found one of their machine-gunners who had died from a headwound. Another body lay across him: that of his ammunition-carrier, killed as he tried to put a field dressing on his partner's head.

As the Argentinian defences stiffened, 2 Para's advance slowed. On the western flank, 'B' company was coming under increasing fire as it encountered the enemy trenches head on. In response, the company's two lead platoons split into smaller and smaller groups, sometimes just two men together, one moving forward with 66 mm anti-tank rockets or grenades while his partner covered him with a machine-gun. One of those men was Ian Aird, a thirty-year-old platoon sergeant from Yorkshire who had served with the regiment for eleven years. Aird found that to use the anti-tank rockets he had to approach within fifty yards of an enemy trench; even closer, fifteen to twenty yards, 'if we were lobbing in grenades or white phosphorus grenades'.

As the sky lightened, Aird began to note, with detached curiosity, the effects of the weapons he was using. No one in a trench hit by an anti-tank rocket survived; but since they were killed through internal injuries caused by the concussion of the explosion, it left their bodies 'looking quite okay'. The white phosphorus was rightly renowned for its frightful effect, adhering to the body and burning right through it; the Argentinians were using it too, and Aird knew that the only antidote was to prize away the phosphorus with a bayonet or a knife. Trenches hit by artillery fire were the worst: the bodies looked like 'hunks of meat', with arms and legs blown off, stomachs gaping open. One corpse Aird saw had half its head blown away by the fountain of debris from an exploding shell. It was only later that Aird reflected on all this. 'When we storm a trench we go in fast. If the guy inside is alive and hasn't given up then it's too bad, if he's armed. You don't have time to play games. If they are just moaning we leave them there and press on ...'

The morning light brought menace to the men of 2 Para themselves. It found both 'A' and 'B' companies short of their first objectives, Darwin Hill and Boca Hill. 'A' company started to attack the complex series of trenches lining Darwin Hill at 6.30 and by mischance, having traversed to approach from the shore, chose the strongest part of its defences, not realising the Argentinians had been expecting the British to come from the sea. In the west, 'B' company was still a mile short of Boca Hill, and had to cross 1,000 yards of open ground before their small-arms would come into range. As Sergeant Aird's 5 Platoon dropped down the bare central ridge towards it, they were pitifully exposed. A private named James Street fell injured when a bullet passed clean through his leg. The two men nearest him, Corporal Leonard Standish and Private Andy Brook, went to his aid, Brook applying a shell dressing to his leg to stem the heavy bleeding before they pulled him into the cover afforded by a slight fold in the ground. Then a private named Hall was shot in the small of the back and lay moaning on the ground. A twenty-year-old private, Stephen Illingsworth, dashed forward under fire with another soldier and dragged Hall back. The platoon was now desperately short of ammunition and on his own initiative Illingsworth went back under fire to retrieve Hall's belt containing one hundred rounds. Suddenly he cried out and fell. He had been shot through the neck by a sniper's bullet which broke his neck and severed his jugular vein. Almost certainly, in the opinion of Sergeant Aird, he was dead by the time he hit the ground. 'It was a bit of a blow to me because I knew him quite well.'

Both 'A' and 'B' company pressed on grimly, neither able to afford the other any support. Helicopters were arriving sporadically, in the teeth of the Argentinian artillery bombardment, to deliver ammunition and remove both British and Argentinian casualties to the field medical station, set up in the disued refrigeration plant at Ajax Bay. By now Colonel H and his TAC headquarters were in a small valley below Darwin Hill, with the beleaguered 'A' company somewhere alongside. To the untutored eyes of BBC reporter Robert Fox, the scene was one of utter chaos. Artillery was being directed on to their position with terrifying accuracy by an Argentinian observation post above them, while machine-gun fire was also arriving from Boca Hill. Two of TAC HQ's radios had broken down. A regimental sergeant major was trying to persuade a group of prisoners to fetch some of the

Argentinian dead, even though there were no body-bags to put them in. It was still raining heavily, and Fox was in tears, 'because of the cold, and the fear'.

Somewhere above them yet another machine-gun post was pinning down a sizeable part of 'A' company. Shortly before 10.30 a.m. H decided to pit his TAC forces against it. Opinions now differ whether that was a sensible move. Fox himself was later to refer to it in a broadcast as 'an act of almost foolish bravery', a judgment with which some British officers agreed, pointing out that H imperilled not only himself but also his whole TAC HQ force. It also accorded with the view formed of H by some other British correspondents on *Canberra*, who found that he did not share most other officers' anxieties about the perils of an opposed landing at the Falklands, and seemed only to be impetuously determined for action. 2 Para's Keeble presents a different view: 'If you go back to the principle that ten men attacking that particular trench would be better than 'D' company an hour later, you can understand ... His TAC HQ consisted of about twelve blokes, twelve men against one trench. One trench collapses and it may be the key to the whole defensive position.'

The machine-gun harassing 'A' company was just over the crest of the rise above H. He took two men with him and ran around the flank while another small group headed directly over the top. They converged, moving fast, thirty yards from their objective. But as they did so they came within the sights of a second machine-gun position to their left, of which they had been quite unaware. The battalion's adjutant, Captain David Wood, was hit first and killed. Then H was shot in the back of the neck. He tumbled unconscious down a gully, mortally wounded. The rest of the group retreated to the comparative safety of the valley. The attack had failed.

In the main HQ 1,500 yards back, Keeble heard only the radioed words: 'Sunray is down'. The code meant that H was out of action – whether he was dead or merely injured was not relevant. It also meant that Keeble had to take over. Long before the battle, 2 Para had prepared its duplicate chain of command which had already been called into play early on, when no fewer than four section commanders had been killed. Now it was Keeble's turn to move into the front line. He says that he felt little emotion. 'We had to keep going. There was artillery coming down, we had a battle to fight. You cannot suddenly burst into tears or anything. You have got to get on. There were people's lives depending on what I actually did at that point – *me*.'

As Keeble evaluated 2 Para's position, the battle seemed delicately poised. 'We had casualties on the battlefield, we needed more ammunition forward, and things were getting to a very dicey stage.' 'A' company, he felt, could keep 'chipping away' at Darwin Hill – a considerable euphemism, for it had been engaged in some lethal hand-to-hand fighting – but 'B' company was in greater difficulty, 'trying to get close to Boca House and unable to do so. I felt that was the *problem*, if you could crack that nut, then you could outflank Darwin Hill.'

Keeble and 'B' company commander Major John Crossland now made an inspired tactical switch. 'D' company was still relatively unscathed in the centre of the isthmus, and Keeble and Crossland decided to bring them forward to 'B' company's aid. In this they were assisted by a convenient feature of the Falkland landscape which until then had told so heavily against them. Where the slopes of the isthmus fell to the west, they terminated in a lip eighteen inches above the beach. Using this as cover, 'D' company crawled along the beach for 1,000 yards until it was level with Boca Hill. At the same time Keeble brought forward some of the battalion's support artillery on to the central ridge. When all were in position, he gave the signal to open fire, hitting Boca Hill from two sides. Milan missiles struck the Argentinian trenches with deadly effect; the British saw an enemy soldier miraculously survive one attack and dive into a neighbouring trench, only for it to be devastated by a second Milan moments later. The attack was over within minutes. 'They just gave up and failed to respond after a while. There was no point in killing them needlessly or wasting our valuable ammunition. Hundreds of white flags came out of the trenches and I stopped the firing.' At almost the same time a radio message came in from 'A' company: 'We have now got Darwin Hill.'

Keeble moved the TAC HQ on to Darwin Hill, with its commanding views over the isthmus, and took stock. The two principal obstacles had fallen; a mile and a half ahead lay Goose Green itself. He decided to ignore the houses of the Darwin settlement – any Argentinians there could be dealt with later – to concentrate on two more important objectives. One was the airstrip just outside Goose Green; the other was School House, a building 400 yards north of Goose Green on the east shore. With fewer intervening defences than earlier, Keeble could adopt the luxury of a three-pronged assault. 'B' company would move down the isthmus beyond Goose Green to approach from the south, while 'D' company would strike from the west, taking the airstrip en route. 'C' company would enter the battle for the first time, joining a platoon of 'A' company to move on School House from the north. It seemed the toughest target remaining, guarding two bridges and the final approach to Goose Green. 'The enemy had based a very strong position there, about fifty men.'

The obvious approach to School House lay across a bridge which, equally obviously, was mined. 'C' company, joined by a patrol from 'D' company, bypassed the bridge and advanced with machine-guns and grenades. As they did so a pair of Argentinian Pucaras dropped three canisters of napalm which narrowly missed a group of men; later they said it had 'put the shits up them'. Soon afterwards one of the Pucaras was shot down as it passed over Darwin Hill. While most of his colleagues were taking cover, a soldier heroically stood up and fired his Blowpipe missile. Keeble saw the missile hit the Pucara's right wing: 'it turned over and hit the ground in a tremendous ball of fire'.

It was now that the most controversial incident of the battle occurred, when a young platoon commander, Lieutenant Jim Barry, and two fellow soldiers were killed as they moved forward after an Argentinian trench had raised a white flag. 'Never trust an Argy!' proclaimed the *Sun*, which wrote of the Argentinians' 'treachery' in luring the three men to their deaths. But Keeble believes it was a mistake in the confusion of battle, with the Argentinians who opened fire not realising that a neighbouring trench was attempting to surrender.

Not one of the Argentinians still defending School House when the incident occurred survived. Was it an orgy of revenge? The paratroopers moved on to the building, launching M 79 grenades and hurling white phosphorus grenades as well. Keeble says: 'You have to appreciate, I suspect, that we had the white flag incident and they were not going to mess about trying to take surrenders any more. They were going in very hard and I suspect there was very little mercy being shown there.' Eventually the building exploded into flames – 'either we hit some ammunition or grain or something and up it went' – and burned fiercely. When the doors were opened all that remained of the Argentinian defenders was a mass of incinerated bodies, twisted and charred beyond recognition.

It was the last major engagement of the battle – and 2 Para had suffered its last deaths. The airstrip proved lightly defended, with no trenches, only tents that housed the Argentinians manning the air control units and the 20 mm air defence guns, and was soon taken. On the far side of Goose Green, on a narrow spit of land to the east, were the radar-guided guns that had plagued 2 Para all day. With the skies clear at last, Keeble called up a Harrier strike. Three Harriers roared in from the west, dropping anti-personnel cluster bombs that exploded with earth-shattering force. 'After that,' says Keeble, 'the whole intensity of the battle fell away. It was then that I first got the feeling that we had won, that victory was ours. They were surrounded – it was just like Custer's last stand.'

Keeble's strategy now was quite simply to conduct a siege, bombarding the settlement and then sending in 2 Para to eliminate all opposition. But his plan was abruptly thwarted when a patrol returned to report that 112 civilians were held captive in the community centre inside Goose Green. 'My "easy solution" was completely screwed up.' If the civilians remained in Argentinian hands, Keeble knew then there was little he as a soldier could do. From then on, 'it was a quasi-political problem.'

Yet Keeble did not give up; and in the quest for final victory, Keeble the soldier became Keeble the diplomat. He decided to make contact with the Argentinian military commanders to offer them a surrender. But he was determined to do so from a position of strength. He had already blocked a company of reinforcements the Argentinians had landed by helicopter to the south of Goose Green. Overnight he brought up extra artillery, ammunition, and reinforcements of his own, in the shape of Major Mike Norman and his company of marines.

It seems that the Argentinians soon grasped the point. In the early morning a senior officer went to the house of the Goose Green settlement manager and asked him to contact the British to discuss a ceasefire. To ensure there were no misunderstandings, Keeble sent two Argentinian prisoners into Goose Green at 6 a.m. bearing the stark message: 'Your military options are as follows: (a) surrender, (b) accept the consequences of military action.' The prisoners were told that if they did not return within an hour, the British would assume the Argentinians intended to fight on. They returned almost at once with confirmation that the Argentinian command wanted to talk.

Negotiations began in a hut at the airstrip shortly after midday. As well as several of his officers, Keeble took with him as civilian witnesses two British journalists, Fox and the *Daily Mail* reporter David Norris, who had been with 2 Para throughout the battle. Fox had advised Keeble to allow the Argentinians to keep their dignity by allowing them a surrender ceremony – 'an exercise in face-saving' says Keeble; 'I thought that was a fairly small concession to make.'

There were three Argentinian officers, one from each arm of the forces; the air force man, Air Commodore Wilson Drozier Pedroza, did most of the talking. They announced at once that they were prepared to let the civilians go; and almost before the British realised it, started talking about a surrender. Pedroza said that he wanted to talk to General Menendez in Stanley and returned to the settlement to make the call. 'We had agreed that if he was successful we would have the formal surrender on a piece of open ground at the top of the settlement. We drifted towards there about 1 p.m. We kept on saying, "Are they surrendering? I think I can see some movement. No. Yes. Maybe they are." We could look down into the settlement and we could see a lot of people packing kit.'

Then some 150 Argentinian men marched out of the settlement and formed up around the patch of ground. The commanding officer made a speech and his men sang the Argentinian anthem. The officer then handed his pistol to Keeble and the men laid their arms on the ground. With a jolt, Keeble realised they all belonged to the air force. 'We started to get a bit twitched and asked, "Where are the soldiers?" He indicated towards the settlement. We moved forwards slightly to look down into the settlement better and there was this huge column of men marching towards us, carrying their weapons.'

Keeble was astounded. By the original intelligence estimates there should have been around 100 Argentinian men left in Goose Green.

Yet here was a group numbering, at a quick guess, 1,000. He quailed at the thought of the odds 2 Para had faced: his 450 men had defeated 1,600 Argentinians. He regained his composure and summoned 'D' company to take the prisoners in charge. Then Keeble hurried to the community hall to free the people of Goose Green. 'They started coming out, they were in fairly good shape, they were jubilant, glad to be alive, and greeted us as the conquering heroes. They broke open their last cans of beer to share with us, they made sandwiches, they were throwing their arms around us. It was an incredibly moving and emotional moment. We really did feel like liberators.'

Keeble has no doubt that the battle of Goose Green did all that was intended, demonstrating British superiority to the Argentinians: not in weaponry, in which he reckoned they were evenly matched, but in determination and resolve. 'We had been given all this garbage about their equipment and their food, and dysentery being rife. All that was really irrelevant. We knew when we got to the Falklands that we would have the same problems, trench foot, shortage of this and that. The question which decides it all is whether they want to fight. There was not a man in 2 Para who did not want to do that operation. *Their* weakness even before we had attacked is that they did not really want to fight. They were not 100 per cent behind their government's action in the Falklands. All this crap about being educated from birth about the Malvinas. If they were that committed, why didn't they fight for it?'

Certainly the prisoners now presented a bedraggled sight. 5 Platoon's Sergeant Aird felt sorry for them, 'especially the young ones, they didn't really know why they were there'. Many were packed into sheep sheds while others were set to work tidying the chaos of battle. Some of the houses had been ransacked, there were discarded weapons everywhere, and ammunition was strewn like litter. It was stacked into small piles before being cleared away – like sweeping up leaves in the garden, Keeble thought.

Although the fighting had stopped, the battle had not yet completed its toll. While a group of prisoners were moving ammunition some artillery shells exploded – whether accidentally, or because they were booby-trapped, was never clear. A British medical orderly dashed into the resulting fire and dragged two seriously injured Argentinians clear. A third man was lying in the flames, his legs blown off and his stomach gaping. Unable to reach him, the orderly fired four shots into his head. A British officer later asked surgeon commander Rick Jolly for his opinion on the incident. 'I just hope I've got the courage to do something like that if it happens to me,' Jolly told him. 'It's the bravest thing I've ever heard.'

The Argentinian dead were buried in a mass grave that was half-filled with water seeping from below by the time the brief service was completed. 2 Para's dead were laid in a broad dry trench on a grassy hillock overlooking San Carlos Water. Keeble marched at the head of the bearers as they carried in the bodies, wrapped in a silver burial sheet, and saluted as they were placed on the ground. Troops stood bare-headed as the names of 2 Para's dead were read out, along with the names of a Royal Marine helicopter pilot and sappers from 3 Commando who had also lost their lives, providing the Paras with support. (The pilot, Lieutenant Richard Nunn, had been on his way to pick up Keeble when he was shot down by a Pucara.)

Even this ceremony reflected the chill calm with which 2 Para had confronted the reality of war, for the burial site had been chosen before the battle of Goose Green began.

CHAPTER TWENTY-ONE

A Bay Too Far

'Thank God it isn't us.'
– Lieutenant Hilarion Roberts, June 1982

The day after the surrender at Goose Green, and as if to celebrate it, the great and now rather rusty liner *Canberra* made her stately return to San Carlos Water. On board were reinforcements from 5th Infantry Brigade – Scots Guards, Welsh Guards and inscrutable Gurkhas – collected from the *QE2* which had ventured no nearer the action than South Georgia. Also on board was Major-General Jeremy Moore, commander of the land forces, and the man charged with capitalising on the paras' victory.

When he came ashore the next day, Moore was in a lively, boisterous mood. He surveyed the command post – which, in more normal times, was the outside lavatory and cloakroom for the Port San Carlos Social Club – and then went on a walkabout to cheer up the troops. He is an angular man, slightly awkward in his movements but not in his views, which are very clear. In a peaked forage cap and camouflage kit, he looked much younger than fifty-one, and he was altogether neat and crisp. He had the habit of folding his arms and staring into the middle distance.

The man most pleased to see the new arrivals, in particular the Guards, was Lieutenant Colonel Malcolm Hunt of 40 Commando. He and his marines had been waiting at San Carlos, holding the bridgehead until 5 Brigade arrived, on the understanding that they would then be freed to join Julian Thompson's general advance on Stanley. They were naturally keen to get forward as soon as possible: 3 Para had already completed an epic march, in full kit and through total darkness, the twenty-six miles to Teal Inlet; 45 Commando had left for Douglas settlement; and advance units of 42 Commando had made the furthest leap forward, by helicopter, to the heights of Mount Kent – from where they could almost see Stanley. (However, 42 Commando's advance had not gone entirely as planned. The first attempt to reach the mountain, on May 29, had nearly ended in disaster when a Chinook helicopter – the sole survivor from *Atlantic Conveyor* – had run into a storm, inadvertently touched down on water, and lost a wheel and a door before limping back to Port San Carlos. The next night, however, the marines and units of the SAS had reached the mountain.) Even General Menendez seemed to accept that time was running out; on May 29, the British had intercepted a signal in which he warned Buenos Aires that his men could not win. Everything seemed set for the final British attack as early as June 6 or 7. 40 Commando was therefore stunned when, on June 1, it learned that everything had changed. That afternoon the order came from the command ship *Fearless*, where General Moore had now taken up residence, that 5 Brigade would move forward; the marines would stay at the bridgehead to defend the Force Maintenance Area – a complex of stores and hospital facilities that had been erected in the derelict refrigeration plant at Ajax Bay overlooking San Carlos Water.

Hunt was furious. As dusk was closing in he went to Moore on *Fearless* to argue as strongly as military discipline would allow that the decision was utterly wrong. He stressed that his marines were trained for the kind of battles that were to come, they were used to working with the other elements of 3 Brigade that had already gone forward – and, if they were now held back, it would seriously damage their morale.

Frankly, Hunt also thought that the Guards were not up to it. Earlier he had watched a Welsh guardsman come ashore at San Carlos with a full pack on his back, walk 400 yards from the jetty and then sit down in the road in tears, saying he could not go on. And the crew of the *Canberra* had been deeply uncomplimentary about the guardsmen, saying that on the voyage from South Georgia they had done no physical exercise but 'sat around all day', had grumbled at the need to share cabins, and had complained when lunch was late. (To be fair to the Guards, the weather on that voyage had not been exactly conducive to running round the decks.)

Moore was unmoved. He told Hunt: 'I hear what you say,' but he was convinced it made no military sense to move a tough unit, familiar with the territory around San Carlos, when there was every chance that the Argentinians might try and launch a counter-attack on the bridgehead, possibly by flying in paratroopers from the mainland.

Hunt returned to San Carlos despondent. He walked round telling his men that Moore would not budge and tried to persuade them that they still had a vital job to do. They were not convinced and Major Andrew Gowan, Hunt's second-in-command, urged him to resign; he thought seriously about it but in the end decided there would be no point. The day ended with the mass desertion of reporters who had been assigned to 40 Commando, but who now felt they should go where the action was. Hunt said he understood.

Brigadier Tony Wilson, the commanding officer of 5 Brigade, a tall

232

and incongruous-looking figure in green wellington boots, did not waste the chance. He set up his headquarters in an abandoned house in Darwin, co-opted the victorious men of 2 Para, and by the evening of Friday, June 4, could report that his brigade had made a startling advance of thirty-six miles, and captured the key settlements of Fitzroy and Bluff Cove.

The circumstances of that advance were rapidly lost in myth. The story that emerged – and went round the world – was that Wilson himself had gone to a place called Swan Inlet, found a telephone box that worked, and made a fifty pence call to Reg Binney, the farm manager at Fitzroy. 'Any Argies around?' said Wilson. 'There were but they've gone,' was the reply. 'Then I think I'll join you,' said the brigadier, ordering an immediate helicopter advance.

It was not quite like that. For one thing, there are no coin boxes at Swan Inlet, or anywhere else on the Falklands. And it was not Wilson who went to Swan Inlet, but 'B' Company of 2 Para. Still, it is true that their commander, Major John Crossland, did telephone Fitzroy, from a private house, and, 'B' Company did, with inspired opportunism, go on and take the settlements. Back at Darwin, Wilson was triumphant: 'I thought it was now or never because they [Argentinian troops] could come back during the night,' he told John Witherow of *The Times*. 'I decided that unless I took that chance I might end up fighting for Fitzroy and Bluff Cove, and only a fool would fight for a place he could have for nothing,' he said.

That achieved, the brigadier now had very ambitious plans. He had found and commandeered a small coaster called *Monsunan* which, he said, 'We'll run as our private navy while it suits us. I've got an enormous stock of huge Union Jacks so no one will mistake us as we go round the corner.'

He added: 'I'm moving people forward as fast as I can and stocks of ammunition to launch what I suppose could be called the final offensive. I've grabbed my land in this great jump forward, and I want to consolidate it.'

There was just one snag: how to get some 1,200 guardsmen from San Carlos to 'my land'.

On June 5, Major Ewen Southby-Tailyour, the task force's connoisseur of Falkland bays, was summoned to *Fearless* to discuss the problem. It was eventually decided that her sister ship, *HMS Intrepid*, would take the Scots Guards from San Carlos that night to Lively Island, near the mouth of Choiseul Sound – but no further because of the risk of losing another ship. (The Argentinians had land-based Exocets on the coastline south of Stanley.) From Lively Island, Southby-Tailyour was to take the Guards to Bluff Cove in four landing craft.

Some of the land force officers thought that the navy's attitude was 'rather selfish' but the plan was agreed, and at 12.30 a.m. on a beautiful moonlit night the landing craft were disgorged from *Intrepid*, through the huge doors in her stern, on to flat calm sea. Southby-Tailyour realised it was the anniversary of D-Day, and his daughter's birthday. As *Intrepid* and her two escorts sailed away, he felt 'very lonely'.

The rest of the journey to Bluff Cove was a nightmare. As the landing craft rounded the south-east corner of Lively Island and headed towards the aptly named Dangerous Point, they came up against a strong tide. The radar in Southby-Tailyour's boat packed up. Flares lit up the sky, there was the sound of mortar or artillery fire and then, four miles astern of the little convoy, two ships appeared, closing fast. Since no British ships were supposed to be in that area, Southby-Tailyour assumed they were the enemy and wanted to make a run for some islands in Choiseul Sound, where the landing craft might be able to hide. He eventually decided there was no point and when one of the approaching ships flashed the 'heave to' signal, he obeyed. She turned out to be *HMS Cardiff*: 'Friend,' came the signal; 'To whom?' replied a by now very angry Southby-Tailyour.

The weather deteriorated rapidly, the wind gusted to seventy knots, and the guardsmen were soaked by flying spray. It took five hours to reach Bluff Cove, by which time three of the soldiers were suffering from exposure. Some of them thought they were lucky they had not all been drowned.

That same prospect faced the Welsh Guards who were due to make an identical voyage on the night of June 6. But during the day Captain Jeremy Larken of *Fearless* agreed to take a risk. He would carry them in his ship beyond Lively Island to Direction Island, a good deal nearer to their destination. Southby-Tailyour was to rendezvous with *Fearless* in his landing craft to carry the guardsmen back into Bluff Cove.

That afternoon in San Carlos, the Welsh Guards embarked on *Fearless*, delighted to get into the warm after five days and nights in waterlogged trenches. The men stripped off their clothes to dry them on the pipes while the officers were taken up to the wardroom and told they could sign for their drinks; they would be billed when they got back to England.

That courtesy, and some hot food, instantly boosted morale, and twenty-five-year-old Lieutenant Hilarion Roberts of 3 Company thought it would be 'marvellous' if something happened to delay the rendezvous so they could stay on *Fearless* one more night 'just to get really dry'.

Something did intervene – the weather. It was so bad Southby-Tailyour could not get the landing craft out of Bluff Cove. He assumed that the operation would be delayed, but he reckoned without the determination to get the men ashore. *Fearless* had two landing craft in her bowels, and they were dispatched into the night with two companies of very gloomy guardsmen. Roberts and his men stayed on board and as he watched the craft chug away he thought: 'Thank God it isn't us.'

Fearless returned to San Carlos Water where it was decided she would not be risked again. Instead the remaining guardsmen would be taken to Bluff Cove by the landing ship *Sir Galahad*, one of five royal fleet auxilliaries named after King Arthur's knights of the round table. Around lunchtime that Monday, the soldiers were trans-shipped to *Sir Galahad*, to be greeted by the smiling faces of her largely Chinese crew. There was slight disappointment as most of the spare cabins had been wrecked by an unexploded bomb on the morning of the San Carlos landings. But there was ample compensation in the news that *Sir Galahad* would go all the way to Bluff Cove.

She would have no naval escorts and therefore no protection, but the theory was that the men would be ashore long before the Argentinians could mount an air attack.

It did not, of course, work out like that. Lieutenant Roberts was woken by a Chinese steward just before dawn, with a cup of tea. He was surprised to find that *Sir Galahad* was heading not towards Bluff Cove but up Port Pleasant towards Fitzroy settlement four miles away. That was because the direct channel to Bluff Cove was too shallow for *Sir Galahad* to navigate. Already at Fitzroy was one of her sister ships, *Sir Tristram*, which had earlier brought round supplies and equipment.

The beaches at Fitzroy settlement were far from ideal as landing sites because they were exceptionally narrow and led immediately to steep banks; at high tide, and for two hours either side of it, getting anything sizeable ashore was virtually impossible.

And so unloading the two ships took much longer than anticipated. The problem was aggravated by the lack of large landing craft. And for the Welsh Guards there was the additional problem that they did not want to go to Fitzroy at all.

On the map, Fitzroy and Bluff Cove are less than four miles apart but they are separated by a deep inlet, and the bridge that crosses it had been blown up by the Argentinians. If the men aboard *Sir Galahad* went ashore at Fitzroy, only 400 yards from where they were anchored, they faced a march of perhaps twelve miles. They therefore stayed on *Sir Galahad* waiting until landing craft might be free to take them direct to Bluff Cove.

Towards lunchtime, Ewen Southby-Tailyour arrived in one of his landing craft to be horrified by the sight of guardsmen still crowded on *Sir Galahad*. He was certain they were in grave danger. He sailed to the beach at Fitzroy to find a major from 5 Brigade and tried to impress upon him the need to get the Welsh Guards on land – any land – just as

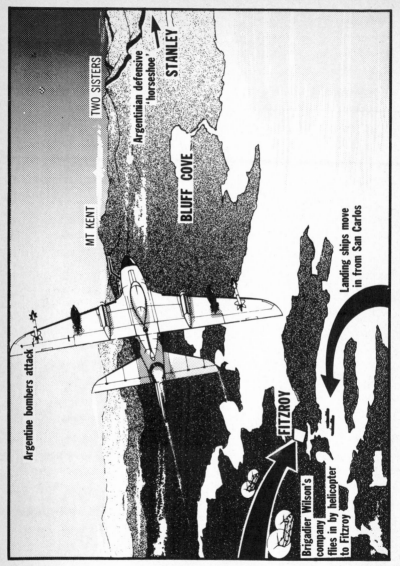

Argentine bombers attack

MT KENT

TWO SISTERS

Argentinian defensive 'horseshoe'

STANLEY

BLUFF COVE

FITZROY

Brigadier Wilson's company flies in by helicopter to Fitzroy

Landing ships move in from San Carlos

Disaster at Bluff Cove, June 8 1982

soon as possible. The major mistakenly insisted there were *no* guardsmen on *Sir Galahad*; he thought they had all been unloaded from *Fearless* the night before.

It was now too late to do anything. At 2.10 p.m., those on the shore at Fitzroy saw a Skyhawk appear at the mouth of Port Pleasant, as if from nowhere, fifty feet above the water; then came a second Skyhawk; then two Mirages. *Sir Galahad* and *Sir Tristram* were too far away for anyone even to shout a warning.

Lieutenant Roberts had gone below to talk to his platoon sergeant. He was about to return to *Sir Galahad*'s deck when the sergeant shouted: 'Get down.' There was a dull thudding bang and then the whole world seemed to explode. All around him Roberts could see people on fire; then he noticed his own hands were melting. It must have happened instantly but his brain registered every millisecond and he saw what was happening as though it was a slow-motion film. As the layers of his skin melted away, the colour of his hands turned from a bright pink to a dull grey. He realised that his hair was on fire and that the flames were licking his face and suffocating him; he tried to put them out with his hands.

The inside of *Sir Galahad* was like an inferno and cases of ammunition were exploding. A lot of men were screaming. But by the stairs that led to safety, others – fifteen or twenty – were lining up as though they were on parade. Roberts told them to go up the stairs one by one, and not panic because if anyone did they would all be trapped. They made it up to the deck where helicopters were already arriving through the swirling smoke to lift men off. Roberts could not get over the fact he was alive. What frightened him was the way people reacted when they looked at his face.

His orderly came and found him and said: 'We'll get you off, sir,' and led him to a ladder. The man wanted to carry him down to one of the life rafts below piggyback style but Roberts was terrified he would fall into the water because he was a hopeless swimmer. So he gritted his teeth and lowered himself down the ladder step by step.

When he finally reached the dinghy, his body felt as though it was in a pressure cooker. Then more helicopters arrived, the pilots attempting to use the draught of the rotor blades to drive the dinghies away from the flames and the continuing explosions. Through that act of extraordinary skill and courage they undoubtedly saved scores of lives at great risk to themselves; all Roberts could think about was the blessed relief which the draught provided for his hands.

By the time he got ashore, it was desperately cold. Even so he could not tolerate the blanket they tried to put around his shoulders. They put him in a helicopter and took him to a field station at Fitzroy where a medic injected him with morphine; he found the effect 'superb'.

Roberts was one of the luckier ones. He has had skin grafts and he will probably recover, in time.

Both *Sir Galahad* and *Sir Tristram* were hit by bombs in that attack. Thirty-three Welsh Guardsmen died. So did five of *Sir Galahad*'s crew and two of *Sir Tristram*'s. So did two Royal Navy engineers, four army engineers, two privates from the catering corps, two medics and a major from the Royal Army Medical Corps. Forty-six men were injured. It was easily the worst disaster the British suffered.

And it caused a great deal of anger among some officers and men of the land forces who felt that the Guards were totally unprepared for air attack. They were also angry at the decision of the navy to send unprotected ships as far west as Port Pleasant where they could easily be seen by sophisticated Argentinian radar positioned on top of Sapper Hill; doubly so because the Rapier batteries which might have provided some protection from land had only arrived at Fitzroy that morning, and were not fully operational.

In short, they believed that the Bluff Cove operation had been too hastily planned and badly executed.

But the navy was right about the threat from shore-based Exocets, as the cruiser *HMS Glamorgan* was to discover when she was hit by one on June 12. Thirteen of her crew were killed.

And, by establishing a second bridgehead at Bluff Cove, the British had created a third front which could attack from the south, thus tightening the noose around the Argentinian garrison. For that advantage, fifty lives may have been an acceptable price to pay.

Certainly, back in London, there was no slackening of resolve; only a stubborn refusal by the ministry of defence to release the casualty figures, on the grounds that to do so might give aid and comfort to the enemy.

Watching the push towards Stanley, the world now became concerned, not so much by whether the British would make it but by how magnanimous they would be in victory. Mrs Thatcher professed not to understand the question: 'Magnanimous. It is not a word I use in connection with a battle on the Falklands.'

The Americans were particularly concerned. For weeks President Reagan had been preparing for the most important European trip of his presidency. He would be attending a crucial summit meeting in the Palace of Versailles, then going on to visit most of the capitals of Europe. It would be disastrous from every point of view if the trip coincided not with a new dawn in American relations with Europe but with a bloodbath on the Falklands.

'I guess that if you guys wipe out Port Stanley as the president stands up to address the Houses of Parliament you can say goodbye to our relations with Latin America for the next decade,' sighed a weary state department official.

The American decision to back Britain with material assistance and impose sanctions against Argentina had not ended the debate about how the United States should handle the crisis. Indeed it had grown more vociferous. Jeane Kirkpatrick, who had remained silent in the National Security Council at the time, now argued that steps must be taken to repair the damage to relations with the rest of Latin America.

The Organisation of American States had held several meetings, some of them addressed by Costa Mendez, at which the United States had emerged as something of a pariah. Haig himself had had to sit through tirade after tirade of abuse, though it was significant that despite the verbal support given to Argentina, her request for military assistance had not met with an enthusiastic response from her neighbours.

Kirkpatrick held several meetings with Brigadier Jose Miret, Enrique Ros and Costa Mendez, though she was careful to clear these in advance with the state department and with the president, whom she briefed. These talks infuriated Haig. In the middle of one of them, enraged by the notion that she was somehow negotiating behind his back, he rang her up and railed at her for undermining his own policies. The conversation was duly leaked to *Newsweek* magazine.

Haig accused her of being 'mentally and emotionally incapable of thinking clearly on this issue' because of her close links with the Latins. She retorted that Haig was for his part incapable of understanding Latin American sensibilities. His team at the state department were just 'amateurs ... Brits in American clothes'. According to one source she viewed Haig's support for Britain as a 'Boy's Club vision of gang loyalty – why not just disband the state department and have the British foreign office make our policy?' she demanded.

In fact all Kirkpatrick had been trying to do was to steer the Argentinians at this late stage towards an accommodation which would save lives. She was struck both by the fact that they were still unable to accept the possibility of defeat, and that the British might now be less keen for a negotiated settlement than they had been before. When President Belaunde of Peru again stepped in to offer peace proposals, the Argentinians accepted them with enthusiasm, and were surprised to find the British giving them only token attention.

This may have been because attention had begun to focus again on the United Nations, where the British efforts to keep the matter from being raised at the security council were finally running out. Spain and Panama had proposed a resolution calling for a ceasefire and withdrawal, and it was proving impossible to stall it. By June 4, as the Reagan party settled down to their talks at Versailles, the debate was getting underway. It was clear that the British would use their veto to 'zap' the resolution, in Parsons' words, but there was some speculation about what the Americans would do. Although one veto is enough, the token value of the United States adding theirs would be considerable.

For most of the day Kirkpatrick had been lobbying the state department for permission to abstain on the vote. But, with Haig in Paris, there was no sign of flexibility. The instructions were that America should veto the resolution. Right up to the moment of the vote Kirkpatrick maintained an open line. Her aides were on the telephone to the state department, while the state department had an open wire to Haig in Paris.

In Paris, Haig, pressed hard by Tom Enders, finally wavered. The argument put to him was twofold: first, the resolution, as drafted, was a reasonable one, calling for a ceasefire and a withdrawal – to abstain on it would hardly be seen as a direct attack on Britain, and it would show a modicum of goodwill towards Latin America. As well as this, it might also just put a little pressure on Thatcher to discover a little magnanimity. Finally Haig agreed.

But the result was disastrous. Haig, who had been attending a dinner with the French, emerged just too late to transmit the change of instructions in time. At the United Nations, Kirkpatrick reluctantly raised her hand to join Britain in vetoing the resolution. Five minutes later a Kirkpatrick aide dashed in with the new instructions, and a startled security council listened as Kirkpatrick explained that America had meant to abstain on the vote. It was too late.

At the height of the hubbub, observers noticed Kirkpatrick passing a note to the phlegmatic Anthony Parsons sitting next to her. Was it an apology or an explanation? The truth is less prosaic. It was in fact a verse from a poem by the Argentinian Juan Luis Borges which Kirkpatrick intended to quote in a forthcoming speech. She was sure Sir Anthony would be interested. He was.

'Of course I'm embarrassed. Anyone would be,' said Kirkpatrick later. But although there were furious recriminations next day as America's alleged duplicity, or indecision, or both, was castigated in the British press, the effect on Anglo–American relations was negligible. When President Reagan flew to Britain three days later, he was greeted warmly by Thatcher, and by the Queen, with whom he went riding in Windsor Great Park. The prime minister described his reception as a triumph. 'This visit has been something more than an ordinary welcome,' she said. 'It has been an extraordinarily warm welcome which I think we must attribute to the way in which President Reagan has appealed to the hearts and minds of our people.'

But the remainder of Reagan's trip around Europe was, to an extent, eclipsed by the crisis. The Common Market's initial enthusiasm for the British case had waned and on May 17 both Italy and Ireland had refused to renew sanctions against Argentina. With all eyes turned to events on the Falklands, the presidential tour never turned into quite the triumph it was meant to be.

CHAPTER TWENTY-TWO

Advance on Stanley

'We are not facing terrifying spectacles
such as those of Hiroshima or Nagasaki,
but each time that we risk men's lives,
we trigger the mechanism that lead to such
catastrophes.'
– Pope John Paul II, June 1982

The church in Argentina had significantly changed its attitude to the war since the early days of the invasion. Writing in April, the Bishops of Argentina had proclaimed: 'We share the joy of our fellow citizens at the reclamation of our territory.' Now, on the eve of the Pope's visit to Argentina, they maintained that 'the defence of our legitimate rights and our national essence cannot be at the expense of others, nor against others'.

That summed up a great deal about the national mood in Argentina. The Malvinas no longer seemed to rouse the enthusiasm of a population that was showing all the signs of war-weariness. The news of the British disaster at Bluff Cove had been received without rejoicing. Even the official propaganda seemed muted, with the triumphal tones of earlier television programmes replaced by more sober calls to save power, fuel and food. The steady stream of bad news had induced a mood of defeat that threatened to become all-pervasive, and the Buenos Aires rumour machine, which had been reporting the *Hermes* or the *Invincible* sunk twice a day, now circulated stories of Argentinian casualties. 'My cousin is a doctor,' said one businessman, 'and he tells me that there were a thousand deaths two weeks ago.' 'Nonsense,' said his friend, 'five hundred at the most.' There was gloom too about another kind of bad news which would not go away. The gross national product of Argentina was down 5.7 per cent in the first quarter of the year; industrial production down 9.4 per cent; salaries down 20 per cent; investment cut back by 23.6 per cent. The ghost of Argentina's economy which Galtieri had tried to lay was back with a vengeance.

It was against this background that Pope John Paul II arrived in Buenos Aires on June 11 for the first visit ever made by a Pope to Argentina. It was a trip fraught with difficulties. Not only had the preparations been very much a last-minute affair, but the delicacy of the mission had exercised the Vatican's diplomats right up to the moment when the Pope stepped from his plane in a sudden shower of icy rain and kissed the tarmac at Ezeiza Airport.

On the one hand it was not intended to be an attempt at mediation – that would be 'a gross defamation of the visit' according to a member of the Curia in Rome. On the other hand, as a senior Argentinian diplomat pointed out, 'the Pope is not coming to Argentina just to pray'. He would have to meet President Galtieri as head of state, but he could not be seen to be supporting the politics of the junta's military adventure. And how would he deal with the plight of 'the disappeared ones?'

The truth, of course, was that the Pope had never planned to visit Argentina at this point at all – and certainly not in the middle of a war. It was a mission he had undertaken in order to balance the long-scheduled visit he had just paid to Britain. With the conflict over the Falklands deepening, he had been on the point of cancelling the British trip altogether, but after long agonising he had decided to carry on, ensuring even-handedness by travelling to Argentina as well.

The British visit had been a joyous occasion, marked throughout by vast singing crowds and full of bursts of spontaneous pleasure from thousands of catholics and non-catholics alike as the Pope preached a consistent message of peace. But messages of peace are, perhaps, more easy to accept when victory is just round the corner. Argentina, facing defeat, might not take to them so readily.

The Pope, however exhausted he appeared, was undaunted. 'I am the pilgrim of difficult moments,' he said, and of course, as soon as he saw the hundreds of thousands of Argentinians lining the route from the airport, braving the torrential rain in the Plaza de Mayo, and standing silently at the national shrine at Lujan, he knew that there was no question about the reception they would give him. The junta's attempts to capitalise on his visit were wrecked by the sheer momentum of the peoples' adoration.

'Allow me, from this very moment,' he said as he stepped up to the airport microphone, 'to invoke the peace of Christ on all victims of both sides left by the war conflict between Argentina and Great Britain.' The crowds cheered. The posters saying: 'Holy Father, Bless Our Just War' were overwhelmed by others proclaiming: 'Your Presence Will Bring Us Peace'. And when President Galtieri knelt to receive the papal blessing, any suggestion that this conveyed the Pope's approval of his invasion was dissolved by the speech that followed it. Galtieri stared rigidly ahead as the Pope said: 'Humanity should question itself once more about the absurd and always unfair phenomenon of war, on whose stage of death and pain only remains standing the negotiating table that could and should have prevented it.'

From then on, although he did briefly meet all three members of the junta, the Pope's attention was for the people who turned to him for comfort. 'Can he help us?' asked one newspaper. The answer, spiritually at least, seemed to be yes. 'Our Father Who Art In Argentina', ran one whole page headline. His references to the 'disappeared ones' were brief and enigmatic, but his condemnations of war were taken to apply to all wars, 'dirty' or otherwise.

At the end of an emotional thirty-two hours, as he prepared to leave Argentina, he stood before the final mass audience of his visit and issued a last appeal for peace: 'I call on those responsible in the two countries ... to restore above all to the families of both nations what they want most: life and serenity for their sons before new sacrifices make matters worse.'

The message fell on deaf ears. Even as the mass was being transmitted live on Argentinian television, it was interrupted by a hurried announcement. Word had come in from London and Buenos Aires that a new attack had been launched. The British, said the reports, had begun a fresh attack on Argentina's positions around Stanley. The final assault had begun. So, as the Pope's plane climbed into the sky, the presidential helicoptèr took Galtieri back to his waiting generals in the Casa Rosada and the focus of attention shifted abruptly back to the Falklands.

President Reagan had made one last attempt to persuade Mrs Thatcher to call off the final push for Stanley and spare the Argentinian garrison a military humiliation. Before returning to Washington from his European tour, he had telephoned her from Luxembourg.

'Now you are about to achieve your objective in Port Stanley...' he began. He never got any further. Briskly, Mrs Thatcher interrupted him. Victory, she said, was never 100 per cent certain. The British objective was to remove the Argentinians from the Falklands, and until that had been done it was pointless to speculate about the future. There was a battle to be fought, she told him, and it was about to begin. 'Let us deal with one problem at a time.' The president attempted one more lame interruption, then made a strategic withdrawal. As he hung up, he turned to his aides and shrugged. There was to be no halting the final battle now.

It was planned, and fought, on the classic lines laid down in the British army infantry manual in which the principles and practice of attacking a well dug-in enemy are those still taught at the School of Infantry at Warminster. They have been the basis for most battle plans since 1940.

'This will be a straightforward, no-nonsense Warminster style attack,' said Captain Mark Stevens, press officer attached to 3 Commando Brigade, as he briefed reporters in a lean-to greenhouse at Teal

Inlet. 'We will get everything together, pound their positions with gunfire, then go in on a night-time attack.'

That, strictly speaking, is what happened. It gives absolutely no hint of the scale and intensity of what was to take place over the next forty-eight hours. Nor can it possibly evoke the extraordinary picture of men fighting a battle using methods and tactics which were not just those familiar forty years ago, but were uncannily reminiscent of the First World War. They left an indelible impression on all who witnessed or participated in them.

Lieutenant Colonel Hew Pike of 3 Para still recalls the image of soldiers advancing at dawn on the morning of June 12, through thick mist – with bayonets fixed. They had stormed some Argentinian positions and had killed a number of the defenders in hand-to-hand combat. Now they were clearing the area. 'With their bayonets on their rifles, these young soldiers looking grim and determined, moving forward through the thick mist of dawn. It is a sight I shall never forget,' he says. 'A lot of the enemy were killed with those bayonets.'

There had been two plans discussed for taking the rough parabola of rugged hills and ridges which lay between the British advance and Stanley. The relative ease with which Mount Kent had been taken fooled no one. All the intelligence suggested that the Argentinians had made full use of the high ground of such hills as Mount Longdon, Mount Harriet, Two Sisters and Wireless Ridge to dig in and prepare the best defensive positions. The area was well within range of the big 155 mm guns which the Argentinians were constantly moving from base to base around Stanley. And the troops manning the trenches were by no means all untrained conscripts. They included hardened marines, armed, as the British were to find, with some very sophisticated equipment.

The first plan, favoured by General Moore and Brigadier Wilson, was for an attack on a narrow front against the peaks of Mount Harriet, Mount Longdon and the Two Sisters, which dominate the land approach to Stanley. It would be a thrust aimed between Argentinian positions using two battalions to establish sufficient momentum to carry them through to Stanley without spreading the troops too widely.

The alternative was proposed by Brigadier Thompson. It envisaged attacking on a wider front, using single battalions to take on specific objectives. These would include Tumbledown Mountain to the south-west of Stanley, and Wireless Ridge to the north, as well as the other heights overlooking the town. It might be slower, but it would be more systematic. Once again, Thompson had his way.

The build-up was agonisingly slow. It took ten days, from the decision taken at Brigade HQ at Teal Inlet, to the final point where Thompson was satisfied with his dispositions. The delay was due

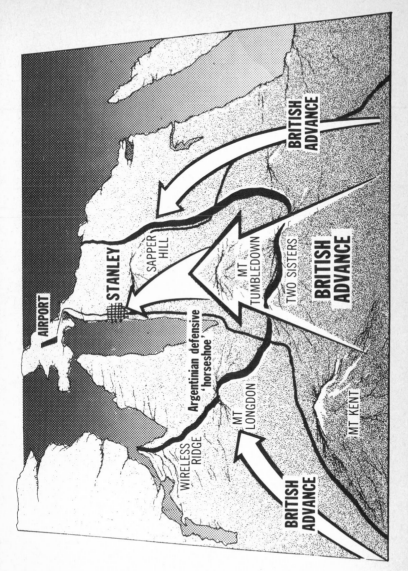

British advance on Stanley, June 12–14, 1982

245

partly to the appalling weather, but was exacerbated by helicopter shortages. After the intensity of the Argentinian artillery bombardment at Goose Green, Thompson was determined to take no chances. He doubled the number of shells for the gun batteries, giving each of the five batteries, with their six guns apiece, a total of 1,200 shells. The helicopters ferrying all this equipment forward from Teal Inlet and Ajax Bay thus had their work cut out, and there was considerable rivalry for their services between 3 Commando Brigade, 5 Brigade and the SAS.

But there was, undeniably, another reason for delay. The disaster at Bluff Cove had not only been a tactical set back, it had been a harsh reminder of the horrors of war. It redoubled the British effort to persuade the Argentinian garrison to surrender before more blood was shed. Radio appeals, read in Spanish by Captain Roderick Bell, were sent out calling on General Menendez to agree surrender terms. For two days Harriers dropped warning leaflets on Stanley spelling out the reality of the garrison's position, and at one stage there was even a plan to send a delegation, which would have included Robert Fox of the BBC, into Stanley to explain personally to Menendez just what was now at stake. It came to nothing.

By Friday, June 11, there had been no response to these appeals, and the effect of the delay, combined with the freezing nights and the sporadic bombardment from Argentinian artillery, had begun to lead to frustration. A Scots Guards platoon was forced to withdraw under heavy artillery fire, and 42 Commando suffered their first casualties since moving forward when they were hit by enemy shells. For 45 Commando there was a greater tragedy. A patrol sent out to reconnoitre enemy positions made what is known as a 'friendly/ friendly' contact (sometimes called a 'blue on blue' contact) and ran into its own mortar section. A fierce fire-fight broke out, leaving five dead and two serious casualties before the mistake was realised and the shooting stopped.

The time came to move forward. The battle plan envisaged two phases. The first was to be launched early on Saturday morning, June 12, and go on to dawn. The second, originally planned for Sunday morning, was postponed until Monday, June 14. There were three main objectives:

1. 3 Para were to take the 600 foot heights of Mount Longdon, five miles west of Stanley. Grouped behind them were 2 Para, the Welsh Guards and two companies of 40 Commando who were to hold back until Phase Two. Naval gun support was to come from *HMS Avenger*. Longdon was considered to be the most heavily defended position and it was felt that 3 Para were in for the toughest battle of all. The prediction was *almost* right – there was to be just one that was even harder.

2. 42 Commando were deployed mainly on Mount Challenger, just to the south of Mount Kent, and thus seven miles from Stanley. Their objectives were to take Mount Harriet and Goat Ridge, west of Stanley, two 900 and 750 foot high hills marked by craggy outcrops of rock. They would be given support by *HMS Yarmouth*. Grouped behind them were the Scots Guards and the Gurkhas who were to see action in Phase Two.

3. 45 Commando were deployed on the far western and northern slopes of Mount Kent. They were to cross the hill and attack the Two Sisters range just west of Stanley with support from *HMS Glamorgan*.

All these units were to be protected by an arc of 105 mm gun batteries ranged in a crescent around the west slopes of Mount Kent facing Stanley. The thunder of artillery fire had begun two nights before the attack and over the next three days it was to be a merciless and sustained onslaught on the Argentinian positions. In the course of it hundreds of shells were to pound down on the trenches, bunkers, dug-outs and caves which sheltered conscripts and commandos alike.

All battle plans, when set out in the crisp and tersely composed language of a military order, have an apparently unassailable logic about them. There seems no possibility that the action can turn out in any way other than that envisaged. It is only when the 'start line' is crossed that things begin to lose coherence.

3 Para were the first to run into the unexpected. For ten days they had been reconnoitring the steep ridges and fortress crags of Mount Longdon, and they thought they had identified most of the deep-running streams, and open areas where anti-personnel mines had clearly been laid. They hoped to mount a swift and silent advance, with 'A' and 'B' Companies moving up the hill in a pincer movement to north and south. 'C' Company was to be held in reserve.

As 3 Para's commanding officer Hew Pike tersely put it: 'That was the plan.'

The surprise was lost when a corporal in 'B' Company stepped on an anti-personnel mine as they were crossing open ground, some 700 yards from the first of the Argentinian trenches. The blast shattered his leg and in the darkness it was impossible to see what lay ahead. Immediately the enemy opened up with a barrage of machine-gun fire, mortars and artillery.

It fell, inaccurately, around and beyond 'B' Company who managed to get a foothold on an outcrop of rocks just 100 feet below Longdon's summit.

In the typically sporting jargon that military men hold dear, the two objectives 3 Para were aiming for were termed 'Full Back' and 'Fly Half', both positions in a rugby football team. 'Full Back' to the eastern side of the summit, was a ridge held by Argentinian machine-gun and sniper units. Here the second unpleasant surprise awaited both companies as they closed on it. It was clear that the Argentinians were equipped with extremely effective night-sights allowing them to shoot with uncomfortable accuracy. In fact, it transpired that they were far better equipped in this respect than the British. They had what are known as passive night-goggles, a form of binoculars which are US-made and give an appearance of bright daylight in the darkest of nights. (The British had a few dozen pairs; the Argentinians had hundreds.) 'A' Company, who had secured a steep ridge to the north-east of the summit, now found themselves pinned down from the direction of 'Full Back'. One soldier was shot dead by a sniper bullet through the head. There was clearly going to be no speedy advance.

The hour needed a hero, and it found one in a marine gunner, Captain Willie McCracken, the Forward Observation Officer with 'B' Company, who now began to direct gunfire from naval guns to complement the 66 mm and Karl Gustav anti-tank weapons which had been brought forward to hit the Argentinian positions. He did it with pin-point accuracy, the shells falling sometimes only fifty yards ahead of 'B' Company's own troops.

'Inevitably, in a battle like this, our own soldiers did become endangered from our own fire,' said Colonel Pike. 'I think they were the closest rounds I've ever experienced. Some of them were *extremely* close. But we had no casualties from our own batteries, and that speaks volumes for the skill of our gunners.'

Pike himself now moved up to join 'B' Company's commanding officer, Major Mike Argue. He found that the firing from the company's second objective, the ridge they had labelled 'Fly Half' was, if anything, even better protected.

One enemy bunker, defended by a heavy 0.5 machine-gun and a number of Argentinian riflemen, was pouring down a stream of deadly fire onto 'B' Company's position below it. A platoon, led by Lieutenant Andrew Bickerdike, moved forward to silence it. Bickerdike was almost immediately shot through the leg. Sergeant Ian McKay, a twenty-nine-year-old from Aldershot, took command. He found himself in a little valley of dead ground, his position raked with heavy fire from a number of positions. Rallying his remaining men, he launched an attack on the bunker which was fifty yards ahead of him.

One of his corporals, Ian Bailey, shot through the legs and stomach, tumbled into the bunker itself, still firing. McKay worked his way round to a position behind and above the bunker, threw two grenades into it, then fell dead across its mouth. Finally, the Argentinian fire was silenced.

Around them other platoons were engaged in similar actions. Lieutenant Mark Cox, another platoon commander, using anti-tank gunfire, grenades and finally bayonets, cleared another position, Cox himself accounting for three of the enemy. 'It really demonstrates the highest possible forms of bravery and determination and tactical skill to close with those kinds of positions,' says Pike. 'Because until one did, the Argentines just went on fighting ...'

By this stage, 'B' Company was in desperate need of reinforcement and 'A' Company, under Major David Collett was moved up through their position. Here, too, there was danger. 'A' Company found itself in a narrow defile with the Argentinians tossing grenades down into it. There was no chance of outflanking the pass because of the snipers with their night-sights. 'The only thing to do was to pass a platoon one at a time, more or less frontally, fighting along it just a bite at a time,' recalled Pike.

The men of 3 Para had been in action for six hours by the time 'Fly Half' was in their hands. 'Full Back' took a further four hours. The fighting by then had become hand-to-hand, and it was as dawn came up in a thick all-enveloping mist at about seven o'clock, that Pike witnessed the almost surreal sight of men moving grimly forward towards yet another position, their bayonets fixed.

By the time Mount Longdon had finally been taken, 3 Para had lost twenty-three men killed and forty-seven wounded. The Argentinians, many of them bayoneted, lost more than fifty. There were thirty-nine prisoners but only ten wounded. It was a very complete revenge.

Argentinian resistance elsewhere that night was not so sustained. 42 Commando, on Mount Harriet, led by Lieutenant Colonel Nick Vaux, used their Milan wire-guided missiles, with mortar flares illuminating the targets, as a means of eliminating machine-gun nests. 'It was a pretty expensive way of doing it,' admits Vaux (each missile costs around £20,000), 'but our job was to get rid of them.'

Even so, advancing up the slopes of Harriet was a slow and bloody business.

Kim Sabido, the IRN reporter, who was watching the action, says: 'For a couple of hours it seemed as if it might all go wrong. Pinned down on the slopes by heavy machine-gun and sniper fire, progress was painfully slow. I saw several men fall with bullet wounds, others were hit by flying fragments from the constant barrage of long distance high-explosive shelling. The men in front of us were not giving up without a bitter fight.'

There was one moment of humour in an otherwise grim night. Sabido had grown friendly with the only Argyll and Sutherland Highlander in the Falklands, Lieutenant Ian Stafford, who was on attachment to the marines. In the middle of the fighting, Sabido saw Stafford being carried down the hill, wounded. He had been hit in the leg, was in great pain, and had been injected with morphine.

'I was standing there, feeling slightly inadequate,' recalls Sabido 'and I offered him some water. I could see he was in a lot of pain and I didn't know what to say, but he looked up and he said, "Stuff this for a game of darts, Kim." And I just broke down laughing and he chuckled, and it seemed to sum up the whole situation.'

In the course of that night Colonel Vaux and others from 42 Commando watched something extraordinary. From a position overlooking Port Stanley they saw a streak of light ('like a car's headlights,' said one witness), moving at first quite slowly, down over the beach, then heading out to sea, picking up speed. It was an Exocet missile fired from an Argentinian shore-based battery towards *Glamorgan*, which was standing out to sea bombarding Argentinian positions in support of 45 Commando. *Glamorgan* saw it too, and fired off Sea Cat missiles in a desperate attempt to shoot it down. The Sea Cats missed, and moments later the watchers on the hill saw a bright flash and a dull explosion. Unlike the *Sheffield*, *Glamorgan* survived, badly holed, to continue her task.

As day broke, Colonel Vaux could see that Mount Harriet was theirs. 'A sergeant major turned to me and said, "There's a good many lads seeing a dawn they never thought they'd live to see," ' recalls Sabido. 'Sadly,' he adds, 'there are quite a few on both sides who didn't.' Argentinian losses were unspecified but heavy. 42 Commando lost only one man, and some 200 prisoners were taken.

On Two Sisters, 45 Commando had already established their position, with the loss of four men. Like the others, as they sank exhausted into their new positions, they found themselves under constant harrying fire from the Argentinians' big guns. Nevertheless, Phase One could be counted an out-and-out success. Brigade Headquarters sent out a message which may not go down in history as supremely eloquent, but said it tersely enough: 'Well done, today you achieved a major breakthrough.' It was by no means over.

That message was one of the last that the main Brigade Headquarters, sited on the slopes of Mount Kent, was able to send. Late on the afternoon of Saturday, June 12, as Thompson and Moore conferred about the next stage of the battle, two Skyhawks came screaming over the top of the hill and dived straight towards them. The major general dived into a hole, and the brigadier dropped in on top of him. Just as he was apologising profusely for the inconvenience, Patrick Bishop, reporter for *The Observer*, dived on top of both of them. Democracy of a kind was established. Main Brigade HQ immediately packed up and started moving forward. The second phase was now about to begin, run by Julian Thompson's Tactical HQ.

This was to involve the taking of the last three hills above Port Stanley, and though by this time the Argentinians were clearly in retreat, the fiercest battle of all was on the point of taking place. Meanwhile, the big 155 mm guns around Stanley were still causing havoc among the British positions. 'Stonking' is not a widely familiar term, but it was one used with some feeling by Major Chris Keeble as, with 2 Para, he started moving forward to take Wireless Ridge, to the north of Stanley. 'These 155s started stonking the area here in front of the company's position,' he said. 'They are nasty, vicious, unpleasant things. They chuck out a huge shell, and they were just stonking the whole area.'

There was no word of what the Argentinians felt about the 'stonking' they had been receiving solidly for the past three days from British artillery which was firing some equally unpleasant bits of hardware including air-burst and phosphorus shells. They also faced, for the first time, the light tanks, Scimitars and Scorpions sent forward to back up 2 Paras' advance. They did not offer an enormous amount of resistance.

'We attacked an objective which had been shelled and continued to be shelled when we arrived,' said Lieutenant Colonel David Chaundler, who had been flown from Britain to take over as commanding officer of 2 Para following the death of Colonel 'H' Jones at Goose Green. (His arrival, by parachute into the sea, caused ill-feeling among some paras who thought that Keeble should have stayed in command.) Chandler added: 'It was cruel because it not only killed a lot of Argentinians but at the end not an awful lot stayed to fight. A lot of them pushed off. They panicked and ran which then had an effect on the others.'

The attack left 2 Para almost within touching distance of Stanley. It was a position they were to take full advantage of.

There was to be no Argentinian retreat, however, on Tumbledown Mountain, eight miles to the south, where, on that same night, the Scots Guards were to face the toughest action of all. There a well trained Argentinian marine battalion was heavily dug into a series of intricate bunkers, cut in the rock. Some of them were sufficiently ingenious to have improvised bunks and a recreation bay, supported by wood and corrugated iron frames. The firepower of the marines was intense and impressive.

Again the tactics used by the British were classic and traditional. Major John Kiszely, aged thirty-four, in command of the 'Left Flank' Company of the Scots Guards, summed up one piece of the action in a terse description which would have been recognised anywhere and any time from Verdun to Vimy Ridge:

'My plan was to have one platoon go up into the crags to take the high ground at the northern section of the ridge and another platoon to take the lower section – both moving easterly in a parallel formation. As the first platoon went into the upper crags, I was with the platoon lower down. We were opened up on from about 300 metres by a couple of machine-guns. The platoon led by Lieutenant Alastair Mitchell put in a section attack but it was beaten back. The section has two groups, one with a general purpose machine-gun while the rest make a flanking attack – that's text book stuff. They have to skirmish through the position and get stuck in with their rifles and bayonets. They had bayonets fixed from the start. They throw grenades into the trenches and then mop up. There is no messing around. It is a question of getting on and keeping going.'

There were some amazing pieces of luck as the Guards moved forward. One platoon found an Argentinian communications cable and simply followed it until it led to an enemy trench where a small unit of snipers was taken unawares. A guardsman, nineteen-year-old Richard Shaw, had three magazines in his top left hand breast pocket which stopped a bullet. The blow knocked him over, throwing him back some ten yards. Shaw thought: 'I'm dying.' But he was unhurt. He still has the magazines. Kiszely himself had a compass hanging over his hip pocket which took the full impact of a bullet and scarcely hurt him at all.

The advance was dogged and slow, from ridge to ridge, with noise and confusion in the dark the predominant features and the continued barrage of artillery fire drowning out orders. At one stage, Kiszely found himself advancing slowly through the night, at the head of his platoon, towards an enemy trench.

'Are you with me, 15 platoon?' he shouted. There was no answer. Kiszely suddenly felt very lonely.

'Come on, 15 platoon, are you with me?' he shouted again, rather more uncertainly.

Then there was a welcome shout on his left: 'Aye, sir, I'm with you.'

And then there was an even more welcome shout to his right: 'Aye, sir, I'm fucking with you as well.'

Kiszely knew they would be all right.

Soon afterwards he used his bayonet, for the first time in his life, to kill a man. It is not something he remembers with pride. It was a matter of sheer necessity. 'We did fix bayonets because I believe bayonets kill people and are useful,' he said. 'It certainly saved my life. As we were charging up, I looked round and saw coming out of a hole in the ground – not a trench, but a hole – this figure with a weapon, almost from behind. I swung round and pulled the trigger. I heard the click. What you're meant to do is count your rounds – twenty rounds in a magazine and you count from one to twenty. Of course, it doesn't work like that. "Click". So there was only one thing to do and without a moment's hesitation you do it. I struck him in the chest and he fell back into the hole. At the time it did not shock me. I was too busy. Immediately afterwards I didn't bother to wonder whether he was dead or anything else and I ran on. Looking back on it now, it is not something I am proud of at all. I knew he was going to kill me but I derive no pleasure from sticking a bayonet into another person.'

Events on that advance grew more and more bizarre – and ever more dangerous. Kiszely, with 'Left Flank' Company, was headed for a ridge overlooking Stanley where he would link up with 'Right Flank' Company. But as his group pressed on it grew smaller and smaller. Several of his men were shot in the back by snipers in positions they had already overrun, but whom they had failed to see in the dark. They took prisoners, shouting 'Manos Arriba' ('Hands Up'), or 'Rindanse' ('Surrender') but each time they did so at least one British soldier had to be left behind to guard them. Still others waited behind to look after the wounded.

As the much diminished 'Left Flank' group finally broke through to their objective, they realised they were looking down onto the lights of Stanley.

'I stood stock still,' said Kiszely. 'It was amazing. I never imagined seeing Stanley lit up. We were so close we could see the grid plan of the streets, with vehicles moving. I could not believe my eyes.' Suddenly, they realised they were a static target. A machine-gun opened up and three men fell badly wounded, including the platoon commander Alastair Mitchell. There were now only four men out of the original company left to hold the ridge until reinforcements arrived. It turned out to be just about enough but it had been an expensive operation. The Scots Guards lost a total of nine killed and forty-one wounded, for an estimated thirty Argentinians killed.

By now other positions were beginning to fall more easily. The Gurkhas, thirsting for action, found to their disgust that Mount William, their objective, had been surrendered almost without a fight, and the Welsh Guards, after an unpleasant night during which they took six hours to cross a minefield, being shelled the whole time, were able to move forward to Sapper Hill without encountering much resistance. John Witherow, staff reporter of The Times, and attached to the Welsh Guards, talked to a young Argentinian prisoner, Antonio, aged twenty, from northern Argentina, who said that for the past week Argentinian soldiers had been moving out of their positions and back towards Stanley. They were in no mood for a fight. Antonio himself was delighted it was all over. As they talked, Harrier jets were launching cluster bombs onto Tumbledown Mountain, using laser-guided bombing techniques. The terrible impact of these weapons tore up hundreds of metres of ground at a time causing huge rolling explosions. Witherow could sympathise with Antonio.

The naval bombardment, too, was both continuous and deadly. On one occasion, it had spelt tragedy for the inhabitants of Stanley.

On June 11, John Fowler, the young superintendent of education, went and stood at his front gate and watched British shells landing in a pattern on the foothills beyond Moody Brook. As the day wore on, the shells got closer to the town. By dusk, the shells were coming over Moody Brook and splashing into the waters of Stanley Harbour beyond it. Fowler thought it was going to be a rough night. He rounded up his neighbours and they settled in to get some sleep on the floor of the front room. They were woken by the louder sound of naval gunfire coming from British ships anchored out to sea. Fowler put the time at around midnight but concedes he could be wrong. 'Everyone was pretty exhausted and confused by that stage of the game,' he said later. Fowler went into the kitchen to make some coffee; Veronica, his wife, stood in the doorway talking to him.

Suddenly there was a thunderous roar and a shell came through the roof into the front room throwing furniture across the house. Two of the people sleeping on the floor – Doreen Burns and Sue Whitney – were killed instantly. The third, Mary Goodwin – at eighty-two the oldest inhabitant of Stanley – sat up with blood pouring down her face. The blast peppered Veronica Fowler's back with shrapnel, and her husband, standing in the kitchen, felt an intense pain as fragments of splintered metal embedded themselves in his lower legs. Veronica rushed into the front room and embraced Mary. They were both in tears. A few seconds later, Mary died in Veronica's arms. The three women were the only islanders to die in the final assault.

A few days later, Major-General Jeremy Moore went to see the Fowler's and apologised for the bombing and the deaths. Moore told them the British had understood there was no one living in the houses west of the War Memorial.

On Monday, June 14, the Welsh Guards began the final approach to Sapper Hill. John Witherow recalls the almost eerie impression they had of deserted positions, with abandoned sleeping bags and equipment everywhere. 'There was so sign of life either on the mountain or the surrounding countryside,' he recalled. 'Nobody seemed to know what was happening. One officer reported a white flag over Stanley, and we began marching, almost running down the road towards the distant Sapper Hill. There was a mood of excitement and apprehension – like the end of term. It was a cold windy day with sleet showers and thin sunshine.'

When they reached the hill, the Guards' commanding officer, Colonel Johnny Rickett, commented: 'I'm very pleased and proud of my men. But I was surprised when this happened. We were expecting at least another couple of days' fighting.'

Just then Brigadier Wilson flew in, in a small scout helicopter, with a celebratory bottle of scotch. He made a small speech as he looked down on the straggling houses of Stanley: 'It is a splendid feeling after this long and tough series of battles on the islands over what has been a considerable distance of singularly inhospitable country that it should come to end like this. There is no doubt that the men against us were very tough, competent soldiers and many died at their posts. We've lost an awful lot of men.'

CHAPTER TWENTY-THREE

Surrender (II)

'There is little point in your continuing the struggle.
A decision to give up should be made now.
This is no reflection on the bravery and skill
of your soldiers.'
– British appeal to Argentinian troops, June 1982

'We always thought Menendez was soft. You could
tell from his photographs.'
– SAS officer, June 1982

At 10 a.m. on Sunday, June 6, Dr Alison Bleaney, a young, redheaded woman from the Isle of Skye, sitting in the radio-telephone office in Stanley's John Street, received the shock of her life. Bleaney was effectively the senior medical officer at Stanley Hospital – her boss, Dr Daniel Haines, had been banished to West Falkland – and each morning answered medical queries from islanders via the Falklands radio-telephone network, the only purpose for which the Argentinians allowed it to be used. She was dispensing her customary reassurance on coughs, colds, and minor ailments when her call was abruptly interrupted by a voice which announced, in faultless Spanish: 'This is a staff officer of the British military headquarters calling Stanley'.

Bleaney's first thought was that a practical joker had come on the line, and she instructed it to get off. But when the voice defiantly repeated its message, this time in English, she realised it really *was* the British. Displaying admirable presence of mind, she telephoned the Argentinian military headquarters and asked the senior naval officer, Captain Melbourne Hussey, to come to the office. Hussey hurried over just as the British voice called back. It explained it wished to discuss humanitarian issues: the safety of civilians, the evacuation of wounded Argentinian soldiers. Hussey listened intently and replied that he understood, but he could not discuss anything until he had talked to his government. In that case, the voice replied, it would call back tomorrow. The line went dead. But the first step in a surrender process that was to last nine days had been taken.

On the command ship *Fearless*, Captain Roderick Bell and an SAS colonel we have named Reid switched off their microphone with evident satisfaction; their plan had taken root. Ever since sailing from Britain, both had argued strongly that psychological operations – 'psy ops' in the military jargon – could help minimise casualties on the way to victory. Bell held that belief with particular passion, for he was the son of a United Nations official, raised and schooled in Costa Rica, and Spanish was his first language: he felt that he understood the Latin American temperament and could 'talk to the enemy as friends'. Reid – aged forty-two, an Oxford graduate in politics, philosophy and economics – shared Thompson's view that the Argentinians could be persuaded rather than compelled to give up. His experience spoke volumes: he had directed negotiations at the Iranian embassy siege in 1980, and two months before leaving for the Falklands had successfully ended a hijack at London's Stansted airport.

Convincing the more orthodox military mind had not been easy. The 'psychological' approach had appeared to suffer a serious setback at Fanning Head, when Bell's attempt to talk the Argentinians into surrender had ended in a gunfight and the apparent escape of most of the enemy soldiers. Thompson had taken a hard line after that, forbidding Bell to try his technique at Goose Green. But when a British patrol found twelve Argentinian bodies on Fanning Head, demonstrating that few if any had managed to escape, Thompson withdrew his opposition. Bell and Reid then argued their case before Moore who, although sceptical, agreed to allow them a second chance.

And so, punctually at 10 each morning from June 6 onwards, Bell and Reid dispatched their appeals, their messages subtly shifting day by day. They began with their simple humanitarian request to assist civilians and casualties, but later hinted at the Argentinians' hopeless military situation. They evoked the Argentinians' sense of honour: they had fought a noble war and could surrender with their dignity intact. Gradually they raised wider issues: Britain and Argentina needed to be friends and a small offshore war should not be allowed to undermine that.

Although Bell and Reid were reasonably confident that their approach was correct, they suffered from one major frustration. They had no idea what effect their campaign was having since, naturally enough, the Argentinians made no response. But Bell and Reid were sure the Argentinians were at least *listening* to their appeals, if only because the rest of Stanley was. Stanley's radio-telephone operator Eileen Vidal, who like Bell spoke perfect Spanish – she was married to a Chilean – had been ordered by the Argentinians not to pick up the calls. She ignored this instruction and even began to interrupt Bell with the words: 'I'm not supposed to be talking to you, but ...' Her preamble became Stanley's catch-phrase of the moment, locals using it to greet each other in the street.

As the British tightened their military grip around Stanley, Bell's appeals became more weighty and earnest. On June 12, with the

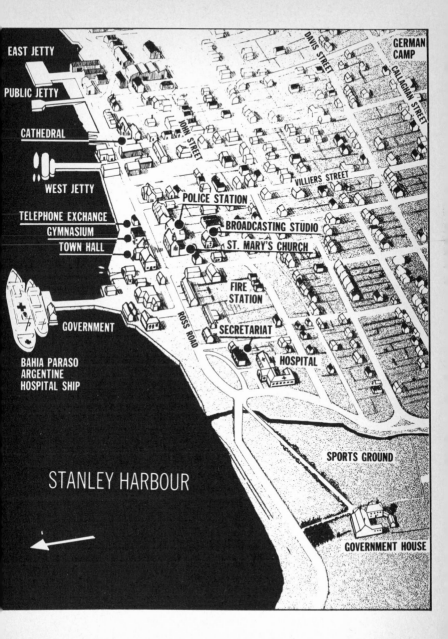

EAST JETTY

PUBLIC JETTY

CATHEDRAL

WEST JETTY

TELEPHONE EXCHANGE
GYMNASIUM
TOWN HALL

GOVERNMENT

BAHIA PARASO
ARGENTINE
HOSPITAL SHIP

STANLEY HARBOUR

DAVIS STREET

GERMAN
CAMP

CALLAGHAN STREET

JOHN STREET

VILLIERS STREET

POLICE STATION

BROADCASTING STUDIO

ST. MARY'S CHURCH

FIRE
STATION

SECRETARIAT

ROSS ROAD

HOSPITAL

SPORTS GROUND

GOVERNMENT HOUSE

257

artillery bombardment intensifying, he announced: 'In spite of our previous efforts, we are now forced to accept the fact that you in the Argentine forces are not going to answer us by this means following the initial contacts. However, it would be irresponsible of us, and history would judge us to be negligent, if we did not at this moment in the battle for Stanley make the following points . . .' Bell then repeated his request for talks over civilian evacuation. There was still no response.

The next day, Sunday June 13, with the British at Stanley's gates, Bell was even more forceful, pointing out that the Argentinians were suffering losses and, since the high ground around the town was in British hands, would be 'unable to prevent these losses continuing'. At noon on June 14 he made a final sonorous appeal. 'The position of the Argentine forces is now hopeless. You are surrounded by British forces on all sides . . . We believe that a meeting should now take place on a link kept open between the two opposing forces. If you fail to respond to this message and there is unnecessary bloodshed in Port Stanley, the world will judge you accordingly.'

For once, there could be no doubt that Hussey heard Bell's words: he was in the John Street office at the time. His presence there was the result of a decisive intervention by Alison Bleaney. Appalled by the events of the weekend – three islanders had been killed by British shells, Moody Brook had been bombed, and machine-gun fire seemed to be 'everywhere' – she had visited Hussey early on Monday morning and implored him to respond to the British overtures. Although Hussey stalled, her words seemed to strike home. When the British called as usual at 10 a.m., Bleaney pleaded with them to call again at noon, and they did so. She now telephoned Hussey and begged him to come to the office. Hussey arrived within moments and although he declined to talk directly to the British, he heard their final dramatic appeal.

Even now Hussey seemed unsure what to do. In desperation, Bleaney intervened again, shouting that he must do *something* or everyone would be killed. Although Hussey repeated that he could do nothing 'without instructions', he said at last that he would speak to General Menendez. At 1 p.m. precisely he returned to John Street with a vital message for the British: Menendez would talk. But just what Menendez intended to say no longer seemed to matter. For outside, white flags were already flying over Stanley.

Events now moved quickly to their conclusion, although not without moments of both humour and alarm. On *Fearless*, as *The Sunday Times* reporter John Shirley noted in his diary, surrender seemed to be 'the one moment no one has prepared for'. A Gazelle helicopter was readied to take Bell and Reid into Stanley for preliminary negotiations but no one could work out how to display a white flag: in the end a folded white parachute was suspended from its belly. Alongside the Gazelle, the Sea King in which General Moore would follow if all went well was similarly prepared with large white squares of masking tape, which only adhered after six weeks' accretion of oil and muck had been scraped away.

When the Gazelle clattered into Stanley it nearly jeopardised the entire delicate negotiating process by landing in the wrong place, 500 yards from the soccer pitch by Stanley Hospital where the Argentinians were waiting. As Bell and Reid crossed fields and crawled through hedges, Hussey came forward to greet them. 'We saw you landing in the wrong place,' he told them. 'We don't know Stanley quite as well as you,' Bell replied. Alison Bleaney was watching from the hospital balcony and caught Reid's eye. 'You Alison?' he called out. 'Yes,' she replied. Reid told her: 'You're doing a great job.'

Bell and Reid went directly to the office Menendez occupied in government house. Although the talks were later described as 'stiff and formal', it did not take long to establish that there would be no more fighting. Menendez at first declined to surrender West Falkland too, but then relented; and both sides agreed to halt air and sea hostilities while the Argentinian forces were shipped home, regardless of overall relations between their two governments. Menendez made a last request: he wanted to remain with his troops until they left the Falklands but Reid, having consulted *Fearless*, said this would not be allowed. Menendez cried a little before pouring himself a stiff consolatory drink. Then he stood stiffly to attention and shook Bell and Reid by the hand.

By now other British representatives were in town. One of them had actually arrived ahead of Bell and Reid, the indomitable Max Hastings, who had made the final advance to Stanley with 2 Para. While 2 Para were ordered to halt a tantalising mile away, Hastings discarded his military clothes, donned a blue sailing jersey, and walked into Stanley with his hands raised high above his head. He said afterwards: 'It was like liberating a suburban golf club.' Reuter's Leslie Dowd, arriving soon after Hastings, met a more enthusiastic reception. Still wearing his camouflage uniform he burst into Stanley Hospital, where he was mobbed by an ecstatic group of nurses. 'It's a British soldier!' they screamed in delight.

Three hours later Major-General Moore landed in Stanley, visibly shaken after his Sea King had flown through a snow storm en route. But he strode boldly up the steps of government house to meet Menendez, surrender document in one hand and a bottle of scotch in the other. Menendez made one of the more celebrated amendments of military history when he deleted the word 'unconditional' before 'surrender', but it was that in all but name. Thirty minutes later an exhausted but beaming Moore reappeared on the steps to flourish the document to the waiting crowd. Then he read out the following dispatch:

'In Port Stanley at 9 p.m. Falklands time tonight, June 14 1982,

Major General Menendez surrendered to me all Argentine forces in East and West Falkland, together with their impedimenta. Arrangements are in hand to assemble their arms and equipment and to mark and make safe their munitions. The Falkland Islands are once more under the government desired by their inhabitants. God save the Queen.'

The crowd surged forward and hoisted Moore on to their shoulders. The elated general was somewhat bemused to find himself swept on a politician's tour of Stanley, kissing babies, shaking hands, and downing tea and alcohol until well into the night.

There were other formalities to attend to. Several flags were already flying in Stanley when Major Mike Norman stepped forward to the flagpole at Government House. In truth, he had had an unobtrusive war, seeming to be invariably consigned to support duties and taking part in no real action. He nonetheless intended to fulfil his pledge that after being ignominiously ejected three months before, he would return in due honour to raise a flag over Stanley. The only slight snag was that the Argentinians had refused to let him take the marines' flag when they ejected him from the islands; but Ewen Southby-Tailyour now obliged. And so, before a battery of cameras, a Falklands flag with a small hole in one corner was raised over Stanley. 'It was very satisfying to be back in Stanley,' Norman said to reporters eager to record his words at this historic moment. 'We said we'd be back.'

That left West Falkland to be dealt with: a consolation prize awarded to Malcolm Hunt, commander of 40 Commando, who had been bitterly disapointed at being left behind to guard the San Carlos beach-head. The surrender ceremony took place on the Port Howard soccer pitch the following afternoon. Afterwards Southby-Tailyour was dispatched with a party of officers, soldiers and journalists, to round up any remaining enemy on the smaller islands. At Pebble Island settlement formalities were dispensed with: the local Argentinian lieutenant was bluntly informed that he had surrendered. He looked sceptical at first but then replied: 'Okay, right, I'll go and tell my men.' After a night's solid drinking with the British settlement manager, the party proceeded to Carcass Island, Golding Island, and Keppel Island to make sure everyone knew the war was over.

It was not the end of Southby-Tailyour's peregrinations. Throughout the campaign he had nurtured hopes of visiting another island, the remote, uninhabited clump of rocks known as Jason West Cay, out beyond the north-western tip of West Falkland. It was an ambition he had held ever since he first visited the Falklands in 1978. As he told everyone whose attention he could capture, Falkland folklore held that an Elizabethan galleon lay wrecked on Jason West Cay – maybe even one lost by Sir Francis Drake on his voyage around Cape Horn. On Sunday June 20, having engaged the interest of a friendly helicopter pilot, Southby-Tailyour realised his ambition and flew to the island.

For fifteen minutes, the helicopter circled while Southby-Tailyour vainly scanned the shattered rocks below. He was about to abandon his search, and his dream, when the pilot spotted what looked like a pile of broken timbers. As they went closer Southby-Tailyour made out the unmistakable shape of a ship's hull against the rocks. The helicopter landed and Southby-Tailyour scrambled out – the first man to set foot on the island since the shipwrecked sailors themselves.

The wreckage was spread over a wide area and, meticulous as ever, Southby-Tailyour photographed and measured it assiduously. He concluded that it was probably not one of Drake's galleons but an eighteenth century vessel – close enough to validate the island folklore, and still quite a find. He lovingly collected samples of the timber and metal fittings and took them back to *Fearless*. When he returned to Britain, he delivered them to the National Maritime Museum at Greenwich. They are there now.

CHAPTER TWENTY-FOUR

The Falklands Factor

'Call off the rail strike or we'll
call in an air strike.'
– Poster hung over the side of
the *SS Canberra* by marines arriving
at Southampton Dock, July 11, 1982

On the day after the fall of Stanley, Sir Anthony Parsons, Britain's ambassador at the United Nations, decided he had earned himself a break. For the first time in nearly three months his time was his own. He decided to go to one of the many parties that take place daily in and around the UN.

As he walked into the crowded reception room he was amazed to find himself the focus of attention. Glasses were raised in his direction, his hand was pumped again and again. 'Congratulations, Sir Anthony! 'Well done!' 'I drink to you, sir! This is a fine day for your country!' The greetings and congratulations came from unexpected people – representatives of third world countries which normally shunned the British delegate.

Sir Anthony was experiencing at first hand what was to become knows as 'the Falklands factor'. Mrs Thatcher, of course, put it bluntly: 'Great Britain,' she said, 'is great again.' The *Daily Mail* echoed her: 'Britain is once more a nation of confidence,' it announced.

As the ships and the men began to come home from their momentous voyage, the scenes of great crowds singing 'Rule Britannia' on the quayside and at airports grew increasingly familiar. There was almost a ritual about it – the Union flags, the balloons, the tears and the embraces. But how transitory was it? Within a few weeks of the end of the war, Britain was grappling with the effects of a national rail strike, and the apparently insoluble causes of mass unemployment. Thatcher's ratings, which had once stood as high as eighty per cent, began to slide towards normality again.

Perhaps the Falklands had indeed touched something deep in the national consciousness, but had victory really changed anything?

Defeat had certainly changed Argentina. The news of the surrender at Stanley marked the end of a two-month dream in which the people had begun to believe the best of their country and its leaders. The disillusionment which followed plunged the country into profound shock.

That night, in the chill dusk, dazed and angry groups gathered in the Plaza de Mayo to shout defiantly at the empty balcony of the Casa Rosada: 'No surrender!' they shouted. '*Galtieri, hijo de puta*' (son of a whore).

The rage they felt was the rage of a nation which had willingly suspended disbelief and given generously of its cash and its faith in a cause it felt to be just. In the process, Argentinians had begun to believe that their troubled and divided nation had achieved unity, maturity and the respect and attention of the world. Their military had at last turned to fight, apparently with honour, a powerful external enemy, and the country had a great national cause. When it turned out to be another lie, there did not seem to be much left.

By the end of that traumatic week, Galtieri was replaced as commander-in-chief of the army by the blustering hard liner, General Cristino Nicolaides, who hastened to assure his troops they had won a great victory. A more realistic note was struck by the mild new president, retired General Reynaldo Bignone, who asked the nation the heartfelt question: 'What is wrong with us Argentinians?'

And as the real casualties of the war trickled home with stories of corruption and incompetence from the front, the men who had led the charge faded into ignominy. Costa Mendez fell shortly after Galtieri. Lami Dozo, who had bid unsuccessfully for the presidency, fell in August, after a vain attempt to recapture some political power. Of the four who had launched the national madness, only one – perhaps the most culpable – remained: the man in whom the ambition to take the Malvinas burned the brightest, whose men had done so little to defend the islands, the man from the silent service, Admiral Jorge Anaya. Of the lessons which a bruised country tried to draw from the experience perhaps one will endure: 'Never again,' ran a letter published in *La Prensa* in July 1982, 'must we let a government we did not elect lead us into a war we did not want.'

Sadly, in the Falklands, where it all began, there were early signs of disenchantment. Simon Winchester of *The Sunday Times*, who had been there when Stanley fell, returned shortly after it was regained. He found that the prospects of being a garrison island for the foreseeable future had not cheered the islanders. He wrote: 'Their attitude to the British is a mixture of continued deep mistrust, disappointment and a sullen acceptance of the military realities of the new occupying army amongst them. Six weeks have passed since liberation and the Falklands people – as distinct from the Falklands establishment – are profoundly disillusioned.'

But the troops will bring benefits – manpower skills for local projects like bridge and road building, entertainment and health facilities, and an enlarged airport, which would have been impossible before the war. Only two years ago the British government baulked at the idea of paying £11 million to lengthen the runway at Stanley to take long-haul jets. Now the decision has been forced on them.

There were the real ravages of war – thousands of unexploded shells and seemingly undiscoverable mines littered the hills and beaches where once the islanders had strolled so freely. Within twenty miles of Stanley there were said to be more than 11,000 unexploded devices. Could mothers ever let their children play on the beaches or in the fields with an easy mind? Could a farmer risk putting his dairy cattle out to graze?

The threat from Argentina, 400 miles away, will continue to be very real. But sooner or later negotiations will have to start again – neighbouring states must learn to live together somehow. At least the war has guaranteed one thing for the Falklanders on their remote rocks in the South Atlantic. No one will ever again underestimate the dangers they face.

Index

FIGHT FOR THE FALKLANDS!

Why and how Britain went to war

JOHN LAFFIN

For more on the Falklands War read John Laffin's FIGHT
FOR THE FALKLANDS! What were we fighting for? How
and why did we win? Using inside knowledge and military
expertise John Laffin tells the full story of the war that
was watched by the world with fear and fascination.

WAR   0 7221 5371 6   £1.50

A SELECTION OF TITLES FROM SPHERE

FICTION

STILL MISSING	Beth Gutcheon	£1.75 ☐
INHERITORS OF THE STORM	Victor Sondheim	£4.95 ☐
NIGHT PROBE!	Clive Cussler	£1.95 ☐
CHIMERA	Stephen Gallagher	£1.75 ☐
PALOMINO	Danielle Steel	£1.75 ☐

FILM & TV TIE-INS

ON THE LINE	Anthony Minghella	£1.25 ☐
FAME	Leonore Fleischer	£1.50 ☐
FIREFOX	Craig Thomas	£1.75 ☐
GREASE II	William Rotsler	£1.25 ☐
CONAN THE BARBARIAN	L. Sprague de Camp & Lin Carter	£1.25 ☐

NON-FICTION

BEFORE I FORGET	James Mason	£2.25 ☐
TOM PILGRIM: AUTOBIOGRAPHY OF A SPIRITUALIST HEALER	Tom Pilgrim	£1.50 ☐
YOUR CHILD AND THE ZODIAC	Teri King	£1.50 ☐
THE SURVIVOR	Jack Eisner	£1.75 ☐

All Sphere books are available at your local bookshop or newsagent, or can be ordered direct from the publisher. Just tick the titles you want and fill in the form below.

Name _____

Address _____

_____

Write to Sphere Books, Cash Sales Department, P.O. Box 11, Falmouth, Cornwall TR10 9EN

Please enclose a cheque or postal order to the value of the cover price plus:

UK: 45p for the first book, 20p for the second book and 14p for each additional book ordered to a maximum charge of £1.63.

OVERSEAS: 75p for the first book plus 21p per copy for each additional book.

BFPO & EIRE: 45p for the first book, 20p for the second book plus 14p per copy for the next 7 books, thereafter 8p per book.

Sphere Books reserve the right to show new retail prices on covers which may differ from those previously advertised in the text or elsewhere, and to increase postal rates in accordance with the PO.